TO OUR BELOVED SON SAMUEL

You are a great student of the teachings of the living prophets of our day. You seem to be most familiar with the teachings of the latest living prophet, whoever it is that the Lord may choose for a season. President Spencer W. Kimball is the one with whom I am the best acquainted and through the closeness to him he permitted me to enjoy, he has had the most profound effect upon my life thus far. We know your love and appreciation for him will be even further increased as you come to know him better through your perusal of this biography.

For your faithfulness to our Heavenly Father, and to our Savior, and to the cause of the gospel and the Church, we are forever grateful. If we could have but one prayer granted, it would be that all our posterity-- our extended family--to the last and latest generation would forever be faithful and gain their exaltations in the Celestial Kingdom of our God. Thank you for doing all that you are doing in working earnestly towards the fulfillment of that prayer.

We love you, Samuel.

Daddy & Mama

Christmas 1995

SPENCER W. KIMBALL

Spencer W. Kimball in 1936

SPENCER W. KIMBALL

RESOLUTE DISCIPLE, PROPHET OF GOD

FRANCIS M. GIBBONS

Deseret Book Company
Salt Lake City, Utah

Books by Francis M. Gibbons

Joseph Smith: Martyr, Prophet of God
Brigham Young: Modern Moses, Prophet of God
John Taylor: Mormon Philosopher, Prophet of God
Wilford Woodruff: Wondrous Worker, Prophet of God
Lorenzo Snow: Spiritual Giant, Prophet of God
Joseph F. Smith: Patriarch and Preacher, Prophet of God
Heber J. Grant: Man of Steel, Prophet of God
George Albert Smith: Kind and Caring Christian, Prophet of God
David O. McKay: Apostle to the World, Prophet of God
Joseph Fielding Smith: Gospel Scholar, Prophet of God
Harold B. Lee: Man of Vision, Prophet of God

All photographs in this book are used courtesy of the Historical Department, The Church of Jesus Christ of Latter-day Saints.

Library of Congress Cataloging-in-Publication Data

Gibbons, Francis M., 1921–
    Spencer W. Kimball : resolute disciple, prophet of God / Francis M. Gibbons.
        p.   cm.
    Includes bibliographical references and index.
    ISBN 0-87579-994-9 (hardback)
    1. Kimball, Spencer W., 1895–1985. 2. Church of Jesus Christ of Latter-day Saints—Presidents—Biography. 3. Mormon Church—Presidents—Biography. I. Title.
BX8695.K53G53   1995
289.3'092—dc20
[B]   95-21428
                                                                   CIP

Printed in the United States of America

10 9   8   7   6   5   4   3   2   1

To the members of the Church
in Brazil, who loved
President Kimball
and who claimed him as
one of their own.

Contents

Contents

Preface

Members of the Church in the United States scarcely can understand the feelings of South American Saints toward President Spencer W. Kimball. While they admire other General Authorities, few other leaders receive the veneration accorded to President Kimball. With some, it borders on worship, reflected in different ways. I saw it in a native Brazilian mission president with whom I conducted a mission tour. Late one night after a week on the road, while driving to our next appointment, he asked quietly, "Tell me about President Kimball." In our seven days together, he had not asked about any of the other brethren with whom I had worked over the years. Now as we had time to visit in an unhurried way, he wanted to know more about this man, and this man only.

The reasons why South Americans have such feelings toward President Kimball are not difficult to identify. He traveled there more extensively and more often than any of his predecessors had done. It was he who organized the first three stakes in South America, in São Paulo, Buenos Aires, and Montevideo. It was he who dedicated the temple in São Paulo, the first one in all of South America. And it was he who announced the revelation on priesthood in June 1978 that had such a profound effect on the growth of the Church in the South American countries, especially Brazil. More than that, South Americans looked on him as children look on a father. He was their champion and advocate. It was he who pleaded their cause in the high councils of the Church, who expressed confidence in their ability to grow and to develop, and who never failed to show his love for them in both his words and actions.

North Americans can be, by nature, somewhat distant and undemonstrative. Soon after his first tour of South America in the late 1950s, after being exposed to the warm and affectionate nature of South Americans, Elder Kimball lost that reserve and began to express his love with a hug and a kiss on the cheek when it was appropriate to do so. The impact on others was astonishing. One woman of my acquaintance—a benign, grandmotherly type—was momentarily surprised to receive a peck on the cheek from the prophet and afterwards was almost awestruck to think she was one of the few to be so honored. And a gnarled Brazilian worker in São Paulo related with tears in his eyes, long after the event, how the prophet had given him a kiss on the cheek as he stood to greet the people. "Imagina! Imagina!" he said with a sense of disbelief. "O profeta me beijou!"

Such was the confidence these people had in President Kimball that they were willing to follow his instructions and example in all things, without question. When funds were being raised to construct the temple in São Paulo, he met with local leaders to discuss the procedure. He emphasized the need for sacrifice in giving to the temple fund, then asked the leaders what they felt their members could contribute in the spirit of sacrifice. The amounts suggested by the leaders were written on the blackboard. After reviewing the figures and complimenting the brethren, the prophet asked them to triple these amounts and to accept that as their goal in fund raising. They did so without dissent or comment, even though it required significant sacrifice by the members, many of whom lived near the poverty level in an unstable economy.

His example was as compelling to them as were his words. Once a regional representative watched President Kimball enter a lavatory in a Brazilian chapel and, without comment, pick up paper towels off the floor and clean the washbasin. Until then, the regional representative had thought it beneath his dignity to tidy up after others. Later, he always inspected and policed the building and grounds of a chapel before a meeting, announcing from the pulpit what he had found, telling the audience what President Kimball had done, and encouraging them to follow the prophet's example. It created a revolution in the way the members regarded and cared for their chapels.

Much of the compassion President Kimball had for the people of South America, and other areas with similar ethnic mixes, derived from the special prophetic charge he received to shepherd those of Lamanite descent. When President George Albert Smith charged him to look out for the Lamanites in all the world, Spencer W. Kimball took it to heart. He interpreted it to apply not only to those clearly identifiable as Indians but to people in any country where there were significant ethnic mixtures. And that view led him to champion the cause of people everywhere who had suffered discrimination or deprivation.

When he received the charge from President Smith, the work with the Lamanites and other minorities was at a low ebb. Through disciplined effort, Elder Kimball imbued them with hope and confidence, aroused the consciousness of the Church to their plight, and spurred Church leaders to take a special interest in them. The results were remarkable. At a meeting to dedicate a chapel in Duncan, Arizona, in 1956, attended by F. Melvin Hammond (now of the Seventy) and other missionaries, Elder Kimball prophesied that the day of the Lamanites had arrived and that from that day the work would flourish among them.

Significantly, only two years before, President David O. McKay had stopped briefly in South America as he returned from a trip to South Africa. At the airport to greet President McKay when he and his party arrived in Santiago, Chile, were Billy Fotheringham and his wife, expatriates from the United States, the only two known members of the Church in Chile. Today there are over 300,000 members in that one South American country alone, fifty-one stakes, six missions, and a beautiful temple. The growth in other South American countries has been equally rapid. In Ecuador, for instance, there are now over 90,000 members, twelve stakes, and three missions, and the construction of a temple has been announced. One of these stakes, the Otavalo stake, had special meaning for Elder Kimball. Here he found what he considered to be direct descendants of father Lehi whose ancestors had not intermarried with Europeans. Their leaders, dressed in sandals, white pants, and ponchos, with their open-faced friendliness and high spirituality, were greatly loved and admired by the prophet. He regarded a meeting he held with them as one of the most unique and moving meetings he ever attended.

The physical ordeals President Kimball suffered over the years and his industrious work habits gave him a special status among members of the Church around the world. What many did not know is that he often endured severe pain and discomfort as he worked. Only occasionally did he part the curtain to reveal his suffering. Once, one of the Brethren went to President Kimball, then serving as the president of the Twelve, to ask for relief in some of his assignments. Before the man had a chance to explain his reason for coming, President Kimball, by way of conversation, mentioned offhand some of his recent physical ailments. Because the visitor's problems seemed so insignificant by comparison, he left without making the request. Another time, a report came that one of the Brethren had been hospitalized because of heart fibrillations. President Kimball mentioned matter-of-factly that he suffered the same problem almost every day but ignored it and went on working. And he worked without interruption through the pain, inconvenience, and embarrassment of numerous boils and carbuncles over the years.

His work habits were so ingrained and pervasive that they sometimes overshadowed other aspects of his life. Once he and Camilla were traveling in Europe with another couple. In Vienna they decided to attend an opera, and tickets were purchased. At the last minute, however, Elder Kimball said he felt uncomfortable going to the opera and that he planned instead to meet with a small group of members, but he urged the others to go on. His sense of duty touched everyone, so all went to the Church meeting. Because of this quality in his makeup, it was anomalous that throughout his life, Spencer W. Kimball avidly took regular vacations with his family, spending two or three weeks each year at different vacation spots, usually in California. In later years, however, he often used these vacations to work on his writing projects.

Although he took his work seriously, President Kimball never took himself too seriously. In relaxed moments with those he knew well, he occasionally reflected the lighthearted sense of humor so evident in his youth. He once boarded the elevator at Church headquarters carrying a briefcase bulging with correspondence. There stood a colleague with a small, thin, leather folder under his arm. Looking at his friend, then the folder, President Kimball asked mischievously, "Are we overworking you?" Another time, when he was on the elevator with a friend named Spencer, someone in the back said, "Spence, will you please push four?" Obligingly, President Kimball pushed the button, saying, "Glad to do it." And seeing his friend Doctor Homer Ellsworth one day, President Kimball carried on this conversation: "Homer, do I understand correctly you have a small farm near Lehi?" "Yes, President." "And is it true you share your harvest with others and can the surplus?" "That's true, President." "And Homer, in time of need would you be willing to share your surplus with others?" "I certainly would, President." "Homer, please give me your address."

Incidents such as these, which were not exceptional, reveal a chief characteristic of President Spencer W. Kimball that endeared him to the hearts of the members of the Church. He was one of us. He was genuine. He was approachable. And yet that approachableness never bred familiarity. He was able to retain a sense of common attachment without in any way compromising his role as the prophet-leader.

During the years of his presidency, except at the end, when he seldom left his apartment, President Kimball often walked around the Church Administration Building, popping into offices unannounced. It was one way to exercise. Regardless of the number of times we might plead with him to just call and let us go to him instead of his coming to see us, he never complied. One never knew when the door would open to reveal the prophet of the Lord standing there. And usually, he would bestow a hug and a kiss on the cheek before taking up the business he had in mind. Who could fail to reciprocate that love? And who could fail to try to measure up to the high standard of achievement he set, to lengthen our stride, to quicken our pace, to extend our reach, to "do it"?

Acknowledgments

G rateful acknowledgment is extended to many people for their valued assistance in the preparation of this manuscript. Thanks are given to numerous associates of President Spencer W. Kimball who provided special insights into his life and work. Thanks also to Elder Loren C. Dunn, Church historian at the time I wrote this book, and to members of his staff, especially Glenn N. Rowe; to the executive and editorial staff of Deseret Book Company, especially Ronald E. Millett, Sheri Dew, and Linda Gundry; and to Ruth G. Stoneman for expert and extensive research assistance. And, as always, thanks to the Mentor.

Chapter 1

From Good Stock

Andrew and Olive Kimball's third son, born March 28, 1895, was almost named Roberts Kimball in honor of B. H. Roberts of the First Council of Seventy of The Church of Jesus Christ of Latter-day Saints. Elder Roberts, a political activist, was at the time a delegate to the Utah Constitutional Convention, as was Andrew. A lively issue then before the convention was whether women should be given the vote. When Elder Roberts stood to argue against women's suffrage, Andrew Kimball was so carried away with the rhetoric that he decided to name his nine-pound baby son Roberts Kimball. That Andrew was a suffragist made no difference. The name would honor the speaker's eloquence, not his politics.

Andrew did not reckon with the opposition of Olive, who was a more militant suffragist than he. She could not abide the thought of her son bearing the name of an individual whose political views differed so much from her own. So, after discussing the matter, the Kimballs reached a

1

compromise. The boy would be named Spencer Woolley Kimball.

Olive's idea of compromise on this occasion was not surprising in light of the character of her father, Edwin D. Woolley, longtime bishop of the Thirteenth Ward and a prosperous Salt Lake businessman who was once the business agent for Brigham Young. It was said of Bishop Woolley that were he to drown, his body would be found upstream. The bishop's tenacity found its way into his daughter but was tempered there by the mild and loving qualities of her English mother, Mary Ann Olpin Woolley, the bishop's fourth polygamous wife.

It must not be inferred that because Andrew Kimball yielded to Olive in naming the baby Spencer, he lacked conviction. It is likely that in giving mature thought to the name, he agreed with his wife's choice of names. But had the issue been vital, involving a question of morality or propriety, Andrew would not have yielded. The quality of willpower in Olive's makeup was no less evident in Andrew, whose father, Heber C. Kimball, was one of the most tenacious of the early Church leaders. Yet Andrew, like Olive, inherited not only the strong-willed qualities of his father but also the mild characteristics of his mother, Ann Alice Gheen Kimball, Heber's seventeenth wife. And some of the traits of these parents and grandparents found their way into the character of Spencer Woolley Kimball.

The new arrival enlarged Andrew Kimball's family to seven: the parents, daughters Clare and Ruth, and sons Gordon, Delbert, and Spencer. Another daughter, Maude, had died in infancy. When Spencer was born, thirty-seven-year-old Andrew Kimball was a man of influence and promise in Salt Lake City, having served as the president of the Indian Territory Mission for eight years. Centered in Oklahoma, the mission area included twenty Indian nations with a combined population of eighty thousand. Before his call as mission president, Andrew served two and a half years as a proselyting missionary, living in the territory among the Indians. The discipline and determination he had shown then prompted the Brethren to call him as the mission president. But because he was married and the father of a child, Clare, Andrew was allowed to live in Salt Lake City and direct the work from there, with occasional trips to the territory to give personal supervision.

Andrew Kimball did not receive a salary as mission president. He was reimbursed for travel and other expenses and was given a small allowance. But this was far from sufficient to maintain his growing family, so he engaged in several different occupations to supplement his income, working chiefly as a salesman. Eventually he traveled in Utah and parts of Idaho, selling a line of goods to variety stores. This brought him into contact with many prominent people throughout the area who knew him as the president of the Indian Territory Mission and as a son of President Heber C. Kimball. They also knew that Andrew's twin sister, Alice, was one of the wives of Joseph F. Smith, then the second counselor in the First Presidency of the Church.

Meanwhile, Andrew was politically active, as his service in the constitutional convention shows. All this, added to the growing influence of the Kimball and Woolley families, gave Andrew significant status in the community. Andrew was part of a large family; his father sired sixty-five children. Andrew was number thirty-five of Heber C. Kimball's fifty-two sons. Another of these sons, J. Golden Kimball, was called to the First Council of Seventy in 1892.

Once Utah gained statehood in 1896, its people seemed destined for an era of significant progress. Many earlier problems that had impeded development were eliminated by the Manifesto published in 1890, which discontinued the teaching and practice of plural marriage in the Church. There was new energy in Utah and a sense of cooperation between the Latter-day Saints and others. Andrew approached the future with optimism, yearning for financial independence and for an expanded role in public affairs. At Spencer's birth, Andrew owned a substantial family home

3

two blocks from the campus of the University of Utah (now occupied by Salt Lake City's West High School). He also owned rental property. These were encumbered by a small indebtedness. He had no other financial obligations and brought in a sufficient though not plenteous income.

Considering his preoccupation with church and family duties after his marriage and the lack of an inheritance from his father's estate, Andrew had done well. When his father died in 1868, Andrew was not yet ten. While Heber C. Kimball had left a substantial estate, his large family, which included forty-three wives, divided the assets, and no one branch received much. The death of the family patriarch had a great impact on Ann Alice Kimball and her children, Samuel, Daniel, Andrew and his twin sister, Alice, and their younger sister, Sarah. Essentially they were left to fend for themselves. And a few years later, when Samuel and Daniel, the older sons, struck out on their own, Andrew had the main responsibility to care for his ailing mother and his two sisters. So, cast in the role of an adult while still a boy, and bereft of the guiding hand of a father, Andrew grew up during the crucial teenage years without secular education and without significant involvement in the Church. He was too busy trying to scratch out a living for his mother and sisters. During his late teens, however, with the gentle nudging of his devout mother, Andrew returned to Church activity, and in 1878, at age twenty, he received the Aaronic Priesthood and was ordained a deacon.

After his mother died in 1879, Andrew, for the first time, was able to give serious thought to his own goals and ambitions. He was employed in the machine shop at the Salt Lake railroad yards. With newfound freedom and a regular income, he turned his thoughts toward matrimony. His attentions centered on Olive Woolley, vivacious daughter of Bishop Woolley. While their temperaments were alike, the physical characteristics of Andrew Kimball and Olive Woolley were markedly different. She had blue eyes and hair with a reddish tint. His eyes were deep brown and his hair dark brunette. She was a petite five feet in height, while he towered over her at six feet. His complexion was almost swarthy, while hers was light and so clear as to seem almost transparent.

There was a solemn earnestness about this pair and a determined sense of purpose. They held common goals for themselves and their family, in keeping with their shared convictions about life's purpose, about the church to which they belonged, and about the obligations they owed to that church. These obligations were confirmed by covenants they made when they were sealed in the Salt Lake Endowment House on February 2, 1882.

It was these religious convictions and the responsibilities they felt from their marital covenants that enabled Andrew and Olive to accept without question Andrew's call to serve a mission in the Indian Territory, even though Olive was then expecting a child and they were without means. And in the same spirit they had accepted his call to serve as the mission president, even though it entailed heavy travel obligations and made the pursuit of financial success very difficult.

After almost eleven years of work with the Indians, and just as things began to look up financially for Andrew and Olive following Spencer's birth, their course was forever altered when somewhat of a bombshell was dropped on the Andrew Kimball family. It was a three-stage explosion. The first occurred at Pocatello, Idaho, in 1896 when Matthias Cowley of the Quorum of the Twelve prophesied that Andrew would be called "to labor among the stakes of Zion." Knowing the man and his spiritual qualities, Andrew had confidence in the prediction. What remained unanswered was the place to which he would be called and the role he would play.

These questions were answered tentatively the following year by another member of the Twelve whom Andrew met in Sevier, Utah. This apostle triggered the second stage of the explosion when, unthinkingly, he told Andrew he was

Andrew and Olive Kimball with their children in 1897. Two-year-old Spencer is seated on his father's lap.

to replace Christopher Layton as the president of the St. Joseph Stake in southern Arizona.

The third stage was completed when Andrew consulted with the First Presidency on his return to Salt Lake City, to receive confirmation of the news the apostle had prematurely divulged. Yes, he was told, the Brethren wanted him to move his family to Thatcher, Arizona, in the Gila Valley, where he was to become the president of the St. Joseph Stake.

In a perfunctory way, they asked about his financial condition, brushing aside quite casually, he thought, the fact he was fifteen hundred dollars in debt. Both he and Olive had thought this indebtedness might dissuade the First Presidency from pursuing the call. Serious reflection would have convinced the Kimballs otherwise. Here they faced Wilford Woodruff, George Q. Cannon, and Joseph F. Smith, men whose combined apostolic service exceeded 125 years, who had endured almost every known privation, including mobbings, burnings, and exile. To these men, a fifteen-hundred-dollar indebtedness was hardly worth mentioning.

When Andrew Kimball left the office of the First Presidency that day, he knew his life had been set, irreversibly, on a course he had never intended or wanted. And Olive's views about Arizona were more pessimistic than his. When Andrew told her of the outcome of his meeting with the First Presidency, she burst into tears. He joined her. After commiserating with each other, they knelt in prayer. "This over," wrote Andrew, "nothing remained but to go to work."

The Kimballs' attitude toward their new home was conditioned by negative reports that had reached Salt Lake City—reports of snakes, centipedes, scorpions, and tarantulas in abundance, of killings by Indians and outlaws, and of malaria epidemics. Also there was the perception that Arizona was so remote that going there was like going to another planet. The facts, however, contradicted this pessimistic view.

The idea of its remoteness was a myth. At the time of Andrew's call, one could board the train at Salt Lake City and, with intermediate changes, step from the train at Thatcher. Indeed, because of the rail connections, it was faster and more convenient to travel from Salt Lake City to Thatcher, Arizona, in 1898, when the Kimballs moved there, than it was to travel from Salt Lake City to many outlying Mormon communities in Utah. As to the danger from Indian attack, the surrender of Geronimo to General Crook on September 8, 1886, had largely removed that threat. Other signs of the growing maturity of the Gila (pronounced Heela) Valley in 1898 included the presence of telephone, telegraph, and postal services; stores that stocked the most attractive and useful commodities to be found in Los Angeles and New Orleans; and a wide range of other services.

Once Andrew and Olive became fully aware of the real conditions in the Gila Valley, their negative attitudes toward the area changed. Moreover, their later enthusiasm for it showed a recognition that here was a place where an industrious and intelligent young couple could plant themselves and their family with the hope of living a full and fruitful life while rendering significant service to their neighbors, their community, and their church.

Later events suggest that there was an even deeper purpose in the Kimballs' move to Arizona, for among the children who accompanied them to Thatcher was the cherubic, three-year-old Spencer, whose nonstop, ever-active mannerisms were perpetual motion personified. Were there insights, impressions, and instructions this future prophet had to absorb that could only be taught him in this faraway corner of Arizona?

Chapter 2

The Move to Arizona

In a meeting held in Salt Lake City on January 22, 1898, Andrew Kimball was set apart by his brother-in-law, President Joseph F. Smith, as the president of the St. Joseph Stake. Elder John Henry Smith of the Twelve assisted. John Henry Smith and the new stake president left immediately for the Gila Valley to attend the quarterly stake conference scheduled for the weekend of January 27 and 28. There they were joined by Elder John W. Taylor of the Twelve. After meeting the local brethren and consulting with Elders Smith and Taylor, Andrew Kimball selected William D. Johnson and Charles M. Layton as his counselors. Christopher Layton (Charles Layton's father), who was released as stake president because of ill health, was sustained as a patriarch.

The release of President Layton, the sustaining of the new slate of stake officers, and the presence of two members of the Twelve endowed the meetings of the conference with much emotion and a high degree of spirituality. One of the highlights about which Andrew Kimball commented was a sermon delivered by Elder John W. Taylor in which he prophesied that one of the most beautiful temples ever built among the Saints in the Rocky Mountains ultimately would be built in the Gila Valley.

At a special stake meeting held before he returned to Salt Lake City, Andrew was presented with the deed to ten acres of land for a homesite. Later, forty-five priesthood brethren cleared the land, removing exactly 459 mesquite stumps by count. Andrew was overwhelmed.

The Kimballs had only six weeks to complete the arrangements for their move after Andrew returned from Arizona. Olive already had done much of the packing during her husband's absence. He helped her to complete it, and with the aid of relatives and neighbors, he crated the furnishings they planned to take with them. Everything else was sold, given away, or left in the home for the new occupants. The family was reconciled to the idea that this was a permanent move and that they would not return to Salt Lake City except as visitors. This reality seemed to affect Olive more profoundly than anyone else. To her, the implications of the move were devastating. It meant she would be separated forever from her family, except for correspondence and for occasional visits when she or they would travel the long distances that would separate them. Meanwhile, she would have the major responsibility to create and to maintain their new home in a strange environment while Andrew carried on with his heavy responsibilities to direct the affairs of the stake and to provide the means to support his family. So as Olive prepared for the move, she shed many tears. And the well-wishing of her sisters and friends, intended to buoy her up, only added to her feelings of deprivation.

By May 3, 1898, all was in readiness. There was a light drizzle that morning, which added another layer of gloom to Olive's feelings. Andrew had gone to the station early to supervise the loading of their furniture and baggage. When Olive arrived later with the children, there was little to do but await the call to board their train. In the hubbub of the cavernous depot, we can imagine Olive's distracted efforts, with Alice in her arms, to monitor the children while bidding her good-byes. In these circumstances, no doubt Clare had the responsibility to supervise the erratic meanderings of her three-year-old brother, Spencer, who probably had never seen such excitement before. At Bowie, Arizona, on the Southern Pacific Sunset Line, which connected Los Angeles, California, with New Orleans, Louisiana, the Kimballs transferred to what the locals jokingly called the Gila Monster, a wood-burning train of the Gila Valley, Globe and Northern Railway. As the Monster chugged north, belching smoke and cinders, Olive and the children probably were unimpressed with the landscape they viewed, if not a little apprehensive. The terrain in the San Simon Valley was dull and sun-baked. It was littered with pockets of volcanic rock, and its vegetation consisted largely of desert weeds, garnished with clumps of small cactus. Such a sight could well have revived Olive's negative perceptions of what to expect in Arizona. Soon, however, the scene changed as the train entered the southern part of the Gila Valley. Here was a verdant, fertile strip of farmland, two miles wide along the river bottom and extending north for many miles, following the contours of the meandering river. Here was evidence of intensive husbandry and intelligent planning, which had created an oasis of greenery in the desert. And here, too, was the place where the Kimball family would be planted, to grow and to mature. While Spencer W. Kimball owed allegiance to Salt Lake City as the place of his birth, it always played a subordinate role in his estimation and loyalties. Throughout his life, any reference he made to "the valley" always meant the Gila Valley, not the Salt Lake Valley.

After the greetings and introductions at Thatcher, President and Sister Kimball, with their children and baggage, were taken to the home of President Charles Layton, second counselor in the stake presidency, where they remained for several days. Then Andrew rented living quarters for his family from Hyrum Claridge until more permanent arrangements could be made. Finally he acquired a three-room adobe house. Adjacent to it, he erected a large white tent which, when partitioned into several separate compartments, served as a dormitory for the older children. This became known as "The White House." The comparatively mild, dry climate made it possible to use the tent throughout the year. With no running water or bathroom, these facilities were spartan by Salt Lake City standards, but they were not unusual for the Thatcher of that day. In time the family's living accommodations were improved to provide all the comforts and some of the luxuries of the day.

Chapter 3

Parental Influences

A t this time, the life of the Kimball family in Thatcher revolved chiefly around the parents, Andrew and Olive. As the president of the stake and as the patriarch in his family, Andrew's role was more visible. All the activities of the stake were centered in him. Because Andrew Kimball's word was final as to all ecclesiastical matters arising in the stake, except those few which were appealable to Salt Lake City, he was regarded by the members of the stake as being, in effect, the head of the Church. All this cast an aura of special distinction around Andrew Kimball, a fact that was not lost on his children, especially Spencer, who idolized his father. To Spencer Kimball, there was no one, absolutely no one, who excelled his father in any way. This attitude was reflected in the undeviating obedience he gave to him. Spencer always responded with alacrity and enthusiasm to even the merest wish of his father. Nor was Spencer's regard for his father shown only in his actions. Throughout his long life, he never missed an appropriate opportunity to extol the virtues of

13

Andrew Kimball. As an adult he was once heard to say that his father was the most important and influential man in the state of Arizona. His wife, Camilla, thinking perhaps that this was a bit overblown, tactfully suggested he limit the area of his father's surpassing distinction to the Gila Valley. Undeterred, her husband added only the qualification *"especially* in the Gila Valley."

Spencer's mother, Olive Kimball, though smaller in physical stature than her husband, cast an equally large spiritual shadow over her son. Indeed, her influence in both practical and subtle ways may have been more profound and lasting than that of Andrew. Part of this is traceable to mere proximity.

Because of Andrew's many duties away from the home, it was generally Olive who prepared Spencer's meals, mended and washed his clothing, supervised his personal hygiene, monitored his studies, and comforted him in illness and disappointment. When Andrew was away from home, Olive supervised and led out in family prayers and Bible study, directed both the outside work and the housework, and was the final arbiter in all matters pertaining to the family. She did all this with calmness and aplomb, with a sense of love and kindness, yet with a firmness which left no room for doubt as to who was in charge or what was expected of the children. The bond that linked Spencer Kimball to this remarkable woman was immutable. As he sought to emulate his father, he flourished with the love, approval, and encouragement of his mother.

On returning home from school on the run, Spencer would burst into the home calling, "Ma, Ma, Ma." When his mother would respond, quietly asking what he wanted, Spencer would answer, "Nothing," an answer which was not quite accurate. In fact, he did want something, and that was to know that his mother was home, available for routine or emergency assistance or merely for the comforting knowledge that she was there. The son's appraisal of his mother's character was no less laudatory than the one he made of his father. "My mother was faultless," wrote he. "She was a Saint, . . . the epitome of perfection. Who could even mention one virtue that she had not possessed?"

These, then, were the parents who nurtured Spencer Kimball and his brothers and sisters into adulthood and whose deeds and reputation far overshadowed those of the children during their formative years.

The move to Arizona, exposing the family to a more challenging way of life, caused the Kimballs to refocus on some of the basic teachings of their religion. Always prayerful, they now found that disease, drought, depression, and other hazards made prayer an essential companion of daily living. The Kimballs always prayed together at mealtime. With their chairs faced outward, they would kneel at the dinner table, and the one called on to pray would not only bless the food but would invoke such blessings as were needful at the moment. On special occasions, the family would kneel together in the family parlor, mingling their hands on the piano stool. While these prayers were sometimes repetitious, they were never offered perfunctorily. There was too much earnestness in this family to allow for that, too much uncertainty about crops, weather, markets, and health.

Perhaps young Spencer's most important instructions about prayer came from his mother, who, during his boyhood, helped him with his personal prayers. As he knelt at her knee, she reinforced the gospel's teachings about God and His relationship to those on earth. She taught her son how to pray, what to pray for, and the attitude one should have when praying. Those intimate sessions between mother and son served an important purpose other than to teach him about prayer. They enabled her to plant in his mind images of what he might become. We gain important insight into that process from a talk President Kimball delivered on April 21, 1979, at the dedication of the Mormon Pioneer Memorial Bridge across the Missouri River at Florence, Nebraska. As the prophet urged every worthy

Latter-day Saint boy to fill a mission, he said, "Every boy should have a picture of the prophet [Joseph Smith] in his bedroom." He then urged mothers to teach their sons to emulate the qualities of character of the Prophet and to become like him. "It works," he told the audience. "That's what my mother did. You couldn't have convinced her otherwise." (*Church News,* Apr. 28, 1979, p. 4.)

Spencer and his brothers and sisters learned many other things from their parents that would help shape their own lives. The willingness of Andrew and Olive to leave their home, family, and friends in Salt Lake City and move to Thatcher was an object lesson in obedience and faith. Through the example of the parents, the children learned abstinence from the use of liquor, tobacco, tea, and coffee, a teaching so profound in the case of Spencer that through his ninety years of life, he never tasted any of them. The family and private prayers, Bible study, and lessons learned at church meetings taught them faith in God. The open-handed, persistent service both parents rendered to others in the stake taught the children love of their neighbors. Reverence and punctuality at church meetings were taught when Olive and her children always sat together in their accustomed place, while Andrew sat in his place on the stand.

The children were taught the principle of tithing in practical, convincing ways. Spencer learned early, as he gathered eggs, that every tenth one was a tithing egg. When he asked his mother to explain the difference between tithing eggs and other eggs, it afforded her a teaching opportunity. Later, when the sons helped the father to harvest the hay, Andrew insisted that the "tithing load" be taken from the side of the field where the best hay was grown. And when Spencer and his sister, Alice, had earned money selling potatoes, their father taught them the most convincing object lesson of all about tithing. When the children failed to mention the bishop in telling their father how they planned to spend the money, Andrew seized upon the omission to teach a principle. He explained that the Lord, who created and who owns the earth, had provided the moisture and the sunshine without which the potatoes could not have grown. And in return for His surpassing contribution to their harvest, He asked only for a tenth of their profit, leaving nine tenths to compensate for their work. Spencer was heard to say later that his father "explained it so convincingly that we felt it an honor and privilege to pay tithing."

The boy Spencer also saw in his father a quality like that of his grandfather Heber C. Kimball, which taught him how to respond to inner promptings. The essence of this quality was to speak out boldly and without equivocation as to matters learned through spiritual insight. Heber C. Kimball, for instance, once prophesied, during the early, struggling years in the Salt Lake Valley, that the Saints would see goods sold as cheaply on the streets of Salt Lake City as in the eastern cities. One of the brethren told Heber he didn't believe a word of it. And Heber seemingly was startled by what he had said. But his statement became fact when travelers streaming to the California gold fields after the discoveries in 1849 disposed of their stores for a pittance in order to lighten their loads before crossing the western desert and the Sierra Nevadas. Suddenly there was a glut of goods in Salt Lake City, which lowered prices as Heber C. Kimball had predicted.

Andrew revealed this same characteristic on many occasions. Once, he met a couple, the Walkers, who had been told they could never have children. As he talked to them about it, Andrew, on an impulse, took Mary Walker by the hand and, while looking at her intently, promised her, "in the name of the living God," that she would have a baby. Then, turning to the husband, Arthur, he said, "You will be a father." Apparently startled at what he had said, President Andrew Kimball left abruptly. Not long afterward, Mary Walker conceived, and thirteen months after the startling conversation on the street, she gave birth to a baby boy. The Los Angeles specialist who had said the wife would never conceive refused to believe she had given birth to a baby. He still believed it was "impossible."

On another occasion, during a dry spring with no snow-pack in the mountains, President Andrew Kimball advised the Gila Valley brethren to go ahead and plant, and promised that if they lived right and had faith, there would be sufficient moisture to grow their crops. Afterward, one of Andrew's associates, Rupert Wixom, asked if he didn't consider his promise "risky." Andrew, conceding the point, said it "scared" him to think about it, but that it would come true. That year there were heavy night dews that provided enough moisture to mature the crops.

Spencer W. Kimball was blessed with this same gift that his father and grandfather had possessed. As we shall see, it was most clearly evident while he presided over the Church.

Of all the things President Kimball learned from his parents, none had a more profound effect on him than the example of their prodigious capacity to work. From infancy, he had seen his father and mother work unceasingly. There were no moments of idleness and few moments of relaxation in their busy lives.

With growing children to supervise and a large household to manage, Olive was constantly occupied with family matters. When the family moved to Arizona in 1898, there were six living children, ranging in age from one to fourteen. During the ensuing eight years before her death in 1906, Olive gave birth to four more children: Fannie, Helen, Mary, and Rachel. For Olive, motherhood was full-time work that began the moment she arose in the morning and ended only when she lay down at night. And sometimes the work did not end then, if there was a sick child or a baby to nurse during the night. She was expecting a twelfth child when she passed away.

Andrew's workload, while of a different kind, was equally arduous. Beginning with his first year in the Gila Valley, he operated a farm with the assistance of his sons.

Since Gordon was only ten, Delbert eight, and Spencer three when the move was made, their help was limited to light chores initially, with the heavy labor falling on their father. This was doubly challenging as Andrew had not farmed before and thus had to learn on the job. Finding that farming alone did not produce enough to maintain his large and growing family, Andrew engaged in other activities to supplement his income. His experience as a salesman in Utah prompted him to handle a variety of products in Arizona, including men's suits and Bible scrolls. He also became an agent for a bank and a loan company, selling insurance as well. Later, as his experience and reputation grew, he organized a farm machinery business that ultimately expanded into a general store, and he also contracted to construct a railway spur track northeast of Thatcher toward the mining operations at Morenci. Besides being active in business, he served a term in the Arizona legislature. All this was in addition to his service as stake president, which entailed frequent visits to the ten units in the stake to train the local leaders and to instruct and motivate the members.

It is not surprising that Spencer Kimball, being reared in such an environment, soon developed the attitude that he should be at work constantly, as his parents were. This attitude was confirmed when, as he matured, he became able to work and found ample opportunity to exert his energies on the endless tasks around the farm and the home. He carried this characteristic into every activity of his life. Spencer was a worker almost without peer. He seemed always to be doing something, whether milking, haying, watering, weeding, or doing chores around the house as a boy and young man or negotiating, counseling, instructing, studying, writing, or planning in his adult years.

When he was later called to the Quorum of the Twelve, he seemed to be abashed by the thought of associating with the men in the quorum who had enjoyed distinguished professional careers. As Elder Kimball compared his qualifications with those of his brethren and wondered what niche he could fill, he concluded that since he "knew how to work," he would become a worker among them.

This is not to say that the others did not work, for in fact they were prodigious workers in their own right. But none of them worked with more diligence, persistence, and pervasive intensity than Elder Spencer W. Kimball. When he attended a stake conference, he was busy from the moment he arrived until the time he left, holding an almost continuous series of meetings, including some meetings the local leaders had never even heard of. If the visit entailed a reorganization, Elder Kimball would work through meals and as far into the night as was necessary to finish. If he became weary, he would ask his assistant to continue alone while he went into the next room and lay down on the floor for a brief nap. Ten or fifteen minutes later, he would return, refreshed and ready to continue the work. And if he could not finish his work in a stake over the weekend, he would stay into the next week until it was finished. Then on returning to Salt Lake City, he would write a lengthy letter to the new stake president, reviewing the things they had discussed and outlining various matters of policy, procedure, and doctrine to guide him in the future.

One stake president who received such a letter referred to it as his "bible," commenting that the letter helped him to adjust smoothly to his new duties and served as a reliable blueprint for future action. A General Authority who accompanied him on one of these weekends reported that Elder Kimball was out of bed as early as 2:30 in the morning, making lists and poring over his notes and the scriptures in preparation for the day ahead. And another one reported, on returning to Salt Lake City, that he felt as if he had been gone for six months.

Thus were the brethren at Church headquarters introduced to work "Gila Valley style." Nor was this vigorous work style a tendency Elder Kimball displayed only on weekends. It suited him every day of the week, whatever the place or the task. It was an obsession with Spencer W.

Kimball always to be busy doing something. And later, when he began to have serious physical problems, the characteristic became even more pronounced. It is reported that then, uncertain about the length of his life, he covenanted with the Lord that he would not waste a minute of any additional time the Lord would grant to him. This was life on the edge. He did not know when the Lord would say "enough" and call him home. In this circumstance, every minute was precious and must not be wasted or frittered away.

This is the attitude President Kimball brought with him into the prophetic office. It soon translated into one of the most productive and action-filled segments of Church history. Showing the qualities of a good sloganeer, he captured this attitude of diligence with the phrase "Lengthen your stride." Later, the imagery was enriched with "Quicken your pace" and "Extend your reach." And eventually all these were combined into the punchy statement, "Do it," which became the motto and the byword of President Spencer W. Kimball.

We need not search far for the genesis of the phenomenal work ethic that impelled Spencer along the path of his apostolic ministry. In an earthly sense, it began in the home of Andrew and Olive Kimball. There the impressionable boy saw the concept of work embodied in the industrious habits of his parents. And because of the love and respect he had for them, he sought to emulate their example. He wanted to be just like his father and mother. This led him at a very early age to develop an enthusiasm for work.

Chapter 4

Growing Up in Thatcher

T
he work demands in Thatcher quickly ended Spencer's babyhood. By the time he was five years old, he had another sister, Fannie, whose birth multiplied Olive's duties. Spencer was then able to assist around the house, performing menial tasks to help lift his mother's burden. Soon he graduated to outside chores, feeding the chickens and gathering their eggs while learning the ropes as an errand boy for Gordon and Delbert, who enjoyed their big-brother status. They took delight in ordering him to run errands or do other things for them. He cooperated willingly, up to a point, until he felt harassed or imposed upon. Then he would resist.

To make Spencer feel grown-up and part of the team, his father fitted up for him a miniature pitchfork with a short handle. Spencer enjoyed playing with it, moving hay from here to there, while imagining himself an equal to his brothers. But at harvest time, his short arms and sawed-off pitchfork prevented him from pitching hay onto the wagon, so he was relegated to the demeaning role of a "tromper." It was bad enough merely to tromp around atop the load, compacting the hay while suffering scratches from burrs and watching out for field mice. But what made the job more irksome was the constant kibitzing from the brothers to tromp the edges as well as the middle of the load, or their tendency, now and then, to fork the hay on top of him. One time Spencer heard the Primary bell ring while he tromped. Seeing an escape with honor, he decided to go to Primary as his father had instructed. Before his brothers could protest, he had slithered off the load and was running like lightning toward the chapel. They never caught him that day. How often this happened we don't know. But later in life, Gordon was heard to say that Spencer "was a great kid for Primary," suggesting it may not have been a one-time happening. The young brother also escaped occasionally from the control of the older ones by retreating to the cool quietness of the family parlor to practice the piano as his father had instructed him to do.

Despite occasional sibling rivalry and disputes about chores, there was love among the brothers and sisters. Gordon remembered with fondness how Spencer, as a little boy, was constantly on the move. A favorite activity was riding a stick horse attached to a makeshift wagon. Spencer would ride this along trails in the cornfield behind the house. Perhaps due to the streak of independence in his makeup, Gordon and Delbert gave the nickname "Spunk" to their little brother. Seemingly unaware of its meaning, Spencer detested the name and bridled whenever they used it.

As he grew and developed strength, Spencer acquired duties independent of his brothers. He daily herded the family cows from the field to the corral. Later he became a milker, milking as many as twenty cows night and morning. He regularly carried slop to the pigs, joking later that handling the heavy pails stunted his growth. He pumped water for the animals, cleaned and oiled harnesses, painted and repainted the house, and helped butcher the hogs. It was a constant job to keep the irrigation ditches clean, to take the water turn during the growing season, and to keep the fences mended. In this way his body became strong and tough.

But he was not only strong, he was quick and agile. And though he was not tall, these attributes, along with a competitive instinct and a desire to excel, combined to make him a good athlete. His favorite game was basketball. He played on the team of the Gila Academy, which once defeated the University of Arizona. That the game was played in the academy's cramped gymnasium, with the noisy, partisan crowd completely filling the building and almost spilling onto the playing floor, could not detract from the significance of the win. And to Spencer Kimball, who was the high scorer and the youngest and smallest member of the team, it was a shining moment whose brilliance never faded from memory. "I have special luck with my shots tonight," he wrote later in reminiscing about the game, "and the ball goes through the hoop again and again. . . . I am on the shoulders of the big fellows of the academy. They are parading me around the hall to my consternation and embarrassment. I like basketball. I would rather play the game than eat."

Spencer Kimball was a well-rounded student, excelling academically as well as in athletics. He also was popular with his classmates, serving as the student body president his last year at the academy and as class president all four years. His friendly, outgoing personality and his ability to play the piano and sing enhanced his social life. One observing Spencer Kimball in this setting could have predicted a life of achievement for him, a life in which he would stand out as a leader. But shielded from view were things in his interior world that carried hints of a kind of leadership the casual observer would not have detected.

Some learned of President Kimball's prophetic identity by spiritual means before he was formally ordained and set apart. Andrew Kimball, his father, knew. When Spencer was

about ten, his father said to a neighbor as they heard the boy
sing a hymn while milking a cow: "That boy, Spencer, is an
exceptional boy. He always tries to mind me, whatever I ask
him to do. I have dedicated him to be one of the mouth-
pieces of the Lord—the Lord willing. You will see him some
day as a great leader. I have dedicated him to the service of
God, and he will become a mighty man in the church."
(*Improvement Era*, Nov. 1943, p. 702.) Judging from President
Kimball's statements about his mother at the dedication of
the Mormon Bridge (referred to previously), she also knew.
And Elder Russell M. Nelson's statement made at President
Kimball's funeral shows that he knew as well. Said Elder
Nelson of the time he performed heart surgery on Elder
Kimball: "I shall never forget the feeling I had as his heart
resumed beating, leaping with power and vigor. At that
very moment, the Spirit made known to me that this special
patient would live to become the prophet of God on earth."
(*Church News*, Nov. 17, 1985, p. 14.) As we follow President
Kimball's progress through the various phases of his Church
experience, we shall see qualities of character and other
hints and suggestions that conform with the reality of his
foreordained role as a prophet.

So his son could easily remember the date, Andrew
arranged for Spencer's baptism on his eighth birthday,
March 28, 1903. It took place in a tub filled with water from
the well. The confirmation was performed in the chapel the
following Sunday. Afterward a technical question was
raised about the baptism because the officiator had not
"gone down" into the water as John the Baptist had done
when he baptized the Savior. To remove doubt, Spencer was
baptized again four years later, this time in the canal.

After his baptism, Spencer endeavored to live every
commandment and requirement of the Church exactly. It
almost seemed that at this young age, he was determined to
be perfect. Yet that aspiration did not create an attitude of
superiority or condescension. He was very much a boy,
rowdy, ruddy, and ready. He was full of good spirits, and he

appreciated humor. Indeed, in the early school years, he was known as a giggler, almost unable to suppress his amusement when something funny happened. And he was not averse to fighting when offended or provoked, although the instances when he did so were few.

There also was a quality in his character that caused the boy Spencer to respond aggressively to challenges. Once, Susa Young Gates, daughter of Brigham Young, asked an audience in Thatcher how many had read the entire Bible. Only a few responded. The speaker then challenged the others to do likewise. Her manner and her explanations about the book infused Spencer with the desire to read it through. He started that night. Then day after day, for many months, he plowed through it, puzzling over unfamiliar words and struggling with tedious parts while thrilling with the poetic beauty of Proverbs and Psalms. It was a significant milestone, being his first serious introduction to the scriptures. And perhaps the tenacity with which he pursued the goal taught him an important lesson about himself, and about human reactions to challenges, which was vital for him to understand.

Later, Spencer read about the prediction of a critic who theorized the Mormon church would go into decline during the third generation from its founding. His rationale was that the Church, being man-made, would begin to wither once the compelling enthusiasm generated by Joseph Smith and his associates had dissipated. He calculated this would occur during the third generation, by which time the masterminds of the movement would be dead or disabled. When Spencer realized he was part of that third generation, his whole being figuratively seemed to rise up in protest and denial. He then vowed to prove the critic wrong. The Church would not wither on *his* watch. That this was another watershed experience for Spencer W. Kimball was shown by the way he perpetuated it, retelling it periodically and reaffirming its significance to him.

To look at Spencer's early life superficially creates the

false impression of an orderly progression toward a fore-ordained goal without serious problems. In reality, those years were marked by a series of events that troubled him and brought sorrow into his life.

The chief traumas he faced as a boy were disease and death. Childhood diseases were rampant as Spencer grew up in Thatcher. Typhoid fever, dysentery, and a variety of respiratory ailments were especially prevalent. These diseases, once they gained a foothold, spread rapidly throughout the community. Lacking knowledge of how a disease was transmitted, and without skilled doctors and effective medicines, the people were powerless to prevent illness or to cure it. As a result, there were numerous deaths from communicable diseases, especially among the children. Few homes escaped death, and none escaped illness. Spencer contracted typhoid fever and spent seven weeks in bed convalescing. Because he survived, he called his a "light case." Other families were not so fortunate, some losing two or three children in an epidemic.

The Kimballs lost a child when five-year-old Fannie died. Her passing was even more poignant for Spencer because she died on his ninth birthday, March 28, 1904. He could remember his mother crying inconsolably as she carried the dying child in her arms. "I shall never forget the anguish and pain which she was suffering," he wrote years later. "We laid her away in the cemetery on the hill in the dry gravel all alone." The remorse of the family at Fannie's death came in the wake of another tragedy. Not long before, Olive's tenth child, Mary, had died shortly after birth. As Spencer put it, she "stayed only long enough to get her body and her name and hurried away."

These exposures to death did nothing to prepare Spencer for the death of his mother. In 1906, Olive was expecting her twelfth child. She became listless and unable to do her work. The loss of Fannie had made her remorseful, and a physical defect in Mary may have created apprehension about the child she was carrying. She went to Salt

Lake City, where she could rest, where she would be near her relatives, and where more skilled doctors and modern medical facilities would be available. It turned out to be a bad decision. The long trip on the train was wearing. Arriving in Salt Lake City, she was hardly able to get around. Separated from her family and worried about the children, she grieved for them. Meanwhile, her physical condition deteriorated, making it necessary that she be hospitalized. There, alone, physically weakened and mentally distraught, Olive Kimball was miserable, perhaps more so than at any time in her life. Learning of her condition, Andrew hurried north to be with his wife. His arrival seemed to lift Olive's spirits, and that in turn encouraged Andrew, who wired home to the children that their mother's condition was improved. This brought a response from Spencer, who sent a newsy letter. "We received the telegram and were very glad to know that Mama was out of danger," wrote Olive's eleven-year-old son. After noting how lonely everyone was without her, he gave a full report about the children: Clare and Ruth were doing the housework and had cleaned everything except the kitchen, Gordon had hauled all the corn fodder from Brother Branham's, and the other children were "very busy." He then reported that Sister Allen, who taught his religion class, had told the students they should be in bed by eight o'clock, "so we could have enough sleep." He then added, "I think I will close for it is . . . nearly half past eight." He ended the letter with "Good bye. Your loving son, Spencer Kimball."

His mother never read this touching letter. The next day she miscarried, and an infection caused her death. She was only forty-six, two years younger than her son would be when he began his apostolic ministry.

To her son, this petite, kindly woman was without fault, a true saint, whose endless charities endowed her, in Spencer's mind, with heavenly qualities. She had always been near in time of need to provide love, solace, or encouragement. And at age eleven, Spencer had assumed she

28

Olive Kimball's eight living children, 1906. Left to right: Alice, Ruth (standing), Rachel (sitting on Gordon's lap), Gordon, Helen, Delbert (standing), Clare, and Spencer.

would always be there. Thus the news of her death, the day after he had written the letter, "came as a thunderbolt." He and the other children learned the dreaded news from Bishop Moody, whom Andrew had contacted to ask that he tell them. There was really no way to cushion the blow. Summoned out of school, the children gathered at home, where the bishop told them their mother had passed away.

Spencer was inconsolable. Not wanting to exhibit his grief in the presence of others, he ran to the backyard, where he sobbed uncontrollably. "My eleven year old heart seemed to burst," he wrote later. Nor did the pain of loss ever entirely leave him. Fifty years later, as he lay in a New York hospital room, his mind reverted to that scene. The same feelings he had then returned with all their agony, and he felt like sobbing again.

Like a fighter hit by a staggering blow, Spencer lived in a

29

daze after learning about his mother's death. He was erratic in attending his church meetings and school. He performed his milking and other chores with leaden disinterest. Occasionally, without warning or apparent cause, he would burst into tears as something he saw or recalled reminded him of his beloved "Ma."

Andrew brought Olive's body back to Thatcher after it had been embalmed in Salt Lake City. Reminiscent of the Kimballs' first arrival eight years before, a large crowd had gathered to meet the Gila Monster as it hissed and clanged to a stop. But this time, all signs of gaiety and happiness were gone. A somber mood prevailed as Andrew greeted his children and as the casket was off-loaded and taken directly to the family home. There it was placed in the parlor, where it remained until the funeral. During that time, Spencer seemed to have made an accommodation with the reality of his mother's death. The lifeless body, cold to the touch, he recognized as merely the shell that had housed his mother's spirit, which had gone to another place. The sermons spoken at the funeral were comforting, as were the complimentary remarks about his mother made by the eight speakers. He always remembered one compliment paid to her at the funeral which capsulized her charitable nature: "When others spoke in condemnation, her lips were always silent."

But the passing of his mother did not end the parade of death in Spencer's family. Only eight months later, his baby sister, Rachel, died of diphtheria. She was only two and a half. At the time, Andrew had gone to Salt Lake City to be sealed to his second wife, Josephine Cluff. He hurried home as soon as he learned Rachel was in peril. Again, the body lay in the family parlor before burial. No formal funeral was held for fear of infecting others. A family service held in the home had to suffice. The little girl was buried in the family plot beside her mother and her sisters Fannie and Mary.

Thus in three years young Spencer had seen four members of his immediate family laid to rest. The last death occurred when he was only twelve years old. Each one was a wrenching experience, creating melancholy feelings of regret. Yet the deaths gave young Spencer a maturity beyond his years and an empathy for others who mourned the death of loved ones. These experiences also helped prepare him for the years ahead, when he would be called on to speak at numerous funerals for relatives and friends. So that the eulogies he delivered would not be marred by a show of emotion on his part, he steeled himself against it by concentrating strictly on the substance of what he was to say, walling out any thoughts about the deceased or the family that might upset his composure.

Two other experiences of Spencer's boyhood taught him the tenuous nature of life and imparted a sense of appreciation for good health. The first entailed a near-drowning during an outing at Cluff's Ranch. Andrew, a superb swimmer, took Spencer on his back for a swim. With his arms locked tightly around his father's neck, the little boy felt secure until Andrew ventured into the deep part of the pool. Then Spencer became fearful and pleaded with his father to take him back to shore. Andrew complied, and on reaching the shallow water, Spencer jumped off his father's back and started to walk toward shore while his father turned and swam again toward the deep part of the pool. Suddenly, Spencer stepped into a hole he had not seen and disappeared from view. Unprepared for a ducking, he sucked water into his lungs and, as he sank to the bottom, began to thrash around, trying to reach the surface. Someone on shore, seeing his predicament, began to scream. "Pa has heard their screams," Spencer wrote later, "and is after me. I am full of water and coughing, spitting, crying for a long time. I thought I was drowned." Spencer never forgot the terror of this experience. And because he thought he was near death in the pool, he looked on his rescue as providential.

While the other experience was not life-threatening, it was frightening. One morning at breakfast, Gordon and Delbert began laughing at their little brother, one of them saying, "Look at Spunk." What caused their amusement was an attack of what was later diagnosed as Bell's palsy, a paralytic ailment that affects the muscles of the face. Of a sudden, Spencer had lost control of the left side of his face, being unable to wink that eye or pucker his lips to whistle. The attack also caused a slight slurring of his speech and a general sagging of the left side of his face, creating a somewhat grotesque appearance. It was this that had caused the older boys to laugh. And later, Spencer himself gave an amusing twist to his condition, saying that his smile became "a one sided affair." At the time, however, it was not a laughing matter. No one knew then what had caused the paralysis or how long it would last. The town physician didn't know. He prescribed a liniment that had no effect. Priesthood blessings given to the boy produced no immediate results. Meanwhile Spencer had to endure the embarrassment of going to school and church meetings, not knowing whether the disfigurement was permanent. His Aunt Alice, conscious of that possibility, wrote from Salt Lake City, expressing the concern the entire family must have felt. "To have that beautiful face of his disfigured through life would certainly be a calamity," she wrote. What Aunt Alice and the others feared did not occur. Over a period of months, the paralysis gradually disappeared, leaving no ill effects. Nor did it ever return, except on two occasions almost seventy years later. On the morning of July 3, 1972, the day following the death of President Joseph Fielding Smith, President Kimball came to a special meeting of the Twelve, wearing a pair of dark glasses and holding a handkerchief to the left side of his face. The Bell's palsy had returned. A few months later, it returned once again. As with the first attack, the effects disappeared gradually over a period of time.

During the weeks of uncertainty over the young Spencer's facial paralysis, consideration was given to taking him to Salt Lake City for examination by specialists. That plan was abandoned, however, when he began to improve.

He later feigned disappointment over this, saying, "Unfortunately my face got well and I could not go to Utah." Whether or not his father intended it as a compensation for this disappointment, a year later, in 1905 when Spencer was ten, his father took him to the general conference in Salt Lake City. They traveled by way of Los Angeles and San Francisco. In Salt Lake City they were the guests of Aunt Alice, Andrew's twin sister, whose husband, Joseph F. Smith, was then the president of the Church. This relationship and Andrew Kimball's status as the president of the St. Joseph Stake opened many doors for young Spencer Kimball. And on the return trip, they saw many of the sights in San Francisco.

Two years after returning from the trip to Salt Lake City, Spencer was ordained a deacon. He was active in his deacons quorum, performing the traditional duties—passing the sacrament, collecting fast offerings, cutting wood for the widows and the aged, and running errands for the bishop. At that time, offerings were often paid "in kind," with flour or bottled fruits and vegetables, for instance. Because these were bulky to handle, Andrew allowed Spencer to take a horse and wagon to make his calls. And if the boy's companion failed to show up, Spencer went alone. He also filled positions of leadership in his quorum, serving first as a secretary and then as its president. Later, at age fourteen, he was called to teach a Sunday School class, and a year later, he became a stake chorister.

These and other activities, and Spencer's inherent helpfulness, began to make a favorable impact on those who knew him and to cause them to anticipate a distinguished future for him. Such was the case with Mrs. Crozier Kimball, a relative by marriage. She once hosted a large crowd for dinner during a conference at St. David. Spencer, who had accompanied his father there, voluntarily pitched in afterward to clean up and help with the dishes, the only guest to do so. Later, in games with his cousin, Eddie Kimball, and others, he was very solicitous and helpful toward them. And the day he left to return to Thatcher, he was careful to follow his father's instructions about packing his things and being ready when his father called for him to leave. Then, while waiting to be picked up, he visited companionably with the family. As he left, the mother put her arm around her son Eddie and said, "Spencer is certainly a wonderful young man. Someday, he will be one of the apostles."

Chapter 5

Gaining Maturity

It soon became apparent to Andrew after Olive's death
that his children, especially the younger ones, urgently
needed a mother. Because of the pressing need,
Andrew did not delay long in seeking another wife.
His attention soon focused on Josephine Cluff, a forty-
seven-year-old divorcée with two children, whose sealing to
her first husband had been cancelled and who, after the
divorce, had retaken her maiden name. Josie, as she was
called by her friends, had taught school in the Gila Valley
for many years before the Kimballs moved there. Well-
educated, intelligent, and self-confident, she had carved out
a rewarding life for herself and her children. Because of her
single status and professional career, Josie was an anomaly
in Thatcher, where practically all the women her age were
homemakers and the mothers of large families. Her distinctive status was enhanced by her flair for fashion, her wide-
ranging interests, and by the articulate and positive way in
which she expressed her views. It would be fair to say that
Josie probably intimidated most of the women in the valley.

And because such an unusual and attractive woman had remained unmarried for so many years after the divorce, it is probably also fair to say she frightened away many would-be suitors. There simply was not an unmarried man in the community with the stature and self-confidence that would have encouraged him to seek Josie's hand—that is, until Andrew Kimball became available.

But behind Josie's facade of independent womanhood lay a character of rectitude who was dedicated to the Church, as shown by her acceptance of a call to serve a mission when she was in her mid-forties. Indeed, she was released from her mission in 1906, not long before Olive passed away. At the time of Olive's death, Josie was serving as a member of the St. Joseph stake YWMIA board.

There are hints that as Olive lay near death, she and Andrew discussed his needs and the needs of the children once she was gone. It is reported that she then referred to Josie, recommending her as one who could help fill those needs.

Not long after the funeral, Andrew undertook the sensitive process of courtship. Having determined through prayer that Josie was the one, and having obtained her consent, he went individually to the children old enough to understand and explained the circumstances and sought their approval. All gave it without qualification. The couple was sealed in the Salt Lake Temple in June 1907.

Life for the Kimball children was far different with Aunt Josie than it had been with their mother. With her large family, Olive had developed a comparatively relaxed style of housekeeping, never having enough time or energy to do everything that had to be done in the perfect way she may have liked to do it. She had made an accommodation with that reality and was content that her house was neat and clean, though not maintained with spic-and-span polish. This had created a relaxed, informal atmosphere in the home; the children felt at ease, without concern about upsetting the decor.

The conditions in the home were different when Josie came into the family. Following Rachel's death, there were only four children at home. The youngest, Helen, was six and in school. This left Josie with a freedom of movement Olive had never dreamed of having. It also enabled her to devote more time to the arrangement and decoration of the home, to the planning and serving of meals, and to the supervision of the children in their studies and recreational activities. To all this, Josie brought a lifetime of training and discipline as a schoolteacher. The different lifestyle she brought to the Kimball home was apparent. And it obviously required a major adjustment in the thinking and deportment of Spencer and his sisters. These adjustments undoubtedly created some moments of tension and discontent. But a peaceful solution was reached, and Josie settled into her substitute role in the family, occupying a place of love and respect. "She was a wonderful woman," wrote a mature Spencer Kimball of his Aunt Josie, "a wonderful mother, and she took good care of us. [She was] a good Latter-day Saint."

During the first three years Josie served as wife and mother in the Kimball home, Spencer was in grade school. Here he did well academically, undoubtedly aided by Josie's tutoring at home. He also was active in sports and well adjusted socially. When Spencer graduated from grammar school in 1910 at age 15, there was no doubt he would go on to the Gila Academy. Not all students did this, however, as many dropped out at this point, there then being no law mandating school attendance beyond the eighth grade. Those who dropped out went to work; many were unable to attend due to lack of means. But there was no alternative for Spencer, even had he not wanted to go. His father was chairman of the school board, and both he and Josie were convinced the children should be well educated.

However, no compulsion was necessary to induce Spencer to attend the academy. He had a natural aptitude for study, as was shown by his record of nearly all A's throughout his four years there, except for one B. He was eager to enroll, although admittedly he had some apprehensions. Because the academy was housed in an imposing two-story building, it had an intimidating aspect. The diverse student body, drawn from throughout the valley, the expanded curriculum, and the more distinguished faculty also made him uneasy. In Spencer's own words, the academy was a "bigger pond." All such feelings left the second week after classes commenced, when he was elected freshman class president. Thereafter, he was at the center of most student activities at the school.

During this period, Spencer's social graces matured and his social activities multiplied. The lack of professional entertainments required the students to be creative in planning recreations. There was an almost interminable series of picnics, hayrides, dances, parties, and swim outings. In season there were watermelon busts and corn roasts. For thrills, the lumber flume at the base of Mount Graham was the place to go. By sitting in the steep water trough designed to slide logs down from the mountain, one could replicate the thrill of a giant slide at the midway, complete with bracingly cold water and occasional slivers. What Spencer enjoyed most were parties that turned into songfests with him at the piano, singing at the top of his voice. He very soon became known as the life of a party, with his music, his singing, and his laughter—a laugh one classmate recalled as the most musical laugh she had ever heard.

Spencer's interest in sports has already been noted. In order of personal preference, sports seem to have stood above either academic or social activities. He loved sports. And while he showed special skill at basketball, he was not a one-sport athlete. He also enjoyed baseball and tennis. And in a pinch, he could be counted on to participate in track events. His most noted venture into track occurred during his sophomore year. The Thatcher athletes had fared badly in a meet involving several schools, having been defeated in baseball and basketball, and they were behind

The Gila Academy basketball team, with Spencer standing at right.

in track. In an emergency, the coach called on Spencer to run the mile. He later told how, as he strained to reach the finish line, all he could see "was a large crowd of people with waving arms and a melee of noise and shouting." Then, as he "fell across the line," a teammate congratulated him on placing third and becoming a bronze medalist. "Of course," Spencer confessed, "I knew that there were only three of us running."

It should not be inferred that young Spencer Kimball was always a model student. He was not free from youthful pranks. Once, for instance, he and some friends concocted a batch of hydrogen sulfide, commonly called rotten egg gas, in a chemistry class. The stench made it necessary to dismiss classes. This "escapade," as he called it, ruined his straight-A record. The chemistry professor gave him a B. Spencer never seemed quite repentant about the prank nor concerned about the smirch on his academic record. Indeed, he reported it later with a sense of enjoyment.

Spencer (seated, center) and his co-workers at dairy in Globe, Arizona, 1914.

On another occasion, Spencer and his friends ran afoul of the principal. It happened on April Fools' Day, 1914, when he was a senior. The day before, the principal lectured the students about April Fool pranks. He said none would be tolerated that year and that classes would be held as usual. Spencer and his friends had different ideas. They conferred immediately afterward and decided to make it a self-proclaimed holiday. The next morning, thirty-two of them headed for the lumber flume on hayracks, with lunches, singing and joking as they went. There they spent the day having fun. Learning what had happened, the principal called an assembly and, pending a hearing before the faculty, expelled the truants, canceled a sports trip to Tucson, and said the seniors who had sluffed would not graduate on time. Then he declared a holiday for the rest of the student body, instructing them to stay away from the lumber flume.

The next morning, Spencer and his friends were barred from class. Still defiant, they planned another escapade, one they apparently thought would strike a mighty and lasting blow for liberty. They gathered at the old livery stable and, having rustled up a camera, had their picture taken in front of a large Bull Durham tobacco sign. It would be difficult to conceive of a more pointed way in which to let the principal know what the rebels thought of his decision. That done, the boys were left to ponder their next move. By now, a sense of reality seems to have seeped into their consciousness as they realized that they had to deal not only with the principal and the faculty but with their parents too. The boys were tilted toward compromise when one of the teachers, John Nash, urged Spencer to apologize. That afternoon, he and his friends did just that. As an adult, Brother Kimball looked back on this incident with a sense of shame. Nevertheless, this feeling did not prevent him, in later years, from sharing the experience with members of his family.

Spencer planned to attend the University of Arizona after graduation. Although he was nineteen years old, he had no immediate plans to fill a mission. At the time, it was not Church policy to urge all young men to fill missions as it was later during the time President Kimball led the Church. Being aware of his son's plans and, perhaps, being a little troubled by Spencer's attitude in leading the April Fools' Day rebellion, Andrew Kimball made an unexpected announcement at the graduation, radically altering his son's plans.

As the president of his class and a good scholar, Spencer Kimball was one of the graduation speakers. He also sang in a quartet and rendered a baritone solo. Everything went according to plan until Andrew Kimball, speaking as the chairman of the school board, announced that Spencer would not attend school the next year because he would be in the mission field. "This took me by surprise," Spencer wrote, "for I had been planning to go to college." A classmate, Lela Lee, said, "I thought Spencer was going to pass out."

Despite the surprise, Spencer unquestioningly accepted

Spencer, age 19, at the time of his graduation from high school in 1914.

his father's decision. He had always planned to fill a mission. The question was not whether, but when. The desire probably grew from the experiences of his father and grandfather and his innate feelings.

With his course charted, money became a major issue. So, four days after graduation, Spencer left for Globe, Arizona, eighty miles northwest of Thatcher, where he got a job working at a dairy. He had done similar work there during the two previous summers. His salary was $62.50 a month, plus board and room. He earned it. Learning that he arose regularly at 8:00 A.M. conveys a false impression about the job. This began an eighteen-hour day, with short breaks for meals and a three-hour period of free time in the middle of the afternoon. The work ended at 2:00 A.M. It included milking fifteen to twenty cows twice during each shift, plus the work of feeding the cows and the cleanup connected with the milking. The routine was broken only on Sundays, when arrangements were made to attend church services.

One of the milking crew, George Lee, was a returned missionary with whom Spencer formed a close friendship. After Spencer received his mission call from President Joseph F. Smith to serve in the Swiss German Mission, he and George Lee spent many hours discussing missionary work and the scriptures, and they often prayed together. During the summer, Spencer was ordained a priest by his father when he visited Globe; and later he was ordained an elder by S. J. Sims. The bishop of the Globe ward twice invited him to speak in sacrament meeting, all of which helped prepare him for the mission field.

Mr. Walliman, who owned the dairy and who obviously had taken a special liking to Spencer, hosted a farewell party for him. The entire Walliman family and all "the dairy boys" were present to give him a royal send-off. He was touched by the gift of an expensive gold watch as a going-away present. "Oh how grateful I was to think my friends cared so much for me to show their kindness and respect by the splendid social and valuable present." The ward also honored him at a party where he sang twice and where the guests donated over twenty dollars for his mission, which, in the meantime, had been changed to the Central States Mission because of the war.

Back in Thatcher, there were other parties in his honor and a hayrack outing to the Hot Springs area with his friends. Then on September 30, 1914, young Spencer Kimball boarded the train at Thatcher, destined for Salt Lake City, where he would be set apart before going to his mission field. "Tears dimmed my eyes," he wrote nostalgically, "as the train rolled out of Thatcher and my friends and sisters [disappeared] from sight."

Chapter 6

The Missionary

The trip was lonely, although brightened by brief visits with Gordon, Ruth, and Clare during stops in Tucson, Phoenix, and Los Angeles. On October 5, Spencer arrived in Salt Lake City, where he would remain for sixteen busy days. He attended the last sessions of general conference with his father, who had preceded him to Salt Lake City. He stayed successively with Aunt Alice, Uncle George, Aunt Fannie, and Aunt Millie, and he visited with President Joseph F. Smith, later attending a play in the Salt Lake Theatre as a guest of the prophet and Aunt Alice and sharing the president's box with them. He attended the Utah state fair, did some final shopping—buying, among other things, a derby hat—and was the guest of honor at a party hosted by Aunt Fannie. He received his endowment in the Salt Lake Temple, where he was impressed by the sacredness of the ordinance. He had dinner with Elder James E. Talmage of the Twelve, whose son Paul he had met in Miami. He received a doctor's examination and was "pronounced sound as a dollar," whereupon he told the doctor

44

Elder Kimball as a full-time missionary, Central States Mission, 1914–16.

he kept the Word of Wisdom *in full.* He was ordained a seventy by Uncle J. Golden Kimball and was set apart for his mission by Elder Seymour B. Young, who promised "that all dread and fear should leave me and that my tongue should be loosed like the pen of a ready writer."

Amidst the customary bustle of the Salt Lake train depot, Elder Kimball left for his mission field at 6:00 P.M. on October 21, 1914. Traveling by chair car to Ogden on the spur line, he was able to get a berth on the Union Pacific from there to Cheyenne, Wyoming. After a three-hour layover in Cheyenne, he caught a train to Denver, Colorado, where he made a good connection for the last leg of his journey to Kansas City. "After a long, lonesome journey," wrote he, "I got in Kansas City at 4:30 and easily found my way to Independence where I was treated well by President Bennion and others at the mission home." Elder Kimball's mission president, Samuel O. Bennion, was called as a member of the First Council of Seventy nineteen years after this meeting and lived long enough to see Spencer W. Kimball called as a member of the Quorum of the Twelve.

Elder Kimball remained in Independence for a month on special assignment to help prepare a new chapel for dedication. He and other missionaries were involved in laying sod, pouring a cement sidewalk, installing benches, scraping and washing windows, and performing other chores around the building. The mission president was anxious that everything about the chapel be shipshape because President Joseph F. Smith and a party from Salt Lake City were scheduled to attend the dedication in late November.

In addition to this manual labor, Elder Kimball also did regular missionary work with a fellow Arizonan, J. Smith Gibbons from St. Johns, as their schedule allowed. Spencer delivered his first talk as a missionary two days after arriving in the field when, at the home of the Turners, where the elders were staying temporarily, he spoke briefly. "My speech was very short," he wrote. "I bore my testimony." A few days later, they tried their hand at tracting, with very minimal success: "The first door I knocked at was slammed in my face." Then, in an apparent attempt to put the very best possible face on what must have been a discouraging experience, he added, "I got along fairly well."

A few days before the dedication, missionaries gathered in Independence from all over the mission. It was a rare opportunity for most of them to meet a prophet in person. "Over a hundred and fifty elders and lady missionaries went out tracting in Independence" on November 20. Independence was the headquarters of the Reorganized Church of Jesus Christ of Latter Day Saints. Its members were well acquainted with Mormon missionaries, and most of them had developed an automatic negative response to their message. Notwithstanding, President Bennion wanted to reach out to them at this time because of the planned visit of President Joseph F. Smith, who was the first cousin of

Joseph Smith III, then president of the Reorganized Church. Before leaving Independence, President Joseph F. Smith paid a visit to President Joseph Smith III, who was very weak and who passed away the following month. Their meeting was cordial and pleasant.

Following the dedication, Elder Kimball was called to serve in the Missouri East Conference, with headquarters in St. Louis. His first conference assignment was to labor without purse or scrip—that is, without any means of financial support except the charity of local hosts—in the Missouri Ozarks south of Jefferson City, the state capital located in the center of the state. He and his companion traveled to Jefferson City by train on November 25 and, arriving there with many hours of light remaining, decided to walk into the country, carrying their grips and seeking hospitality as they went. It was a new and humbling experience for Elder Kimball. In the late afternoon, they began to ask for a place to stay and something to eat. They asked and were turned away twelve times. Finally, long after dark, a farmer grudgingly provided them with a bed but no food. The following day, which was Thanksgiving, saw improvement. They tracted all day, and toward evening they found a place to stay in a friendly atmosphere, where they shared a Thanksgiving dinner with their hosts.

During the next six weeks they walked through the surrounding country, tracting and holding cottage meetings and street meetings while depending on the hospitality of the people for food and shelter. They became acquainted with the many small villages in the area and even better acquainted with the numerous farms in between, farms whose owners were merely eking out an existence. Most farmhouses were unsubstantial dwellings, poorly furnished and lacking modern conveniences. Many of them were infested with insects and rodents. Some of the farmers were friendly, others were cold and indifferent, and a few were belligerent. "I wouldn't keep anybody free," they were told at one farm, "even if they would all turn to apostles." Others were suspicious and distant, believing the Mormons still practiced polygamy and that the purpose of the missionaries was to find plural wives.

The cool reception was more than matched by the weather. The high humidity, heavy precipitation, cold temperatures, and biting winds of Missouri posed a major challenge for the missionary from Arizona. "We walked fifteen miles through miry, sticky roads without a bite to eat from early morning until late at night" was not an unusual entry in Elder Kimball's journal. And when the wind was up and the temperature down, the cold seemed to sink into their very bones. "Oh it is cold," Spencer complained as a heavy snowfall began, "minus 6 degrees Fahrenheit with sharp, cold wind."

Conditions improved when, near Sullivan, the missionaries found a hospitable family named Strausser with whom they spent Christmas. They bought a few trinkets in town and, on Christmas morning, exchanged gifts, receiving from their hosts handkerchiefs, garters, armbands, and straps for their grips. Later in the day, they enjoyed a dinner of "turkey, duck and all other dainties," followed by games, including sledding in the snow. "What a glorious Christmas. A most happy one. No thought of home, hardly."

Elder Kimball was transferred to the conference headquarters in St. Louis the first week in January 1915. There he lived in the conference house with eleven other missionaries. They shared expenses and took turns cleaning the home, shopping, and cooking. They also did the custodial work at the hall where the branch held its meetings. This was an enjoyable change from the hard country work. There was a spirit of congeniality among the elders, who were given special consideration by the members of the branch. The elders also accepted teaching assignments in the branch; not long after his arrival, Elder Kimball was sustained as the teacher in the intermediate class. He also was able to use his musical skills to good advantage, singing in a quartet and playing accompaniment.

*Elder Spencer W.
Kimball in the
mission field, 1915.*

The main missionary activities were tracting and holding follow-up meetings with those who showed an interest.
The missionaries distributed small tracts free of charge, but
where appropriate, they tried to sell copies of the larger
tracts or of the Book of Mormon. Elder Kimball approached
this work with his customary diligence. "Tracted alone it
being too cold for my companion." The next day, when it
was still too cold for his companion, Elder Kimball sold nine
books, the most ever. "It was so cold I would walk around
the block to get warmer." And two days later, when his

49

companion was still indisposed, he reported, "It began to snow very hard. But, I worked on until I had given away all my tracts."

But there was a negative side to his tracting experiences—times when he was "very discouraged" or when there were "no results in tracting." Once, he and his companion met a belligerent old man, whom Elder Kimball called "an old Mormon hater," who cursed the missionaries "shamefully."

After two months in St. Louis, Spencer was transferred to Hannibal to labor with Elder Henderson. He was "very blue" to leave the companions he had "learned to love." Because of Hannibal's status as the home of Samuel L. Clemens, or Mark Twain, who wrote *Tom Sawyer* and *Huckleberry Finn*, it is not surprising that soon after arriving in Hannibal, the missionaries visited the old Clemens home.

At the time, however, something other than Mark Twain dominated their thinking. They were out of money. The cost of transportation and getting settled had exhausted their funds before the monthly allowance from home arrived. It seemed it would be necessary to sell some of their books and pamphlets to help tide them over. Then, unaccountably, Elder Kimball received a letter, forwarded from St. Louis, from his old friend Clell Haynie, one of the dairy boys in Globe, which contained two one-dollar bills. In that economy, it was enough to buy food for a while. "The Lord will provide," Elder Kimball wrote appreciatively.

Elder Kimball soon met a relative in Hannibal named Rose Kimball Bradshaw, a niece of Heber C. Kimball. A close friendship developed with this relative, whom Elder Kimball later called Aunt Rose. That friendship grew when the elders rented a room in the Bradshaw home and began to teach the gospel to Aunt Rose and her adopted daughter. This culminated in their baptism shortly before Elder Kimball was transferred. Meanwhile, the elders performed five other baptisms in Hannibal.

Elder Kimball suffered serious infections in his ears and

throat while he worked in Hannibal. They persisted for several weeks and cleared up only after he consulted a specialist at the insistence of his father. It also was in Hannibal that he suffered the first reported attack of boils. These would bother him intermittently for years.

Before he was transferred from Hannibal, Spencer and his companion were assigned to conduct a funeral service for a prominent member in northeastern Missouri. Because they were only across the river and upstream a few miles from Nauvoo, Illinois, they visited there before returning to Hannibal. Here Spencer saw the large two-story red brick home that had been built by his grandfather, Heber C. Kimball. He also inspected other homes belonging to early Church leaders: Joseph Smith's Mansion House and the home of Brigham Young nearby, adjacent to which stood the home of Bishop Vinson Knight, whose widow, Martha McBride Knight, was married to Heber C. Kimball after Bishop Knight died. Most of these and other homes the elders inspected were badly deteriorated and hardly portrayed the true appearance of the city when the Latter-day Saints occupied it.

A few days after returning from Nauvoo, Elder Kimball and his companion went to St. Louis for a district conference. While there, Spencer was assigned to remain in St. Louis to work out of the conference house again. By then spring had come, which opened up the opportunity to hold many more street meetings. A favorite place for them was at the corner of Twentieth and Franklin. While some questioned the value of these meetings, Elder Kimball never did. They gave him a sense of exhilaration unmatched by any other kind of proselyting. They also provided memorable moments such as the time when, at the end of a meeting, with not a soul in sight except the missionaries, the elder conducting solemnly announced, "If you'll all give your attention, we'll dismiss," or when Elder Kimball ended his talk in midsentence when the only people he could see were his three companions.

Tracting and follow-up cottage meetings continued to be the staple of Elder Kimball's missionary work. In time he developed skillful door approaches. Once, for instance, seeing a new Kimball piano through an open door, he asked if the family would like to hear their Kimball piano played by a Kimball and was invited in immediately. At another home he "tamed" a person who was belligerent and was finally invited in, where he "sang and played for them." Such tact and persistence created many friendships and produced some converts. So, within four months after returning to St. Louis, he baptized, or was instrumental in baptizing, five additional converts, this in an area where, at the time, baptisms were not plentiful. Other baptisms followed.

Elder Kimball never attached special significance to his role in baptizing people. Later in life when questioned about it, he tended to minimize it. Yet he was intensely interested in the conversion process, valued his role in it, and later as an apostle and then as president of the Church gave strong emphasis to it.

Shortly before Christmas 1915, Elder Kimball and a companion, following a tour in the country, returned to St. Louis to attend a missionary conference directed by President Bennion. On the last day of the meetings, the conference president was honorably released and Elder Kimball, to his surprise, was "appointed to remain in the city and take charge until a new president is appointed." Was this temporary appointment the means President Bennion used to test the mettle of young Spencer Kimball before he entrusted the direction of the conference to him on a permanent basis? After all, he was only twenty years old, still younger than most of the other thirty-five missionaries in the conference. And while Elder Kimball had been in the field for fourteen months and had proven himself an effective proselyter and a diligent worker, there still would have been the maturity factor to consider in making a permanent appointment. For whatever reason, Elder Kimball was placed in charge of the conference on only a temporary basis, which put him in an awkward position, especially in relation to the elders who lived with him in the conference house, all of whom were older than he and some of whom outranked him in the length of their service. The two and a half weeks that followed may have been among the most challenging of Elder Kimball's mission.

"Not much like Christmas," he reported on the twenty-fifth, although later in the day he and several elders enjoyed a turkey dinner at the home of a member family. Then commenced ten days of intensive work, interspersed with numerous administrations to the sick among both the members and the missionaries. The work consisted entirely of tracting, it being too cold to hold street meetings. Before the end of the year, Elder Kimball spent three days of hard tracting in "bitterly cold" weather. On the thirty-first it was so cold that he "shook and ached." His discomfort was aggravated by a painful foot on which minor surgery had been performed a few months earlier to remove an ingrown toenail. Meanwhile, he "got the elders out early to tract," joining with them while scurrying about with a companion to take care of the sick. Two of these were lady missionaries, Sister Titlow and Sister Mackay. When her condition worsened, it was decided to hospitalize Sister Mackay. Elder Kimball informed President Bennion, who promptly came to St. Louis. The two of them administered to her in the hospital on January 7. The next day, President Bennion called Elder Kimball as the permanent conference president.

While it was not totally unexpected, the call came as a shock to the young elder from Thatcher. "I feel terribly weak, small, young and inexperienced," he wrote. "But having been called by proper authority, I cannot but accept and do the best I can. Heaven help me."

As the conference president, it was his responsibility to deploy the missionaries as he saw fit; to train and motivate them; to receive, compile, and analyze their reports; and to help them in times of illness and build them up in times of discouragement. Given the difference in the ages of the missionaries, this was a heavy responsibility to give to a young man not yet twenty-one. But these were only part of his duties. As the conference president, he also presided over all the officers and members who resided in the area and therefore had the responsibility to train others, to motivate them, and to direct their activities as well.

At the outset, another spate of illnesses and the normal pressures of adjusting to his new duties created a sense of crisis: "At 3:00 A.M. I came home, slept for a couple of hours, cooked breakfast and went to class, then tracting. It was so terribly cold that I went revisiting. Visited Mrs. Loughlin in the North Baptist Sanitarium and Sister Mackay at the St. Johns Hospital, then to MIA. I was worn out." Two days later he worked "about 43 hours without being in bed." In time things settled down into a manageable routine.

A major leadership challenge for Elder Kimball was to correct the missionaries when it was needful yet avoid being overbearing. He was not averse to good-natured fun during times of recreation; at a summer outing at Pea Ridge, a few miles southwest of St. Louis, he joined enthusiastically in games and harmless antics with the missionaries, which included a water fight and taking a series of comic pictures. But he drew the line when a spirit of levity crept into the daily work. "In priesthood meeting," he reported, "I made as strong a play as possible for the elders to refrain from light mindedness and so much frivolity which I had noticed of late." At other times he was more direct with the elders, as when he "started them up as they have been shirking." But he was equally hard on himself when he detected a letdown on his part. "I have come to the conclusion," he wrote a few months before his release, "that the conference is running down. I am losing enthusiasm. I also realize that I have not many months in the field now and must get the work better in hand or it surely will not be much honor to me." He did not delay long in taking remedial steps: "I started the elders evening tracting. Some of them almost balked; but they went out and had some success."

Elder Spencer W. Kimball (left) and a missionary companion.

He was buoyed up by conference meetings in June attended by the mission president and Elder James E. Talmage of the Twelve. The apostle made a profound impression on Elder Kimball. "Dr. Talmage recognized me and gave me a hearty handshake and said his son Paul sent best wishes to me. Several times during the day he talked with me as man to man, now giving suggestions, now complimenting me on the work, etc., which confidence I truly appreciated, for in my estimation, Dr. Talmage is one of the greatest of men for with all his great intellect, his knowledge, etc., he yet is as humble as can be."

During the last few months of his mission, Elder Kimball was heavily involved in the acquisition and renovation of a church building located on Maple and Clarendon streets. The members of the Church in St. Louis met in their "new" building for the first time on September 4. Elder Kimball was pleased that he conducted the first meeting and preached the first gospel sermon there that day.

The renovated chapel was dedicated on November 26, 1916, by Elder James E. Talmage. On the same day President Bennion advised Elder Kimball to come to Independence in two weeks to be released prior to his return home. "I was overjoyed," he wrote. But it was not a joyous thing to sever ties with missionaries and members whom he had come to love. "With tear filled eyes," he wrote two days after the dedication, "I bade good bye to most of the elders who were going to the country." Then, during the next week and a half, he bid farewell to the missionaries who had remained in St. Louis and to the members. This accomplished, he left for Kansas City, from where he found his way to the mission home in Independence.

He participated in a missionary conference in Independence over the weekend of December 10 and 11, then had a long interview with his mission president. "President Bennion said many good things to me. Putting his arm around me, he said I had done remarkably well, [he] was proud of me and disliked to lose me. I felt like my tears, prayers etc. had not all been in vain."

Encouraged by these words of commendation, Elder Kimball boarded the train on December 12, 1916, "and with Elder Dalton started homeward." Arriving in Salt Lake City two days later, he began a stay of nine days, during which he was honored and feted by his many relatives.

The most important event that occurred while Spencer was in Salt Lake City was an interview with the First Presidency—Joseph F. Smith, Anthon H. Lund, and Charles W. Penrose—during which he reported his mission. At the time, the offices of the First Presidency were housed in the annex between the Beehive House and the Lion House on East South Temple. The new Church Administration

Building, immediately west of the Lion House, had been completed except for some final cleanup. It would be occupied by President Joseph F. Smith and his counselors and the other General Authorities four months later.

It is easy to imagine the trepidation of twenty-one-year-old Spencer W. Kimball as he faced these three distinguished-looking men, whose average age was seventy-eight and whose combined apostolic service totaled eighty-nine years. They were kind and friendly, however, and sought to put the young elder at ease. As coherently as he could, Elder Kimball described his service and responded to questions asked by the Brethren. He also outlined his plans for the future and then, after being admonished "to keep up my missionary work," was excused.

Spencer boarded the train in Salt Lake City on December 23, 1916, bound for home via California. It actually was the first time he had had any significant time alone since he left Missouri. Any plans for the future he may have reflected on then or previously discussed with the First Presidency were nebulous at best. His desire to continue his education was shrouded with uncertainty. The Allied blockade of German ports had prompted retaliatory German submarine attacks on Allied shipping, which later extended to all shipping within a "war zone" designated by Germany in 1915. While Germany later softened this stand through diplomatic initiatives, there were signs toward the end of 1916 that it would harden again, which would bring the United States and Germany into direct conflict, making war inevitable. (Indeed, this became a reality on January 31, 1917, when Germany announced it would attack any shipping within the war zone. Three days later, the United States severed diplomatic relations with Germany and on April 6 of that year declared war on her.) Because Spencer was a prime candidate for military service, his plans, at the moment, could not have extended rationally beyond renewing his acquaintances at home and, if possible, picking up the threads of his pre-mission plans of enrolling in the University of Arizona at Tucson.

Because of an unexpected train delay, Spencer did not arrive in Los Angeles until Christmas Eve. He spent Christmas Day with his sister Clare and her family, enjoying, by contrast with frigid Missouri, "the roses which were in bloom, the green grass, the oranges on the trees and the sun shining brightly." During the following two days, the returned missionary had a nice visit with the family, did a little sightseeing, and tested the surf at Venice Beach. He caught the Sunset Limited on the twenty-eighth, laid over in Tucson to visit his brother Gordon and his family, and arrived home at 5:00 P.M., December 31, 1916. A week later he gave his homecoming report, in which he talked about the Resurrection.

Chapter 7

College, Courtship, and Marriage

I t was decided Spencer would enroll at the University of Arizona. Armed with a transcript of his record at the Academy, he traveled to Tucson on Saturday, January 27, where he was met by Gordon and his wife, Clara, in whose home he had been invited to stay to reduce expenses. Their home was in Binghampton, a suburb of Tucson, where many Mormon refugees had settled following their expulsion from Mexico a few years before. He spoke in their sacrament meeting the next day.

Assisted by his friend Ralph Bilby, who would later become a prominent Arizona attorney, Spencer registered for classes the following day. He signed up for English, German, American history, English history, economics, and military training. Some of the professors tried to play a little game of academic intimidation. "The Profs made such a big bluff that I was almost frightened to death," he wrote. "I was very much discouraged." His reaction to the challenge was typical. He dug in and studied with furious intensity. "Working hard in school, night and day," he wrote in mid-February. And the following week he added this note of optimism: "I feel quite encouraged in school." And the week after that, in an apparent attempt to increase his academic momentum, he "stayed home from [Sunday] meetings to study." This began a practice that continued for several weeks. It paid off academically, earning him high grades in all classes and accolades from his professors. His history professor, for instance, gave him the best grade in the class for his theme on the Revolution of 1688 and later used it as a standard in grading other papers.

At first Spencer seemed not to mind missing his church meetings in order to study. After several weeks, however, introspection convinced him it was wrong to miss church. Afterward he discontinued studying on the Sabbath and instead spent the day in worship, as he had been taught and as he had taught others.

After the United States severed diplomatic relations with Germany on February 3, 1917, there was high expectancy on the university campus that war was imminent. Spencer's military training then took on new meaning. On April 1, he participated in an American Day parade, marching with a crowd he estimated at seven thousand. Feelings against Germany ran high, as did patriotism for the cause of America. Five days later, the United States was at war. "Today war was declared against Germany," he wrote on that day. "It is probable that I shall soon be forcibly enlisted in the army and killing my fellow beings. Horrors!" While this prediction never became a reality, the prospect of its coming true would agitate Spencer's feelings for months.

Since many of this year's graduates who had enlisted were scheduled to leave in early May for the Presidio near San Francisco, the baccalaureate services were held on April 29, a month early. The speaker was the silver-tongued pacifist William Jennings Bryan, whom Spencer had heard in St. Louis the year before.

Afterwards, there were courses to complete and examinations to take before the summer recess. Spencer buried himself in his books during the "dead week" preceding the exams. These commenced May 28 with a German exam, which included submitting a sixteen-hundred-word composition that Spencer stayed up until 2:30 A.M. to complete. Possibly his interest in German was keyed by the call he had first received to serve in the Swiss-German mission. Later, he would occasionally use a German word or phrase in communications with his wife, whose father was of German descent. Spencer's last examination was taken on June 1. After collecting his things and saying good-bye, he returned to Thatcher three days later.

The semester Spencer spent at the University of Arizona, though short, was an important phase of his development. Except for a few days spent at Brigham Young University the following autumn, it was the only university training he would receive. The content of the courses he studied probably was the least important thing he learned. Of greater importance were the knowledge that he could excel in higher academic studies, the increased discipline and improved study methods he developed in mastering his courses, the lesson of ordering his priorities by placing his religion ahead of his university training, and the skill gained in managing his slender resources.

By the time he returned to Thatcher, Spencer had decided not to enlist but to register for the draft and await his call-up. He registered on June 5. After a few days at home, during which he worked around the house and the farm, he decided to go to Los Angeles to seek employment for the summer. He boarded the Gila Monster on June 13 with his sixteen-year-old sister, Helen. There was the usual stop in Bowie to transfer to the Sunset Limited and a brief stop in Tucson to say hello to Gordon and Clara before arriving in Los Angeles the next day. There they were met by Clare and her husband, Hyrum, who took them home. Spencer was amazed that on the way, Hyrum bought a crate of sixteen dozen oranges for only fifty cents.

With good references, Spencer had little trouble finding

work at the Southern Pacific freight depot unloading freight cars. It paid only twenty-two cents an hour, but he felt fortunate to have any kind of work. Meanwhile, he and Helen went to Redondo Beach with Clare and Hyrum for a swim in the surf, apparently Helen's first. And on July 4, they visited Venice Beach, where, on this holiday, Spencer estimated there were 175,000 people. "We had a time elbowing our way through thousands on every side."

The physical toughness Spencer had developed before his mission had been partially lost through inactivity. He was not quite prepared, therefore, for the rigors of his new job. It took a while to adjust to handling the heavy cargo. "My eleven hours of work nearly exhausted me," he wrote a few days after starting on the job. "But I could tell I was getting hardened." The strenuous work did not trouble Spencer, as he had done hard work for many years. He was, however, troubled by the foul language and the vulgar stories of his co-workers. When he discovered some of their stories occasionally coming to his mind involuntarily, he resigned. When the supervisor, who was impressed by his hard work, learned why Spencer had quit, he offered him a job checking the cargo in boxcars. Since this removed him from the source of his annoyance, he accepted.

However, this job was short-lived too. Less than two weeks after starting it, he received a telegram from his father: "Bring Helen home. Come Monday night. Better job waiting." This terse directive is all that was necessary to cause twenty-two-year-old Spencer Kimball to quit his job immediately and return to Thatcher with his sister. Obviously his habit of obedience to parental direction did not end when he reached maturity.

Yet in another context, when it was a matter of parental advice, not direction, Spencer felt justified in declining to follow it. Thus when Andrew published an open letter to his son, advising him to enlist in an Arizona regiment rather than wait for the draft, Spencer declined. In such an important personal matter, he went his own way.

The job Andrew had in mind was helping drill a water well on the Gillespie Ranch. Spencer worked there for five weeks. It was dull and unexciting, but it was in the open and he had a congenial co-worker, his stepbrother Wallace Jones. However, an incident that occurred there was far from dull. During Spencer's retellings of the story, his memory may have sometimes confused some of the surrounding facts, but the key spiritual element of the incident never changed. At the ranch house one evening, he read an article in the *Graham County Guardian* that listed the names of the faculty at the Gila Academy for the coming year. On the list was the name of Camilla Eyring, whom he had met casually at a dance shortly before he entered the mission field. He had not danced with her then, nor had he seen her or corresponded with her since. As he read the article, the spiritual impression came to him that Camilla Eyring was to become his wife. Recalling the incident years later, he wrongly remembered that her picture accompanied the article. Nevertheless, the remembrance of the spiritual impression remained unaltered. That this young couple, whose only prior acquaintance was an informal introduction at a dance three years before, would be man and wife within three months after Spencer's spiritual impression suggests that something out of the ordinary was at work here.

Spencer finished his job at the ranch in time to attend the stake conference in Thatcher on August 25 and 26. As he had not previously done so, he was called on to report his mission at that time. He also sang in the choir and in a quartet. Four days later, he and Camilla Eyring had their first personal conversation. They met on the street in Thatcher waiting for the jitney bus to Pima, she to go home and he to visit his friend Lawrence Holladay, who lived there. Taking the initiative, Spencer reintroduced himself. He need not have done this, because Camilla remembered him distinctly since he had not invited her to dance when they first met. Moreover, everyone knew him as the stake president's son; nor could she easily have forgotten that she had heard him speak the previous Sunday. They took seats by each other on the jitney bus and talked all the way to Pima. Consistent with his earlier practice of making very brief diary entries, Spencer merely noted he had "met Miss Camilla Eyring and [had] accompanied her home." Camilla's account of this historic meeting is more extensive and infinitely more interesting. "We sat together on the bus," she reported, "and discussed Shakespeare and similar high-brow subjects, each trying to impress the other." She remembered exactly what she was wearing—a white voile dress with blue design—and wished she had worn something nicer. She remembered, too, that he was wearing white socks, but she "forgave him" for that. Arriving at Pima, Spencer walked her home from the bus stop and, lingering at her front door, asked if he could call on her later. When she said yes, he seemed to take that as a carte blanche invitation to be exercised at any time and without notice.

A few days later, he appeared unannounced at the door to pursue what he obviously considered to be a monumental program of courtship. It was a most inopportune time, as Camilla, preparing to go on a date, had her hair up in curlers and was wearing a kimono. After more highbrow conversation, it became apparent to Camilla that this eligible young man had not dropped by just to say hello but was there to spend the evening. Not wanting to discourage Spencer nor disappoint her date, she solved the dilemma by explaining that a "crowd" had planned to go to a dance and asked if Spencer would like to go too. "He seemed delighted," wrote Camilla. However, her date did not share that enthusiasm. "All the way to the dance," she wrote, "he drove as if the devil was after him." And once there, he didn't ask her to dance. Camilla had mixed feelings about the incident. On the one hand, she felt "terribly guilty" about the "shabby trick" she had played on her date. But on the other hand, she obviously was pleased to become better acquainted with Spencer Kimball.

Seemingly, Spencer was oblivious to any undercurrent

of tension during the evening. He may have thought the young man at the wheel naturally drove in that intense and reckless way. Nor did it seem to make an impression on him that the driver failed to dance with Camilla, since he understood she was just one of the "crowd." To him it was an entirely satisfactory evening, which he recorded with customary brevity. "In the evening," he wrote on September 3, "I went to Pima to see Miss Camilla Eyring. Two other couples came in a car and we all went to the Layton Pavilion to a farewell dance for the soldier boys. I stayed with Lawrence."

At this time, Spencer had made plans to enroll at Brigham Young University for the fall semester. Indeed, he had made arrangements to leave Thatcher a week after the dance at the Layton Pavilion. If he were to court the young schoolteacher, he knew he would have to move with alacrity. He did so. He apparently spent every available free moment with her. It did not take long for their conversations to go beyond discussions of Shakespeare. Nor did it take long for Spencer to drop the formal "Miss Eyring" from his diary, substituting "Camilla" instead. On September 9, the night before he left, he was "with Camilla and a group of young people for a social hour of music and conversation." After he departed, Camilla wrote, "I was very much in love." He obviously was of the same mind, but was reticent to record that in his diary. She gave him a box of homemade fudge as a going-away present and later sent him her picture. He cut out the head from the picture and put it in his pocket watch.

Spencer was gone only a month. During that time, he and Camilla corresponded frequently. In the beginning, his letters were merely factual recitals of what he had seen and done. Later he felt comfortable sharing personal things about his military status and plans for the future. After receiving a summons from the draft board to appear for a physical examination, he wrote in detail about the various options available to him, then added: "Pardon me for

Spencer, age 22, near the time of his marriage in 1917.

bothering you with my troubles but I [thought] you might be glad to know. If I am to leave soon I am not unwilling to go but, of course, it is hard to have one's plans so broken into, that's all."

This brings into clear focus the uncertainties young couples like Spencer Kimball and Camilla Eyring faced in this month of September 1917. Spencer's plan at the time was to complete his education so he could teach. This goal now seemed blocked by the demands of the war. It had been five months since the United States entered the conflict, and the government efforts to draft and enlist personnel were rapidly building a major American military force for service in Europe. Those already in the service and those, like Spencer, who seemed destined soon to enter it were

66

reminded daily of the perils of the war. At the moment, the British and French forces were locked in a grim battle with the Germans around Ypres, Belgium. Torrential rains had turned the battlefield into a quagmire, and the Germans' use of mustard gas had added a note of terror to the offensive. Moreover, the successful negotiation of the German-Russo peace accord threatened a major intensification of hostilities on the western front.

Thus, not only were career plans put on hold for healthy young men like Spencer Kimball, but the prospect of being injured or killed on a bloody European battlefield was a gloomy possibility. And for one such as he, who had recently completed a mission where he taught principles of Christian love and peace, the prospect of killing men toward whom he had no personal animosity, men to whom he might have taught the gospel had not his assignment been changed, was repulsive. Yet loyalty to country and the perception that the Allied cause was just overrode all these considerations and gave Spencer and others like him justification for military service. And uncertainty about the future caused many of them to seek a moment of happiness while it was available and to accelerate plans for marriage. As we shall see, this is what happened to Spencer Kimball and Camilla Eyring, who were married when Spencer's induction into the army seemed imminent and in less than three months after their first highbrow conversation on the jitney bus.

Despite the uncertainties of the moment, Spencer had come to Brigham Young University to pursue his educational goals. He registered on September 18, signing up for English 1 and 3, mathematics, theology, and physical training. He then obtained part-time employment picking peaches to help cover his expenses. However, less than a week after registering, he received notice from his draft board in Safford, instructing him to report for a physical examination. At his request, approval was given for him to be examined in Provo, with the understanding he would leave Safford for his training base on October 3 or "soon after." With this turn of events, he withdrew from school and went to Salt Lake City, where he visited relatives for several days and attended the general conference with his father, who had traveled there. Andrew also gave his son a special blessing in anticipation of his induction into the army. Spencer then returned to Safford. Meanwhile, the date of induction had been set back.

Alerted to the date and time of his arrival, Camilla had arranged to spend the night in Thatcher with a girlfriend so she could greet him. This began an intensive courtship that culminated in their marriage on November 16. During that interval, they were together every evening, and over the weekends they spent most of their time together. Many of their evenings were spent in the Eyring home in Pima, where Spencer occasionally played and sang for the family. This endeared him to the Eyrings, who were already impressed with his good looks, his genial personality, and the aura of distinction surrounding the Kimball name.

"This was a very auspicious occasion," wrote Spencer on November 10, "as Camilla promised to be my wife. On account of the likelihood of my leaving soon for the training camp, we decided to be married in a short time. Father being in the east, we planned to await his return and have him perform the ceremony." The time constraints, the expense of travel, and Camilla's teaching commitments ruled out a temple marriage at the time. That would occur later, as routinely happened at that time among Latter-day Saint couples who lived a long distance from a temple.

After sharing their decision with Camilla's parents, who gave their approval, the young couple set their wedding date for Friday, November 16, so that they would have the following weekend for a brief honeymoon. It was assumed that President Andrew Kimball would be home from the East by that time so he could perform the ceremony. This assumption was correct, as he and Sister Kimball returned on the fourteenth. What Spencer and Camilla did not know was that Andrew had made a previous appointment to meet with a group of men in Phoenix the evening of the sixteenth, an appointment he could not easily break on such short notice. Under these circumstances, it was decided that the wedding would go forward as planned, with the approval and blessing of Spencer's parents, but with the ceremony being performed by Bishop Merrill.

The Eyring home had been selected as the site of the wedding. Camilla, sensitive about the appearance of her home compared to the Kimball home, was anxious that everything look especially nice, as she knew that Sister Kimball—Aunt Josie—would be present. Accordingly, several ragged places in the wallpaper were masked by tree branches ostensibly there as decorations. This touch, which compensated in part for the lack of flowers this late in the season, added to the thorough grooming the room underwent, provided an attractive setting for the ceremony.

The guest list had been pared to a bare minimum. It included only Camilla's parents and her teenage brothers Henry, sixteen, and Ed, fourteen; Aunt Josie; and Spencer's sisters, Alice and Helen. The Kimball sisters had offered to host a bridal shower, but Camilla had declined because she did not want to publicize the marriage in advance. Moreover, she did not want anyone to feel "obliged" to give her anything.

The morning of the wedding, Spencer and Camilla went to the clerk's office in Safford together to get the marriage license. He had six dollars in his wallet, the total of his earthly possessions other than his clothing and other personal effects. After paying the two dollar and fifty cent license fee, he and his fiancée had three dollars and fifty cents with which to begin their married life. At the moment, the excitement of the coming nuptials seemed to erase any concern about such mundane things as money. Meanwhile, Camilla had had second thoughts. She went home to Pima from the clerk's office to get ready for the ceremony. As she reflected on the speed with which everything had

Camilla and Spencer near the time of their wedding in 1917.

happened, their short acquaintance, and the uncertainty of the future, she was "ready to back out." She went into the bedroom and cried. "Yet," she wrote, "I also loved him desperately and decided I was willing to go ahead despite my fears."

Although the thought of backing out never occurred to Spencer, he experienced major distractions as he went home and prepared for the evening, so much so that he forgot the hot water as he got into the tub and had to have it handed to him.

The ceremony was scheduled for 8:00 P.M. Spencer, Aunt Josie, and the girls drove to Pima in the Chevrolet, arriving ahead of Bishop Merrill. While they waited for him to arrive, Spencer and Camilla went to a room adjacent to the living room where they could be alone. Without knocking and unannounced, Henry came barging in to find them kissing, with Camilla sitting on Spencer's lap. Showing at age sixteen the aplomb which was his trademark throughout life, Henry assured them, "I'll be as silent as the tomb."

As the young couple stood before Bishop Merrill, Camilla wore a pink party dress and Spencer his khaki army uniform. There was no bridal bouquet and no music. There was a piano in the room, but no one except the participants knew how to play it. The ceremony was short but beautiful in its quiet simplicity. By omitting publicity of the marriage, the newlyweds avoided being shivareed, a practice President Kimball always condemned as being crude and insensitive. They spent their honeymoon weekend on the Eyring farm, using Mother Eyring's own bedroom, which she had fixed up for them. The next issue of the local weekly newspaper carried an announcement of the wedding on the front page under the caption "Popular Young Couple Married." Reporting that Camilla was a member of the faculty of the Gila Academy, the article noted as to Spencer, "He is one of the drafted boys from this county and is certified for duty in the National Army. His name appears among those called for service in the next contingent from this county."

These then were the modest circumstances under which Spencer and Camilla Kimball began their married life. It brought together two young people of intelligence and achievement who had come from solid Latter-day Saint homes and who had aspirations for self-improvement and service to others. It will be interesting to trace the path, sometimes wide and smooth and sometimes narrow, rocky, and steep, which led them from this beginning to a place of high eminence in the Church.

Chapter 8

Early Years of Marriage

A s the newspaper article announcing the nuptials explained, Spencer was among the next contingent of those scheduled to be called up in the draft. This no doubt created an element of uncertainty for the newlyweds, who were unable to make definite plans for housing. Assuming Spencer would be gone soon and that Camilla would then live with her parents in Pima, they accepted the invitation of the Kimball parents to live temporarily with them. Camilla continued to teach at the academy and to try to hold up her end of the household work, while Spencer busied himself with work around the farm. At the stake conference held over the weekend of November 24 and 25, Spencer "spoke briefly as one of the soldier boys leaving for war." The next day, he was surprised to receive word from the draft board in Safford that a change in quotas would indefinitely delay his call-up. Learning of that change, Spencer and Camilla decided to seek housing for themselves, even though there was still uncertainty about his status. The scarcity of the kind of housing the newlyweds could afford made them thankful for an offer from Spencer's sister Alice and her husband, George Nelson, to rent part of their small house. Their part was partitioned off with outing flannel curtains. With odd pieces of furniture donated by their parents, they moved in on December 3 and "had their first meal alone together." Here they had more privacy and were able to begin functioning as a family. And here, although they had no child of their own, they had their first exposure to baby care. Alice had a five-month-old baby boy, Kimball Nelson, who was colicky and cried a great deal. The thin partition separating the two apartments enabled the Kimballs to share the crying with the baby's parents. This challenge, coupled with Camilla's desire for a place where she could demonstrate the principles of domestic science she taught at the academy, caused them to look for better accommodations. After the first of the year they rented, for fifteen dollars a month, a furnished house from Mr. Wakefield, across the street from the old Thatcher hotel.

When it became apparent that Spencer's call-up would be further delayed, he sought employment. He was hired by the Citizens Bank for seventy-five dollars a month, the same amount Camilla received for teaching at the academy. At first his duties consisted of posting accounts. Later he worked in the teller cage, learned to process contracts, and acquired experience in negotiating loans. Impressed with Spencer's work, his supervisor, Williams McRae, soon increased his salary to eighty dollars a month and gave him the title of assistant cashier.

This was a stressful time for Camilla. She had conceived a month after the marriage. The normal discomforts of a first pregnancy may have been accentuated by a sense of embarrassment that she had conceived so soon, by questions about her status at the academy, and by uncertainty about the future should her husband be drafted. These factors caused her some distress and produced frequent mood swings and bouts of crying.

Adding to the upset, Spencer broke out with smallpox, "monstrous and thick." He reported that the only spot free of the pox was on the upper left part of his forehead, "so my wife can kiss me there." He appreciated her kindness. "Camilla is so good to me, waiting on me hand and foot. She is so wonderful." Then, despite their infirmities, he added, "We are so happy in our little home." By the time school was out at the end of May, the Kimballs had saved enough money to travel to Salt Lake City to have their marriage sealed in the temple. Leaving Thatcher on June 2, 1918, they arrived two days later and were welcomed into the home of Aunt Fannie. The sealing took place in the Salt Lake Temple on June 7, giving assurance that the child Camilla was carrying would be born in the covenant of their sealing.

The visitors spent eight days in Salt Lake City after the sealing to enable Camilla to see some of the sights and to meet some of her many in-laws.

Soon after returning from Salt Lake, Spencer was reclassified because of his married status and Camilla's expectancy. He had mixed feelings about the change. He was happy because he would be able to care for Camilla and their child without interruption. But he was anxious, worrying that some might think he had married to avoid the army. But apparently the issue was never raised, given Spencer's unquestioned reputation for integrity.

On her return, Camilla worked with John Nash, the county agent, giving extension training in home economics to women living in rural areas. This involved driving over rough, unsurfaced roads, something hardly suited for one so near to childbirth. It is not surprising, therefore, that Camilla went into labor three weeks earlier than expected. It was an agonizing, painful birth, complicated by the inexperience of the young attending doctor, whose training was in osteopathy.

This first child, a baby boy born August 26, 1918, was named Spencer LeVan Kimball. In his maturity, he would distinguish himself as a Rhodes Scholar at Oxford, England; an attorney; a law professor and dean; and an author.

Camilla was bedridden for many days as she recovered from childbirth and adjusted to nursing procedures. As for Spencer, he now had the challenge to make up for the loss of Camilla's salary. To take up the slack, he resumed playing the piano for dances, which netted from two to five dollars a night. He also kept books for the People's Department Store, wrote as a stringer for the local weekly newspaper, and sold Brown Herb Pills, a laxative his father had handled as an agent. The extra care Camilla required increased when she contracted the flu. This was in October, near the beginning of the influenza pandemic of 1918 that took thirty million lives. Camilla's weakened condition following childbirth made her especially vulnerable, and fear of infecting LeVan caused major concern. After weeks of struggle, she began to recover, and in time she recovered completely. Meanwhile, Spencer added nursing and housemaid duties to his already crowded schedule as he learned the juggler's art.

A happy note sounded during this period of trial when, on November 11, the Armistice was signed, signaling the end of the war in Europe. This removed any chance Spencer would be called away from his family and left him and Camilla free to chart their future without interruption.

Soon after Camilla recovered from the flu, the Kimballs moved into a larger place owned by William McRae. They bought some new furniture and, using Camilla's sewing and artistic skills, hung new curtains and decorated the home tastefully. They also purchased their first automobile, a used Buick, open on the sides with transparent curtains for use in case of bad weather.

Wanting to test the Buick and to get away for a while, they decided in July 1919 to drive to northern Arizona for a vacation with two other families, the Wesley Taylor and Burt Hoopes families, traveling in the Kimballs' car and a second car. Their destination was St. Johns, about a hundred and fifty miles north over a winding, mountainous, unpaved road that roughly paralleled the Old Coronado Trail.

The Buick and its companion had low horsepower. This made it hard to negotiate the steep hills without help. When it became apparent the cars could not make it up a hill on their own power, everyone but the drivers and babies piled out to push. This reduced the distance covered to about sixty miles a day. If this seems slow to us, it didn't to them. Indeed, for that time and place, given the limitations of early automobile travel, it was good mileage. And the tedium was eased by the camaraderie, the singing, and the ready laughter, which turned trouble into triumph. The travelers carried their own bedding and food, sleeping out while on the road, except one night in the forest when rain drove them inside at a sawmill where they were welcomed by the owners, the Copelands.

They stayed with friends in St. Johns. Here they celebrated the 24th of July. The festivities commenced early when a stick of dynamite was exploded on the church square. There was the usual children's parade reenacting the arrival of Brigham Young and the pioneers in the Salt Lake Valley. Then followed competitions on the church grounds, a rodeo in the afternoon, and a dance at night.

On the return trip, they drove through the Petrified Forest. Because of recent rains, it was a quagmire of mud. When they reached San Carlos, the Gila River was in flood. They hired Indians to tow the cars across the river with horses. Then the cars wouldn't start because the water had flooded the motors. As their food was gone, Spencer and Burt Hoopes walked upstream, removed their trousers as they stood behind some bushes, and, holding the trousers above their heads, waded the river, dressed, and bought food at the San Carlos store. "Vacations were real adventures," Camilla wrote of the experience.

This was the first of innumerable trips taken by the Kimballs. It became a tradition for the family to go on vacations together, although occasionally the parents went alone.

These outings were conducive to family unity and loyalty as the family planned the trips together and afterward took pleasure in reminiscing about what they had seen and done. On the road they avoided boredom by singing and playing games. And after Elder Kimball's call to the Twelve, traveling became a way of life for him and Camilla.

At the time of the outing to St. Johns, LeVan was only eleven months old. Soon after, the parents were excited when they learned Camilla was pregnant again but were devastated when she miscarried. Later she conceived again but miscarried at six weeks. It was a dark time for the Kimballs, brightened somewhat by Spencer's progress at the bank and his growing influence in the community.

In 1920 his monthly income was roughly $250, which included $175 at the bank. He was well respected, was broadening his knowledge of banking procedures, and was learning about the intricacies of business dealings. Moreover, he was multiplying his acquaintances and friendships, both inside and outside the Church. His growing prominence was recognized that year when he was appointed to a two-year term on the Common Council of the Town of Thatcher. Unknown to Spencer, events were then in motion that prevented him from fulfilling this appointment.

These events soon surfaced when it was announced that the Citizens Bank would undergo a reorganization. This entailed changing the name of the bank to the Arizona Trust & Savings Bank, constructing a new building in Safford, and shuffling some of the personnel. In the shuffle, Spencer was transferred to the main office in Safford with the title of assistant cashier and with a pay raise to $225 a month, a substantial income in that day for a young man in his midtwenties.

With an assured salary added to income from other sources, he and Camilla decided to buy a house in Safford. It was a three-room, white frame house with a bath, located on Central Avenue, which they purchased for $2,400 with a small down payment and payments of $25 a month. "It seemed like a palace," wrote Camilla. She lavished all her skill and ingenuity on decorating and furnishing it, always with three-year-old LeVan at her side.

Influenced, perhaps, by the serenity of her new home and the security she seemed to feel there, Camilla conceived again toward the end of 1921. Because of the two miscarriages, the doctor advised that she severely restrict her mobility during the first five months. After that, she moved about more, but with care. These precautions were rewarded when, on July 31, 1922, the Kimballs' second child was born, a petite little girl with blue eyes and a reddish tint to her hair. This attribute, which reminded him of Olive, prompted Andrew to urge that the baby be named after her grandmother. The parents assented but added the name Beth.

Olive Beth's birth added the crowning touch to the young couple, who seemed to have everything going for them—a new home, a car, a comfortable income, status in the community and the Church, a host of friends, love for each other, and now two children, a boy and a girl. Spencer also had an enjoyable outlet for his athletic bent, playing on a basketball team sponsored by his employer and appropriately called the Bankers.

Sadness intruded on the Kimballs' lives on October 12, 1922, when Josie passed away at age sixty-two. Her passing was not unexpected, as she had had heart problems for several years. Yet it was a blow, especially for Andrew, who loved and admired her and who was ever grateful for the way she had come into the family at a crucial time.

When Josie died, she was eulogized as much for her own achievements as for her role as the wife of the most prominent man in the community. The students of the academy and the public schools came en masse to pass by her coffin in the Kimball home, in recognition of her contributions to education in the Gila Valley. After appropriate funeral services in the chapel, she was interred in the cemetery, near but not next to Olive. Between the two graves was a vacant plot reserved for Andrew.

With Josie's passing, Andrew experienced another trial of readjustment. After considering the alternatives, it was decided that Spencer and Camilla and their children would move into the family home in Thatcher, where they could help Andrew adjust to his loss. This, of course, entailed a move from their new home in Safford and a rearranging of the Thatcher home to accommodate the needs of a young family while preserving the ambience suitable for the ecclesiastical and social obligations of Spencer's father. It was not an easy thing to do. But after making the move to Thatcher, Spencer found a renter for their home for an amount that covered the mortgage payments.

This arrangement lasted ten months. In August 1923, Andrew returned from Salt Lake City with a new bride, Mary Connelly, an attractive and accomplished woman in her late forties. Never before married, she was a member of the general board of the YWMIA and the editor of the *Young Woman's Journal*. Andrew had met her when Mary visited the stake as a representative of the Young Women general board. At the April general conference in 1923, Andrew contacted Mary Connelly to renew their previous platonic acquaintance. When it was found there was a mutual personal attraction between them, Andrew courted her over a period of months, won her, and was sealed to her in the Salt Lake Temple. Upon Andrew and Mary's arrival in Thatcher, Spencer, Camilla, and their children moved back to Safford.

They returned to the town in the midst of an economic depression. The surge of prosperity which followed the end of the war and which had fueled the optimistic expansion of the bank had begun to subside in 1922. This caused a lag in bank business, which in turn resulted in a reduction of Spencer's salary, first to $175 a month and then to $150. Yet, because many were much worse off, he felt fortunate—at least until December 17, 1923. On that day, his friend and supervisor, William McRae, told him in tears that the bank examiners were closing down the bank. Plunging prices and soft markets had created chaos among the farmers and cattlemen, causing widespread defaults on their bank loans. With that source of money cut off, the bank had foundered. The news shocked Spencer and Camilla. Suddenly, their sense of security vanished with the loss of Spencer's job. Also gone were shares of bank and other stock purchased with their savings. The prospects for this Christmas were dismal indeed. The gloom deepened when some depositors berated Spencer for not warning them about the bank's impending collapse.

The blow was cushioned when the bank examiners employed Spencer for two weeks to help wind up details of the closure. Also, he was able to satisfy a debt to the bank by offsetting it with deposit credits he had purchased at a discount. This left him debt-free except for the mortgage on his home.

Within a week after completing his work with the bank examiners, he received three job offers, two of them from competitor banks and the third from the People's Store. He accepted the job of chief teller with the Bank of Safford at $150 a month. The work was similar, though in time it became more varied, which broadened his knowledge of the banking business. Here he became better acquainted with the procedure for negotiating loans and for dealing with correspondent banks in New York and other major cities. Moreover, he became better acquainted with people from all over the area, people of every occupation and economic status who had need for banking services. And because he was always friendly and helpful, taking time to inquire about his customers and their personal interests, he created a great reservoir of goodwill toward his bank and toward himself personally that would be invaluable later when he started his own business with a partner.

Little did Spencer realize that at the time he was learning his duties at the Bank of Safford, one of the great challenges of his life was in the making. A few months after

Andrew Kimball's marriage to Mary Connelly, Andrew became ill. Because he was only sixty-five and until then had seemed to be in comparatively good health, there was no inkling his illness was life-threatening. Thinking the better practitioners and medical facilities in Salt Lake City could help cure him, Mary took Andrew there in the early months of 1924. It was easy for the doctors to identify the symptoms of his illness—painful joints, infected teeth, and high blood pressure—but they were unable to give it a name, much less prescribe a cure. From early spring on, his condition worsened until August, when it appeared the illness was terminal. Mary notified the children of their father's serious condition and that the end might be near. Spencer went to Salt Lake immediately, obtaining a leave of absence from the bank.

He was deeply stressed by what he found. His father, wracked with pain, was unable to get relief, even with medications. Spencer and other members of the family took turns staying with him. But he was so distraught by the pain he could not converse with them but could only cry out, over and over: "Oh! my Father, let me die." His fervent wish was granted when he passed away on August 31, 1924. It was difficult for Spencer to see his father die in this way, to see his ideal, who was always so poised, so kind, and so self-assured, totally dominated by the pain that afflicted his body.

Funeral services were held for Andrew on September 2, 1924, in the Twenty-seventh Ward chapel in Salt Lake City. Present were many relatives, including Andrew's brother J. Golden Kimball of the First Council of Seventy, and his twin sister, Alice, together with many friends with whom he had been associated during the twenty-six years he had served as the president of the St. Joseph stake. The main speaker was President Heber J. Grant, who was only two years older than Andrew. They had grown up together in Salt Lake City, the sons of Heber C. Kimball and Jedediah M. Grant, who had served as counselors to President

Brigham Young. As a mark of the respect he had for Andrew and his family, President Grant accompanied the body to Thatcher by train, where he spoke at additional funeral services. After the funeral, Andrew's body was interred in the city cemetery between the graves of Olive and Josie. There at the graveside, Spencer, under stress from the suddenness of his father's passing and the remembrance of the agony he had endured at the end, began to weep openly while clinging to Camilla. Aunt Alice, who had seen many trials and dark days, came to him quietly and whispered, "Now, Spencer, you pick up. Stand up." There can be little doubt he obliged.

It had been announced earlier that immediately after the burial a special meeting would be held where the stake presidency would be reorganized. Ordinarily, action such as this would not have been taken so soon after the burial because of the tender feelings of the family. In this case, however, President Grant considered it unwise to wait, presumably because of the long distance involved and because the stake had been without the direct leadership of a president for several months.

Emotionally drained by the funeral and burial of his father, Spencer was hardly prepared for what took place at this meeting. Surprising the men involved and the congregation, President Grant presented for sustaining vote Harry L. Payne as president, John F. Nash as first counselor, and Spencer W. Kimball as second counselor. Trained as he was in Church procedures, Spencer accepted the call without hesitancy or qualification. However, it was not something to which he had aspired. He had no illusions about the job nor about the pressures it would exert on him and his family. From infancy he had seen how service in the stake presidency had dominated the life of his father and, indeed, the lives of the entire family. And for six years as an adult, his role as the stake clerk had shown him that the pressures exerted on his father were shared by his counselors, the three of them bearing the responsibility for the spiritual and temporal welfare of the members of the stake. It was a responsibility he would never take lightly.

It has been said that some people grow in a job while others merely swell. Spencer Kimball was always a grower. He immediately assumed his duties as a counselor and continued serving as stake clerk. He worked with customary diligence in these dual responsibilities, without pride or a sense of self-importance, while developing good relationships with Harry Payne and John Nash that lasted throughout life. They were wholly compatible and worked with unity for the betterment of the stake and its members.

When Spencer was called as a counselor, the St. Joseph stake included more than seventeen units located in the states of Arizona, New Mexico, and Texas, with a Latter-day Saint population of more than six thousand members. The precise boundaries of the stake had never been defined since its creation in 1883. The letter to Christopher Layton creating the stake, dated February 20 of that year, merely stated, "As regards the boundaries of your stake, we cannot specifically define them at present. Circumstances hereafter must determine this matter." On this account, for many years the members of the stake had merely referred to it as "The Big Chunk of Real Estate." From the stake's beginning, units had been added or eliminated as the needs of the members required. In 1924 when Spencer was introduced to the administrative work of the stake, it required travel of two thousand miles to visit each of the units. Unsurfaced roads made travel slow and arduous, so that when a community had rail service, stake members often traveled there by train, as with El Paso, Texas, the easternmost unit of the stake, which was more than two hundred miles from Thatcher. Within this vast area, President Kimball had responsibility to supervise priesthood and auxiliary organizations, to see that they were fully staffed and trained, to conduct worthiness interviews, and to instruct, motivate, and inspire leaders and the general membership. During much of the time Spencer served in the stake presidency, Camilla served in leadership positions in the auxiliaries, so it was not uncommon for them to travel together.

While the Kimballs were acquiring prominence in the community in church and business affairs, they were also developing a full and satisfying social life. There were many couples their age during these early years with whom they created close social ties. They enjoyed dances, picnics, group dinners, hayrides, and other activities with these friends. In time some of them built rustic cabins on Mount Graham, where, with their families, they enjoyed summer outings. The Kimballs also enjoyed mingling socially with the Rotarians and their wives, a more diverse group that included some who were not members of the Church and some who were only nominal members.

Of all their socializing, however, Spencer and Camilla enjoyed nothing more than their regular gatherings with the Eyring family. The patriarch of the clan, Edward Christian Eyring, was a polygamist who married sisters, Caroline (Camilla's mother) and Emma Romney. After the expulsion from Mexico, Edward Eyring settled his two families in Pima, ultimately building a large farmhouse with separate wings for each wife and her children and a large connecting living area shared by everyone.

From the beginning of their marriage, Spencer and Camilla regularly went to Pima to visit the Eyrings, to eat with them, to ride horses, and, in the case of Spencer, to milk cows or otherwise work around the farm. In time, as the Kimball children came into the family, it became a frequent ritual on Sundays and holidays to travel to Pima to have dinner there. The Eyrings had "adopted" Spencer, making him one of their own, admiring him and taking pride in his achievements. The Eyring children sought to emulate him. As for Spencer, he received from Caroline Eyring, who was partial to him and was one of his staunchest supporters, some of the mothering he had missed following his own mother's death. And after Spencer's father died, the Eyring farm in Pima really became the focal point for his ancestral feelings.

While he seems to have been content with his situation following the call to the stake presidency, in a short time Spencer became restive and dissatisfied with his employment at the bank. By the end of 1926, he had been in the banking business for nine years but had little to show for it in a material way. While his family lived in a comfortable home, he had some savings, and his salary of $175 a month was adequate for their needs, there seemed to be little future for him there in a monetary way. It was then he began to cast around for alternative employment. The opportunity he finally took was an offer from Bishop Joseph Greenhalgh to go into the insurance business with him. Since the bishop, who was old enough to be Spencer's father, had a variety of business interests in the community, Spencer had dealt with him in financial matters as well as in church matters. Indeed, they had collaborated earlier in buying commercial paper—unsecured short-term loans—from automobile and other businesses that did not want to handle the installment payments. In this way Spencer had learned that the bishop was an able businessman and was meticulously honest.

The insurance agency, which handled mostly fire and casualty policies, had been started some time before by Mr. Greenhalgh and two partners. One partner had pulled out and moved to California, and now the other one was ill and wanted to sell his interest. After agonizing over the decision, Spencer bought it for $150 and gave notice at the bank he would be leaving May 1, 1927. In today's economy, the sum seems insignificant. It was not so then, especially since the three original partners each invested only fifty dollars to start the business.

It was a crucial and in some ways frightening decision to make. Until now, Spencer had always had an assured income, something he could definitely depend on. He was not sure how he would react to an unstructured situation where income could fluctuate or might even disappear. He had discussed the prospects with Camilla, who had given her unqualified approval. Yet there was another concern when their third child, Andrew Eyring Kimball, was born on March 5, 1927. Was Spencer gambling with the security of this infant, his siblings, and Camilla? Despite the uncertainties and the hazards, Spencer took the leap and on May 1, 1927, went into business with his partner, Joseph W. Greenhalgh, under the name Kimball-Greenhalgh Agency. In addition to handling fire and casualty policies, which was the heart of their business, they also wrote some life insurance policies and security bonds while dabbling in real estate. Meanwhile, they continued to acquire commercial paper from local merchants as well.

The order of the names on the agency's masthead is significant. While Bishop Greenhalgh was one of the founders of the agency and was much older than Spencer and more experienced in the business, the name Kimball was a household word in the Gila Valley, a name that stood for honesty and integrity. Therefore, the partners wisely decided to utilize that name to their advantage, placing it first on the masthead. Moreover, it was intended from the beginning that Spencer would play the major role in the business, under the tutelage of his partner. Mr. Greenhalgh was nearing retirement, suffered from arthritis, and had other business interests. It was decided, therefore, that Spencer would take charge of the agency's small office, located at the rear of a bank building across the street from the bank from which he had just resigned. There he would be responsible to handle all the records, process claims, review or prepare applications for insurance or bonds, correspond with insurers or claimants, take care of any walk-in business, and respond to questions or resolve any complaints. As the volume of business justified their employment, he would also direct the work of an office secretary and an assistant. Meanwhile, with his self-taught typing skill, Spencer could bang out letters, make reports, or fill out forms as necessary. Because these and other duties would keep him anchored to the office during working hours each weekday, it was agreed Spencer would have a regular drawing account at the agency to cover his family expenses, with a ceiling that could be lowered when the agency became pinched financially. Then, after deducting all expenses including Spencer's draw, the partners divided the net proceeds, fifty-fifty.

For his part, Bishop Greenhalgh worked in the field on a flexible schedule, writing renewal or new policies and checking on investment opportunities for himself and his partner, whether as to commercial paper they might acquire or real property they might buy, sell, or serve as broker for.

It was an unusual partnership that worked from the beginning. Its foundation was the mutual trust and admiration the partners had for each other. In time, their business arrangement progressed from a partnership to a corporate form. But that did not change the method of dividing their profits, nor was that formula altered by the bishop's diminished contributions because of infirmity or age or by Spencer's increased contributions as he matured and grew as a businessman. Their financial arrangement remained unchanged until 1941, when Mr. Greenhalgh passed away.

Spencer's entrance into his own business produced a powerful surge of energy and widened the horizons of his financial goals. His was no longer nine-to-five employment, but it was a job that dominated his waking hours, except for personal, family, and church commitments. And time constraints made it necessary that these be compressed into short but meaningful segments. It was during this period that President Kimball's habit of nonstop, fast-paced work permanently took root. He had always been a worker, but now it became an obsession that impelled him forward each day, pushing him from here to there to keep ahead of the imaginary tide of work that seemed poised to engulf him. It was the perception of a father always on the move, seldom at rest, never idle, that dominated the remembrances of the Kimball children as they grew up. Yet he could never be charged with neglect, for he was always near, a looming and comforting presence, and he was always at their side in times of need or emergency, to provide support, encouragement, and motivation.

Spencer created an atmosphere of friendliness and efficiency in the office of Kimball-Greenhalgh. His desk was near the door, and anyone who entered received his prompt and cordial attention. It was a repetition of the treatment he had given to customers at the bank, intensified now by the personal stake he had in their satisfaction and goodwill. The interest he showed in others by inquiring about their families and personal affairs was no facade but was a reflection of the genuine interest he had in the welfare of others. Through personal and family contacts, his work at the bank, his musical involvements, and his prominence in church and Rotary affairs, Spencer was acquainted with practically everyone in the valley. This wide acquaintance was a key to the success of the business. When Val Webb was brought into the office as an assistant, Spencer was freed to work more often in the field with his partner in servicing their clients and soliciting new accounts. He systematically contacted his acquaintances asking for their business. Those found to be insured through other agencies were not written off but were contacted later in follow-up visits to show a continued interest. And those who never gave Kimball-Greenhalgh their business were still treated as friends.

In time, the persistence of the partners and their policy of fair dealing resulted in a steady growth of their insurance and bond business. Recognizing that the small population base in the valley restricted the growth potential in that field, they began to expand their activities in real estate. Encouraged by success in building several small houses on lots they had purchased and selling them profitably, they launched into the development of a twenty-acre tract they had purchased in 1928 for $20,000. The economy seemed solid at the time and the prospects for success most promising. Spencer's optimism showed when he purchased a new

Studebaker in June 1928 and took Camilla and the three children on a trip to British Columbia via Salt Lake City and Yellowstone Park. Spencer and his family returned home in a leisurely way, stopping in San Francisco to visit Camilla's brother Ed and his new bride, Evelyn, and in Los Angeles to visit brother Del Kimball and his family.

To the relatives in Salt Lake City, San Francisco, and Los Angeles, the Kimballs, driving a new car and traveling in a leisurely fashion over a period of weeks to places most people only heard about, must have appeared to be a family with ample means and a prosperous and happy future ahead.

Chapter 9

Times of Trial,
Testing, and Trauma

For a year after their Canadian vacation, the reality of the Kimballs' financial situation seemed to coincide with the outward perceptions of prosperity. The partnership, thriving in a booming economy, subdivided its twenty-acre tract into eighty-two building lots. Located in a desirable part of Safford, almost surrounded with other homes, it seemed to be an ideal place for a high-quality subdivision to serve the needs of an expanding community. Among Spencer's friends in Rotary, there was no hint of an impending downturn in the economy, only unbridled optimism for the future of Safford, the county seat of Graham County and the business and financial center of the Gila Valley. And Spencer's personal finances were bolstered at the time by his service as the secretary of several canal companies and the Cotton Growers Association, from some of which he received fees for keeping their books.

However, all was not well. As summer approached in 1929, the United States was caught up in an orgy of speculation in the stock market. Many investors, confident about the future of the economy, had made large purchases on margin, believing that as stock prices rose, they could make a killing by acquiring stock at the lower margin price and selling at the higher current price. And many of these purchasers bought the stock with borrowed money. In order to put a brake on this inflationary spiral, the Federal Reserve Board raised its discount rate in the summer of 1929. This automatically produced an increase in interest rates by member banks, creating anxiety among those who had bought on margin, and anxiety turned to fear in the autumn, when Great Britain also raised its discount rate, which helped bring on a worldwide market crisis.

The collapse of the American economy was swift and devastating. The stock market crash, beginning with "Black Thursday" on October 24, 1929, was the most spectacular and highly publicized element of it. Between then and November 13, the average price of the major securities dropped to less than half the previous price, with a loss in stock values of more than $30 million. But there were other factors in the collapse that more directly affected the residents of the Gila Valley and businesses like Kimball-Greenhalgh. For years before the collapse, U.S. agriculture had been in a gradual decline caused by a loss of foreign markets as the production of wheat and cotton increased in other lands, by a reduction in domestic consumption through changes in dietary habits and clothing styles, and by lower prices due to agricultural surpluses. Moreover, the farmer was handicapped by the need to sell his products in the open market while he purchased his farm machinery and tools in a protected market. This put the squeeze on the farmer's buying power and profits. And the increase in interest rates, designed to cool down stock speculation, acted as a further brake on agriculture, as most farmers financed their operations with borrowed money. Because the economy of the Gila Valley rested on agriculture, these factors cast a pall over every aspect of its business and personal life.

The firm of Kimball-Greenhalgh suffered along with all the others. Business began to decline almost immediately. The first to fall off were securities and real estate transactions. Furthermore, people lacked the money to make down payments on automobiles and household appliances, or, if they had money, were generally unwilling to spend it this way when the future was so uncertain. This almost dried up the business of purchasing installment sales contracts. And it dried up the sales of real estate completely. No one was buying, a sad situation for a firm like Kimball-Greenhalgh, waiting to sell eighty-two choice city lots whose purchase represented its major asset and investment. It was also a consuming asset that continued to accrue taxes and utility assessments. Prudence dictated the lots be sold as soon as possible, even if at bargain prices. The partners decided on an auction. To stir interest, they strung decorations at the tract site, hired a band, and announced there would be refreshments and prizes. Unexpected rain put a damper on the gala event, keeping all away except a determined few who came to claim the prizes and drink the punch. Not one lot was sold. The partners were distraught. However, they continued to work day after day.

What kept President Kimball afloat financially was the income from keeping books for the canal companies and the Cotton Growers Association, from insurance policy commissions, and from an occasional installment contract. The shaky economy made insurance vital in certain transactions, as with some bank loans. But other policies were allowed to lapse when the holders did not consider them essential or when holders lacked the money to pay the premiums. "It is hard to keep optimistic," President Kimball wrote during this period. "After a good night's rest I rush down to work all pepped up and ready for anything. In the first couple of hours about 6 or 8 policies are returned (can't pay for them) and down drop my feathers. And by night time you feel like everything is gone to the bad." Then, showing the cheerful bent of his character, he added: "But while conditions are certainly at a low ebb, and prospects look mighty gloomy and unfavorable, yet so far we have not actually been stinted in food, so we feel mighty thankful for that."

As the income of the agency declined, so did Spencer's drawing account. And with money in short supply, bartering became prevalent. Camilla shopped where the family had credit, not where the quality or the prices were best.

Although the economy remained bleak, the year 1930 brought a ray of sunshine into the Kimball family when, on September 23, their fourth child, Edward Lawrence Kimball, was born. Named after his maternal grandfather, Edward C. Eyring, this child, who as an adult would distinguish himself as a law professor and as one of his father's biographers, bore his Grandmother Kimball's mark of red hair. The fact that Eddie, as he was known in childhood, represented added expense in a crucial year of the Depression was swallowed up in the love his parents had for him, a love that would intensify as they later nursed him through a serious illness.

Because of their frugality, the Kimballs entered the Great Depression in fighting trim. They were not burdened with heavy debt; they owned their home, had a garden and a cow; and though it was crippled, had the family business. The economic crisis did not, therefore, ring down the curtain on their financial future. They went on as before, although on a scaled-down basis. They continued to enjoy the social diversions life in Safford offered and to travel occasionally. Early April 1930 found them in Salt Lake City, where they attended the general conference and enjoyed the Church's centennial pageant. The pageant, titled *Message of the Ages,* was staged in the Salt Lake Tabernacle. It depicted the influence of the gospel from the beginning, while the conference addresses portrayed the struggles the Latter-day Saints had confronted and overcome. All this provided a sobering perspective against which the Kimballs could appraise the significance of the economic problems they faced.

On the way home, they spent several days in Los Angeles, visiting Del and his family and playing at the beach. Then in Phoenix, beginning on April 15, they attended the Rotary state convention.

The crash of the stock market and the attending upheavals in the American economy played havoc with the U.S. banking system. Falling prices, tight money, bloated inventories, and sluggish sales resulted in wholesale bankruptcies and bank foreclosures. Often the property taken in a foreclosure had far less value in the depressed economy than the amount of the loan the property was originally given to secure. There was no market for the foreclosed property, which, encumbered by taxes and utility assessments, hung like a dead weight around the necks of the banks. In addition, the higher interest rates imposed on banks by the Federal Reserve discouraged further borrowings, which are the lifeblood of banking. Thus the banks were stalled by an economic gridlock from which they could not be extricated easily. Given these conditions, it is not surprising that bank failures in the United States became epidemic.

It did not take long for the infection to reach Safford. The victim was President Kimball's former employer, the Bank of Safford, which failed on May 28, 1932. Before the closure, there had been widespread rumors the bank was in trouble. In checking them out with friends who still worked there, Spencer was told that the rumors were false and that the money of the depositors was safe. From his experience with the failure of the Citizens Bank, he knew how fast a bank could go under without a warning. And because of that experience, it may have been prudent to withdraw his funds from the Bank of Safford. Out of loyalty, however, and concern that withdrawal by a person as prominent as he might produce a needless run on the bank, causing it to fold, Spencer rode it out to the end. He and the entities for which he handled banking transactions—Rotary, the stake, the canal companies, etc.—lost a total of about nine thousand dollars. Only about 30 percent of this was ultimately recovered. It was learned later that the collapse of the bank was hastened by a dishonest officer who had embezzled twenty-three thousand dollars, for which he was convicted and imprisoned. Spencer was outraged by the revelation. "The more I think of it, the worse I feel about it," he wrote, "to think that he could be living high and spending our money and causing an entire community to suffer by the falling of their air castles."

As America's commercial structure seemed to crumble, many insurance companies also began to fold, a threat that struck at the very heart of the business of Kimball-Greenhalgh. On November 24, 1931, Spencer received a message he and his partner had feared might come. "I had a phone call from Phoenix that one of our insurance companies had failed," he wrote on that day. Hurriedly gathering the records on policies the agency had written with this company, the Home Fire and Accident Company of Arkansas, he left early the next morning for Phoenix. Over the next three days, he worked feverishly with his friends J. R. Price and George F. Price, who also brokered insurance, to cobble together an arrangement that would provide alternate insurance coverage for the Kimball-Greenhalgh customers affected by the Arkansas company's failure. The complicated transaction was completed on November 28, and the issue of the *Arizona Republic* the next morning contained an article detailing what had taken place. One senses that while President Kimball was enormously relieved to have dodged this bullet, he was wary about others that might be aimed his way in the future.

The Kimballs enjoyed a "very conservative" Christmas this year, although "the children were happy." And following a New Year's Eve party, Spencer made this summary of the second full year of the Great Depression: "And thus ended in mirth a year of trouble for the country, depression, famine, drouth, floods, . . . extremely low prices for raw materials, bank failures and financial ruin to many; and yet, there were many joys and the year brought much of happiness."

There would be two more years of deep depression before the economy began to turn around in Safford. As far as the Kimball-Greenhalgh agency was concerned, the year 1932 was a repeat of 1931. The business continued to limp along, producing barely enough to keep the partners going and to pay their employees, eating into the agency's principal when necessary. They managed to weather the bank failure, fortunately having on deposit enough in the Valley Bank to cover their checks drawn on the Bank of Safford that had not cleared when the bank failed. This bolstered their reputation in the community for judgment and integrity and built goodwill for the future.

By careful planning, the Kimballs were able to save enough to take a two-week family vacation in August 1932. They arrived in Long Beach, California, on the eighth, renting a furnished apartment near the beach for ten dollars a week. It was the first time the entire family, with all four children, had enjoyed an extended vacation together. Eddie, almost two, was toddling and talking by this time; LeVan, age fourteen, was big enough and strong enough to ride the breakers; and Olive Beth, ten, and Andrew, five, were the right age to enjoy building sand castles and wading in the backwash of the breakers. Long hours were spent in the sun on the beach. Spencer and Camilla watched as their children played, while they intermittently read, napped, dipped in the surf, or merely gazed at the sea, whose rhythmic poundings eased away thoughts of the Depression or bank failures. While the Kimballs knew how to work, they also knew how to play. It was a tempering quality that enabled them to handle life's pressures with poise.

The Kimballs returned home as the presidential campaign was heating up. The Democrats had nominated Franklin Delano Roosevelt, governor of New York, at the Chicago convention held in July. His Republican opponent was President Herbert Hoover. The Depression was the overriding issue of the campaign. Governor Roosevelt's focus was two-pronged: to blame the Republican administrations of the past twelve years for the Depression and to call for change, for a "new deal." He never defined the new deal precisely, saying only that he would seek to adapt "existing economic organization to the service of the people." President Hoover saw something ominous in this. "Dominantly in their spirit," he said, "they represent a radical departure from the foundations of one hundred fifty years which have made this the greatest nation in the world." President Kimball, an avid, lifelong Republican, supported Herbert Hoover. That the Democratic platform included a plank to repeal the eighteenth amendment cast him even more decidedly for the Republican candidate.

The outcome of the election was hardly a surprise, given the deadening effect of the Depression and the widely held view that a change was necessary. Franklin D. Roosevelt won by a landslide. Immediately following his inauguration on March 4, 1933, President Roosevelt began pushing through Congress a host of new bills, several of which were a short-term boon to farmers and which soon began to have a positive impact on the economy of the Gila Valley. Farm prices rose when production decreased due to agreements that subsidized farmers for limiting production. Other legislation aided farmers by giving them protection against foreclosures and subsidizing some mortgage payments. With brightened hopes for the numerous farmers around Safford, other elements of the community shared in the optimism and the economic benefits, including the Kimball-Greenhalgh agency. We can imagine Bishop Greenhalgh, a confirmed Democrat, gently ribbing his partner because of the improved conditions created by *his* party. The bishop was once heard to say he believed the country would go to pot were a Republican elected president, and Spencer felt the same about the election of a Democratic president.

Near the dawn of the "Roosevelt Revolution," the Kimballs faced a devastating personal challenge. It came in the form of illness to their youngest child. At first, it did not seem to be serious. In early September 1933, Eddie came indoors from playing to complain that his legs hurt. Asked why, he said he had sat down hard on a block. Later symptoms, a fever and vomiting, discounted that as the cause and led to Camilla's initial diagnosis of tonsillitis, an ailment he had had before. This seemed wrong when, a few days later, Eddie fell as he arose from a chair. Alarmed, Camilla took him to the doctor, who decided he had rheumatism, perhaps the result of a mild case of diphtheria. The next day, the doctor came with a colleague to examine the child again. They had nothing further to offer. Camilla questioned them, fearing the possibility that Eddie had infantile paralysis, but they flatly rejected that suggestion. When soreness in the legs persisted, Eddie was taken to a chiropractor, whose treatments only aggravated the pain. After several visits, which were pure torture to the child, the chiropractor said he thought Eddie's illness might be polio. "We were terrified," wrote Camilla. Immediately, Spencer called Del to make an appointment with a specialist, loaded Eddie in the car, and, with Camilla, left for Los Angeles. The specialist confirmed the parents' worst fears, diagnosing the ailment as poliomyelitis. He put Eddie's legs in splints, ordered him quarantined, and chastised the Kimballs for needlessly exposing others along the way by traveling before the three-week period of contagion had ended. Burdened now with feelings of both guilt and fear, the parents began an odyssey of eight years during which they struggled with their child to try to repair the terrible physical and emotional damage the disease inflicted.

In some ways, the three days of the quarantine were the worst of all. Eddie, already stressed by the pain, was terrified to be isolated from his parents. He cried almost incessantly for them until he was hoarse. They were powerless to do anything except pray for him and endure the anguish his pitiful cries aroused. They were allowed, during brief visiting hours, to peer at their son through a small crack in the door, a privilege that was more of a penalty. It only increased their feelings of helplessness and escalated their small son's frustrations.

They rented a room in a home across the street from the hospital so as to be near. There was nothing for them to do, really, except wander the yards and the halls of the hospital in order to be available to respond promptly, if needed, or to peer through Eddie's door during the awkward visiting hours, occasionally singing to him or telling stories. Once the quarantine was lifted and it was certain the boy was not near death, Spencer returned home to supervise the other children and take care of church and business responsibilities. Camilla remained in Los Angeles for ten tedious weeks, spending every possible minute during the days at her son's bedside as he began to recover and then watching as he underwent painful therapy. Fearful, perhaps, that he would again be separated from her, Eddie was insistent that his mother hold him constantly or that she always be at his side during the day; when she left to get food or some rest, he would immediately begin calling for her, crying, "Mama, Mama," over and over again. It was a frightening thing for a three-year-old to experience, isolated in such a strange place, so far from home, and conscious that something terrible had happened that prevented him from walking like other children. It was not surprising, therefore, that he would cling to and incessantly call for the one familiar figure among all the giant, white-robed people who inhabited his new world.

At home, assisted by Camilla's sister Mary, Spencer endeavored to be both mother and father to the other children. Because Andrew, the youngest of the three at home, was six, all were in school, which simplified the problems of care during the day. Conscious of the gravity of the tragedy which had descended on the family, the children were generally helpful and cooperative, though occasional disputes seemed to arise between Olive Beth and Andrew. The big sister complained that "Andrew is like a stubborn mule." It turned out he had refused to go with his sister to eat dinner with neighbors, though he had been invited. Andrew's defense never found its way into the record, although it is probable he didn't like being bossed by one who was only five years older than he, and so he apparently took this means to declare his independence and to strike another mighty blow for liberty.

The anxieties and loneliness caused by the ten-week separation and Eddie's agonizing struggle bound the Kimball family more closely together. Almost daily correspondence between Safford and Los Angeles kept everyone posted about the happenings at both ends. And the loneliness induced by separation prompted reflections about the nature and depth of the love the parents shared.

President Kimball lacked catastrophic insurance to cover Eddie's high medical costs. The initial bills were staggering for one struggling during a depression while supporting a large family. A tentative payment schedule revealed monthly installments to be almost equal to Spencer's monthly income. Nor did these include charges for future medical services, which were projected to extend over a long period. These mountainous debts threatened to crush the Kimballs' financial stability and impoverish them for years. Happily, the March of Dimes intervened to prevent this. Through subsidies it provided, the Kimballs were able to handle the expenses and avoid financial ruin. The family was grateful for the timely aid the March of Dimes provided and afterward contributed generously to its annual fund drive by way of appreciation. It still was not easy to pay for the remaining portion of medical care, and the cost of Eddie's illness represented a major item in the Kimball budget for many years.

The brunt of this family trauma was, of course, borne by the son. However much his parents may have wanted to shield him from it, it was he who had to bear the pain, the indignity, the inconvenience, and the lifelong physical limitations his illness imposed. Recognizing this, the family and others lavished attention on him in the early years to such a degree that he could have become permanently dependent on others. Spencer and Camilla sought to avoid this danger by insisting from the beginning of their son's convalescence that he do things for himself, if at all possible, rather than expecting others to do them. Sometimes it was difficult to refrain from helping when the little boy struggled so hard to perform simple tasks another could do effortlessly. However, the parents exercised disciplined restraint, and the son similarly became disciplined in doing things for himself. The result was the best one under difficult circumstances. Through numerous operations and seemingly endless therapies, Edward Kimball eventually was able to walk without braces or canes, though not perfectly, and in time he grew to maturity and became a husband and father.

There were times, however, during this long process when both parents and son must have wondered about the outcome. Such a time occurred three years after polio struck, when Eddie started the first grade. He was out of braces by then and was recovering nicely from the first series of operations. While walking in front of a slide on the playground, he was struck accidentally by a schoolmate who failed to see him in time to avoid the collision. The impact broke Eddie's right leg just above the ankle. Stoically, he wore a cast for weeks until the bone healed.

Some friends of the Kimballs speculated why such an exemplary family should reap such misfortune. The Kimballs never considered it to be a mark of heavenly indifference or retribution. To them it merely represented the natural consequences of living in a hazardous world. They expected problems, setbacks, and difficulties throughout life as the natural legacy of mankind. At the same time, their belief was that through divine agencies and influences, earthly burdens could be made light and endurable and, in some instances, through invincible faith could be lifted entirely. The numerous illnesses and ailments that later afflicted Spencer, and the manner in which he endured them or cast them off, suggests the importance of these concepts in President Kimball's life.

Chapter 10

The Emerging Leader

From the time he was called to the stake presidency in 1924, President Kimball played a vital role in the administration of the St. Joseph Stake. But it was a subordinate role. His function was to assist the stake president, Harry L. Payne. Whatever Spencer Kimball did during the twelve years he served as a counselor, he did it as delegated by Harry Payne. However, there were some assignments that gave him broad discretion, enabling him to demonstrate his initiative and his executive ability. One of these was his appointment to serve as the chairman of the St. Joseph Stake's golden jubilee. It was to be the most colorful event in the history of the Gila Valley since the creation of the stake in February 1883.

The advance planning for the four-day gala, scheduled for February 23, 24, 25, and 26, 1933, began in early 1932 with the appointment of nine prominent people to serve with President Kimball on the committee. To add special stature to the celebration, President Heber J. Grant was invited to attend as the guest of honor and to be the featured speaker at a priesthood session and the four general sessions. The prophet willingly accepted, as the trip would provide a welcome break from a cold Salt Lake winter.

President Kimball worked feverishly on the jubilee program while he struggled to save his business. He worked with each committee chairman to make sure everything was just right. Nothing was left to chance. Every detail was checked and rechecked. Every assignment was reviewed and re-reviewed. Taking special interest in the music, he organized a chorus comprised of the stake presidency and high council that sang at the priesthood banquet. His quartet also sang there. Meanwhile, Spencer and Evan Madsen, the music committee chairman, worked together arranging for various choirs to sing at other sessions.

The celebration began with a parade on Friday. After the parade, the throng divided into two groups for the field events, the children eleven and under going to the meetinghouse grounds and everyone else going to the alumni field at the academy. All afternoon, they enjoyed a variety of sporting events—tug of war, foot races, wheelbarrow races, relay races, pioneer races, costume change relay races, donkey polo games, team pulling, ring picking, and a greased pig chase, among others. It is easy to imagine that thirty-eight-year-old Spencer Kimball, then at the height of his physical powers and brimming with energy, enlivened these events with his sunny disposition and musical laughter. Because the other members of the stake presidency were in their sixties and lacked his physical vigor, there can be no doubt that Spencer Kimball was the life of these proceedings, as also of the dances held that night.

The general sessions, held over Saturday and Sunday, provided a spiritual uplift for the stake. The participation of President Heber J. Grant guaranteed that. He was a forceful, eloquent speaker whose accomplishments in learning to play baseball, to sing, to write well, and to do other things against heavy odds were legendary in the Church and highly motivational to his listeners.

This celebration showcased Spencer Kimball's organizational and leadership abilities as few things could have done. Nor could the President of the Church have failed to notice the special spiritual qualities he exhibited. Another participant in the jubilee, Eli Abegg, recognized them, as many before him had done. He is reported to have said, "I want to tell you in the name of Jesus Christ that Spencer Kimball will one day become an apostle of the Church."

By now the economy had begun to turn around in the Gila Valley. Loans and subsidies to farmers, higher prices for farm products, and mortgage loans insured by the Federal Housing Administration had broken the financial gridlock. As new housing starts increased, lots in the Kimball-Greenhalgh subdivision created six years before began to sell. The agency's business in insurance and bonds picked up proportionately, as did the sideline business of purchasing and servicing installment contracts. Meanwhile, Spencer qualified as an FHA appraiser, which provided additional income.

All this translated into financial gain and increased prominence in the community's business and civic affairs, so much so that a group of fellow Rotarians urged Spencer to run for the Rotary Club's district governorship the following year. The district included most of the state of Arizona. This encouraged Spencer's supporters about his chances because of his prominence among Latter-day Saints throughout the state. Moreover, he was friendly, honest, personable, and successful, qualities that would have had uniform appeal among Rotarians. Having obtained Spencer's consent, his backers announced at the annual convention in Prescott, Arizona, in May 1935 that he would be a candidate for district governor.

Spencer entered into the campaign with enthusiasm. He was devoted to Rotary not only for the enjoyable and profitable associations it afforded but for its goals of service, reflected in his club's projects of helping the Boy Scouts and providing free lunches for children. Moreover, he believed his election would be an honor to his club and to the Church since no Latter-day Saint had ever served as district governor of Rotary in Arizona.

Spencer and his supporters approached the district conference in Prescott with optimism. The campaign manager, Louis Long, who was not a member of the Church, had contacted the other Rotary clubs in the state, furnishing biographical data about the candidate and, by word of mouth, assuring them that Spencer Kimball's strict religious beliefs would not hinder his effective service as district governor. While his opponent was the nominee of a club in the Phoenix area and could hope to profit from that, he had been defeated twice before, which improved Spencer's chances.

Soon after the Safford contingent had arrived in Prescott and had set up for the final campaign push, it received word that the campaign manager of Spencer's opponent had dropped dead on the golf course. A meeting of key members of the Safford group was convened immediately to appraise the effect of this on the campaign. It was the consensus that to continue an aggressive effort to win votes might be viewed as a graceless attempt to take advantage of a wounded candidate. And merely to mark time could be interpreted as a lack of real interest in the job. In these circumstances, it was decided that to concede the election would be in the best interests of all concerned.

As the delegates assembled for the final campaigning, to be followed by the vote, Spencer arose and, being recognized by the chair, formally withdrew his candidacy, then nominated his opponent and moved that he be elected by acclamation. That motion was seconded by Ben Blake, president of the Safford club, and unanimously carried. The favorable reaction to this concession was prompt and unanimous. The Rotarians at the convention, who were aware of the circumstances, thronged around Spencer to laud him and to express their admiration. The news accounts, written without full knowledge of the background, focused on the drama of the concession and on the sacrifice made by Spencer Kimball and his supporters. Many who were close to the withdrawn candidate and yet were unaware of the background were left to speculate about the reasons for the concession. One of these, seventeen-year-old LeVan, offered an explanation his father would always treasure. The son was reported as saying that whatever prompted his father to concede, it was the right thing to do.

This idea of personal rectitude lay at the heart of the perceptions others had of Spencer W. Kimball. In all his dealings over many years, no one ever accused him of dishonesty or sharp practices. He was always a straight arrow, delivering what he promised and negotiating with candor and without devious motives. This is not to say, however, that he was an easy mark, either in the negotiation or the execution of a business transaction. He insisted on fairness and promptness in others, even as he showed those qualities in his own conduct. He was therefore strict in collecting amounts owed him. This attitude was driven by two main considerations: that it was only fair his debtors should pay and that delinquent debts soured personal relationships. In one notable case, he frankly told a debtor he intended to pursue him relentlessly until he paid so there would be no permanent rupture in their personal relationship. When the debt was finally paid, the friend stopped avoiding him and renewed business contacts, something he probably would not have done had the debt remained unpaid.

Soon after conceding the Rotary election in 1935, Spencer decided to be a candidate the following year. To show his interest in and commitment to the cause, he felt it necessary to attend the international Rotary convention that year in Mexico City. Although it required careful budgeting, the Kimballs went at their own expense. It proved to be an unusual experience. For Spencer, it was a clinic in the operation of an international organization and extended his acquaintance with Rotarians from around the world. For

Camilla, it was like a pilgrimage to her native land, providing insights into Mexican culture she had never gained in the Mormon colonies in Mexico where she was born and reared. And for both, it was a revealing introduction to the architecture of the civilizations that had successively dominated the land—the Aztecs, the Spaniards, and, more recently, the Mexicans, some of whom were remnants of a people whose ancestry extended to the Holy Land as chronicled in the Book of Mormon. Little did Spencer and Camilla Kimball realize in 1935 how intimately their future would be intertwined with this country and its people and with other countries and peoples in Central and South America.

Because of his unexpected concession at Prescott, Spencer was unopposed in the Rotary district governor's race in 1936. Elected by acclamation, he began a year's service that took him to all the Rotary clubs in Arizona and introduced him, on a first-name basis, to key business and professional leaders throughout the state. In the process, he practically wore out an automobile as he traveled to instruct the leaders of local clubs and to speak to the general Rotary membership at special meetings.

Camilla accompanied him on most of these assignments, meeting when possible with the Rotary Anns, the women's auxiliary, and joining her husband for the social events. They maintained their own standards about not drinking alcoholic beverages, while respecting the right of others to do so. There was, however, one point at which Spencer Kimball's attitude toward alcohol influenced his administration. He insisted that those who drank must pay for their own liquor so that abstainers did not subsidize the drinkers by having the liquor tab paid out of Rotary funds. This was an equitable arrangement to which no one objected and which raised no issue about Mormon influence on Rotary affairs.

The administration of district governor Spencer W. Kimball was successful and personally rewarding. During the year, four new Rotary clubs were organized, a record for

Arizona. The district was effectively managed within budget, and Spencer's efficiency and enthusiasm raised the esprit de corps to a high degree. At a personal level, it was satisfying to know he could succeed in an organization of able men of such diverse backgrounds and convictions. The acquaintances he made developed into friendships that lasted throughout life.

During the year President Kimball was district governor of Rotary, a major change occurred in his church responsibilities. It had its genesis the previous year, when he again became the stake clerk while retaining the position of second counselor. Because he had efficiently handled both jobs before, he was surprised by a suggestion the first counselor, William Ellsworth, made in the autumn of 1935. President Ellsworth suggested that Spencer should be released as a counselor while continuing to serve as the stake clerk. His reasoning was that Spencer's knowledge of stake affairs and his closeness to the presidency as the clerk would enable him to serve as a de facto counselor while making it possible to call another counselor, providing "four instead of three" men to administer the affairs of the stake. Spencer was stumped to understand what prompted this suggestion. "I can hardly think of any selfish motive on his part," Spencer wrote to his stepmother, Mary. "If there is one, it is well hidden, at least I have not been able to fathom it." Once the shock had passed, he began to see merit in the suggestion. "As I think about it a lot I seem to feel a great relief from responsibility and it seems good to contemplate that there will be few or no more funerals, no more responsibility in manning the organizations, signing recommends, attending meetings, etc., and I welcome it." But there was a downside that Spencer was frank to acknowledge. "Still, I wonder how I shall feel shorn of the honor and responsibility and all, to which I have become so used. I am wondering just how I shall feel when the change takes place." When the suggestion surfaced with President Payne, he demurred at first. But when he learned Spencer was willing, he agreed.

The change was made at the stake conference in early 1936. The visitor was Elder Melvin J. Ballard of the Twelve. President Kimball broached the subject with Elder Ballard in a typical way. "It is hardly right, is it," he asked the apostle, "for one little man to have two big jobs?" When Spencer explained the situation, Elder Ballard asked which job he would prefer to keep. He answered that he wanted to serve where he was called. When pressed as to his preference were he able to choose, he opted for the clerk's job. And so after twelve years in the St. Joseph stake presidency, Spencer W. Kimball was released. His friend Jesse Udall was called to replace him.

No doubt the unexpected release from the stake presidency aroused speculation as to the reason. The strange conclusions some reach in these matters is illustrated by a woman who accused President Kimball of choosing the clerk's job because of the modest stipend it carried. After making the accusation, she predicted he would be an apostate in six months.

Events of the next summer suggest it was fortunate Spencer was released from the stake presidency. As a reward for his service as district governor, Rotary offered to pay his expenses to the international convention in Nice, France. Because he had no confining church duties, he and Camilla decided to convert Spencer's trip into a once-in-a-lifetime grand tour of Europe and England for both of them. They mapped out a ten-week tour of ten countries and, estimating Camilla's costs and the extra costs for Spencer, decided they could handle it financially by dipping into their savings and borrowing on their life insurance policies. With LeVan in the mission field, arrangements were made for Camilla's sister Mary to stay with the other three children. Bishop Greenhalgh would guide the business in Spencer's absence, and his secretary would handle routine stake clerk matters. With all bases covered, the attractive young couple, now forty-two years old and brimming with health and enthusiasm, boarded the Gila Monster, bound for their grand tour.

The first leg of their journey took them by rail via Chicago to Montreal, Quebec, Canada, where LeVan was serving in the Eastern Canadian Mission. They spent a week here, visiting their son and touring the city, whose predominant French and Catholic influences were reflected in its language and architecture.

The travelers boarded their ship, the *Duchess of Athol,* at the Montreal docks, though the ship did not reach the open Atlantic until it had traveled a thousand miles down the St. Lawrence River, passing en route through the city of Quebec and other major cities in the province of Quebec.

Spencer and Camilla proved to be good ocean travelers on this, their first voyage. They did not miss a meal, although they ate sparingly of the tasty French cuisine. Fresh flowers always decorated the tables. At night there was dancing to the music of a good five-piece orchestra. Walking the decks provided good daily exercise.

There were more than two hundred Rotarians on board, drawn from all parts of the United States and Canada. Their common interests in Rotary fostered the formation of new friendships. Indeed, one couple the Kimballs met became fast friends with whom they maintained a close relationship for forty years.

The *Duchess* docked at LeHavre, the French port on the English Channel closest to Paris. They boarded a train there for the 110-mile trip. This took them through the fertile lower valley of the Seine, past Rouen, a bustling port upriver fifty miles, and on to Paris, the famous city that never sleeps. That they arrived near midnight did not deter them from beginning their sightseeing immediately. They rented a hotel room, parked their bags, freshened up, and began a walking tour of the downtown area. They wanted to see everything. They returned to their room near dawn, napped briefly, freshened up again, then caught the train for Nice. This leg of their journey took them diagonally across France to the Riviera in the southeast corner of the country.

Located between Cannes and Monte Carlo, Nice is a city

devoted almost exclusively to catering to the wants of tourists. Rotary selected it as the international convention site that year to provide the delegates with a taste of French luxury while conducting the necessary business of the convention. The couple from Safford gained an important insight into the local culture when, at their first formal dinner, they found seven goblets of wine arranged behind their dinner plates. Their companions, who by now had learned about Mormon dietary rules, understood perfectly why the Kimballs' wineglasses remained untouched.

But they did not abstain from other features of the convention. They enjoyed the delicious French food; the dancing; the sightseeing, which included a visit to one of the ornate gambling casinos at Monte Carlo; and the spectacular fireworks displays on the beach.

After the convention, the Rotarians separated and went their own ways, some to return home and others, like Spencer and Camilla, to pursue their own travel itinerary. Since Italy was just across the border to the east, they began their tour in that pleasant land. Their first stop was at Genoa, on the Ligurian Sea. Italy's greatest seaport, the city attained fame chiefly as the birthplace of Christopher Columbus. They visited a house on one of Genoa's narrow, winding streets reputed to be the birthplace of the great navigator.

Angling in a southerly direction along the west coast of the Italian boot, the travelers stopped in Pisa to inspect the campanile of the cathedral, commonly called the Leaning Tower of Pisa. By climbing to the top of the cylindrical white marble structure by means of a spiral staircase in its hollow center, the visitors found themselves almost two hundred feet above the ground at a point where Galileo Galilei, a native of Pisa, is said to have made his experiments with falling objects. Reared in an area where the two-hundred-year-old San Xavier Mission was the oldest structure built by Europeans, the Kimballs were intrigued to realize that the famous tower in Pisa was begun almost eight hundred years before their visit. They also inspected the adjacent marble cathedral, whose interior was richly decorated with beautiful paintings, sculptures, and mosaics. From the center of the dome of the cathedral hung a bronze lamp whose movements, it is said, conveyed to Galileo his understanding of the regularity of pendulum oscillations.

Their sense of awe at the ancient character of Italian civilization was heightened when the Kimballs reached Rome. Here were remnants of a civilization that flourished almost three thousand years before, its most ancient, identifiable ruins being part of the basement of the Temple of Jupiter, built on the Capitoline Hill. More recent ruins were the Forum and the Colosseum, whose interior view revealed the animal cages, the subterranean passageways, and the supports beneath the floor of the arena. Here in ancient times, gladiator slaves fought with lions and other beasts for the entertainment of the Roman crowds.

The Kimballs were astonished by the Catacombs, a labyrinthian complex of underground burial crypts on the outskirts of Rome, extending for miles in all directions. During periods of persecution, the early Christians in Rome used these as clandestine places of worship, adorning some of them with pictures of fish and other symbols from Christian art. In contrast were the impressive aboveground structures of Vatican City, including a number of its palaces; St. Peter's Cathedral, the largest church in the world, covering nearly four acres and featuring the great dome designed by Michelangelo; the Sistine Chapel with its ceiling and *Last Judgment* frescoes by Michelangelo; and the sweeping Colonnade and Piazza San Pietro of St. Peter's Basilica. What human intuition could have foretold that this obscure American businessman, walking with his equally obscure wife amidst the splendor of Vatican City, would one day wear the same apostolic mantle once worn by Peter of old, for whom these impressive buildings were named?

The next stop was at the ruins of the ancient city of Pompeii, twelve miles southwest of Naples. Situated at the base of Mount Vesuvius, Pompeii was buried in A.D. 79 during a forty-hour volcanic eruption of Vesuvius. The speed with which the lava and volcanic ash covered the city provided a delayed snapshot of an ancient culture and lifestyle once the city was excavated hundreds of years later. Shielded from the atmosphere, the decorations of the buildings were preserved, as also the colors of the paintings on their walls. The inspection of these ruins was made more meaningful for Spencer and Camilla Kimball by reading *The Last Days of Pompeii.* Like thousands of tourists before and after them, they had their picture taken standing in front of the central court of the luxurious Pompeian home of the Casii.

The Kimballs also hiked to the top of Vesuvius, where they succumbed to the cajolery of two Italians who, for a fee, extracted a small bit of hot lava through a fissure and fashioned it around an Italian coin as a memento.

Spencer and Camilla felt the reputation of Florence had been overblown, so this art center did not appeal to them. A detracting factor was a temporary siege of homesickness on the part of Camilla, who had been away from her children for a month without word from them. This was soon swallowed up in excitement when they reached Venice, the Queen of the Adriatic, many of whose buildings rest on piles driven into the bed of the lagoon. The more than a hundred small islands within the city were formed by the colliding forces of the ocean tides and the river flowing into the lagoon. Bordering the islands are more than a hundred canals that provide the main source of travel within the city.

Caught up in the romantic mood that pervades Venice, Spencer wrote almost poetically of a gondola ride he and Camilla took one balmy evening when, following a light, refreshing rain, a bright moon intermittently broke through drifting clouds. "How romantic," he wrote, "to sit cozily in a comfortable upholstered seat under a canopy with someone you love and glide smoothly through the water, down little side canals, under bridges, hearing voices from the houses as you pass along."

Leaving Venice, the Kimballs traveled to Budapest, Hungary, sometimes called the Queen of the Danube, passing through upper Yugoslavia en route. Here the travelers found traces of oriental influence, derived from Turkish dominance of the area for 155 years during the sixteenth and seventeenth centuries. They also became conscious of the dominating influence of the Danube River on the history and the culture of Budapest, a city that straddles the river and is a composite of three independent cities, Buda and Obuda on the right bank and Pest on the left bank, that were consolidated into one city in 1872. Accustomed to the meandering Gila, the Kimballs found that the Danube, extending more than seventeen hundred miles from its head in the Black Forest of Southwestern Germany to its mouth on the Black Sea, stretched their imagination.

Their imagination was stretched even further, but in a different way, when they reached Vienna, Austria, 135 miles upriver from Budapest. Here the Kimballs hired a guide, Mr. Schmertz, to show them the city, famed as probably the most outstanding musical center in the world. Because of his love for music and his musical ability, Spencer was intrigued by Vienna, the native or adopted home of many of the world's most distinguished composers—Joseph Haydn, Wolfgang Mozart, Ludwig van Beethoven, Johannes Brahms, Franz Schubert, Anton Bruckner, Gustav Mahler, and Arnold Schoenberg, who was then still alive. The guide, Mr. Schmertz, was so attached to the Kimballs that he saw them off on the train the next morning. Thereafter, they kept in touch with each other periodically, and when Elder and Sister Kimball toured the European missions in 1955, they contacted their friend and took him to a church meeting.

News received in Vienna about Hitler's aggressive demands and the nervousness those demands had created throughout Europe cast a temporary shadow over the Kimballs' tour as they traveled to Switzerland. However, in this tiny country noted for its traditional neutrality, any concerns they had were eased away by the friendliness of the people and the majesty of the Swiss Alps. And a boat trip down the Rhine after entering Germany, where they saw numerous ships plying the river, laden with equipment, raw materials, and foodstuffs, brought home the reality that this was the busiest waterway in Europe.

Leaving the boat at Rotterdam at the mouth of the Rhine River, the travelers spent several days in Holland, visiting Amsterdam and The Hague.

Because their stop there en route to Nice had been brief, the Kimballs now returned to Paris for a longer visit. Traveling via Belgium, they saw vivid scars that had been inflicted on its cities and the land during World War I that had not healed. In Paris they took the time to visit the key points of interest—the Eiffel Tower; the museum at the Louvre that contained the *Venus de Milo*, the *Mona Lisa*, and other masterpieces; the Ile de la Cite, the small island in the Seine River, shaped like a ship, where the early Roman governors built their palaces and their administrative offices; the Cathedral of Notre Dame, reputed to have been built on the site of an ancient pagan altar to Jupiter; the site of the Bastille, the prison whose capture on July 14, 1878, became the symbol of the French Revolution; the Arc de Triomphe, commissioned by Napoleon in 1806; and Napoleon's Tomb.

After France, only England remained on their itinerary. Their ancestral ties and church connections there perhaps should have made this part of the tour more satisfying than any other. Their arrival in London, however, was not attended with the kind of enthusiasm one might have expected. By this time, after more than two months on the road, living out of a suitcase, they were tired. That they had sometimes slept on the train so they could devote their days to sightseeing had added to their weariness. And frankly, though they had enjoyed the tour immensely, they had had enough of touring and of tourists. "I have seen so many tourists," wrote Camilla after viewing the scene at Trafalgar

Square, "all herding around to see the same places and do the same things, that I am quite fed up with them. I shall be most happy to go home to my own little niche and let the rest of the world go by."

There was still another factor that made their arrival in London less than the happiest time of the tour—they were running out of money. They had been caught in a common tourist trap of spending more than they had budgeted. On learning that the charges at the hotel where they had planned to stay were beyond their means, Camilla waited in the lobby, and later on a bench at Trafalgar Square, while her husband looked for a more reasonably priced room. "I am so downright homesick tonight I just had to cry a bit," she wrote. "I wish I could fly home. I have seen so much I have reached the saturation point. Nothing seems interesting anymore. Our expenses are so high, I am quite in the dumps."

However, a good night's sleep in a room they could afford and a hearty breakfast the next morning put things in a new, optimistic light. They were ready to see London. Despite Camilla's comments about the herding instincts of tourists, they went to see the things that attract most tourists—they witnessed the changing of the guard at Buckingham Palace and visited Hyde Park, the Tower of London, the British Museum, the Palace of Westminster, where Parliament is housed, and Westminster Abbey. They traveled to the Midlands to visit Shakespeare's birthplace. While there, they attended a performance of *Hamlet*. The last stop before embarking for home was Brighton, the resort on the English Channel south of London.

They recrossed the Atlantic on the *Berengeria*. After sleeping away the weariness that had built up over the weeks, they enjoyed every aspect of shipboard life. Seven days at sea, free from the hassle of tight travel schedules, enabled Spencer and Camilla to digest what they had seen, heard, and felt during the tour and to reflect on their meaning. Certainly, their perceptions of the world had changed forever, as also their attitudes toward other cultures. The

Berengeria berthed at New York City. As she entered the harbor, the Kimballs were moved by the sight of the Statue of Liberty and the towering Manhattan skyline. This was their first exposure to the throbbing energy of New York City. The conditions at dockside seemed chaotic to them.

The Kimballs, gathering their bags and other belongings, engaged a cab that took them to the train depot. The long trip across the country gave them a new appreciation for the vastness and richness of the United States and for the efficiency and comfort of its trains. At home, all was in order, although Eddie was pale and thin from a siege of the whooping cough. And both he and Andrew had "hair like lions' manes," not having had access to their father-barber for almost three months. Mary had managed things efficiently and, with Olive Beth's help, had spruced up the house so that Camilla did not have a backlog of unfinished work. The same was not true of her husband. It took some time for Spencer to bring everything current and return to a normal work routine.

Few people in the Gila Valley, if any, had made a grand tour of Europe. There were, of course, some who had served missions there, but no one had toured as extensively and as long as had Spencer and Camilla Kimball. When they returned, they were much in demand to share their experiences and to show their film and the keepsakes they had brought home. Because Spencer had been released from the stake presidency and had completed his service as district governor of Rotary, both he and Camilla seemed to feel that this round of talks about their travels was the culmination of their service in the limelight and that they could now settle into their "little niche," as Camilla had put it, finish rearing their children, and enjoy life with their family and friends.

Chapter 11

Mount Graham Stake President

Spencer's enjoyment of his "little niche" was short-lived. Only a few months after the Kimballs returned from Europe, Elder Melvin J. Ballard returned to Safford to preside at another conference of the St. Joseph Stake. This time, he came with instructions to divide the stake, which had grown so large as to make administration of it unwieldy. The event, the first of its kind in fifty-five years, created intense interest in the Gila Valley and busy speculation as to the division line and the makeup of the two presidencies. The suspense ended February 20, 1938, when, following a long series of interviews conducted by Elder Ballard, Jesse A. Udall was called as the new president of the St. Joseph Stake, and Spencer W. Kimball was called as the first president of the new Mount Graham Stake. The new stake included the Safford Ward and all Church units to the east, and the St. Joseph Stake included the Thatcher Ward and all Church units to the west.

The choice of these two men provided the Church in the Gila Valley and surrounding areas with the kind of experienced, vigorous leadership needed to ensure its continued growth. They were near the same age, Jesse Udall being two years older than Spencer Kimball. They were schoolmates, had been close socially, and had common interests in business as investors in a proposed radio station, KGLU. Both their fathers had been pioneer stake presidents in Arizona. On the day of the division, Jesse Udall was in St. Johns attending the funeral of his father, David King Udall. Elder Ballard contacted him there by telephone to tell him of his call.

Initially, President Kimball was hesitant to accept his call, being concerned that members with whom he had had business disagreements would not sustain him. At Elder Ballard's suggestion, he went personally to each of these people, in company with Camilla, to apologize for any offense he had given and to resolve any existing problems. This cleared the way to begin his ministry without feelings of enmity or discord.

His long training as a counselor and clerk simplified President Kimball's assumption of the work as a stake president. He knew what to do and how to do it, yet his competence did not breed overconfidence or arrogance. He was typically humble about his new calling. "I find I am weak and too small and too lazy and too inefficient," he wrote after being installed. "Maybe they will release me after a year or two. I really hope so. I could step out today with the best of feelings and no misgivings, but I guess I'll have to go on until an apostle comes down to see how poor it is." However, beneath that unfeigned humility lay a basic self-confidence and an assurance of the divine source of the call. With that, he moved forward with confidence to complete his organization of the new stake, to identify the needs and resources of the stake, to define goals and map out a strategy for their attainment. Once this had been done and delegations of authority made, he went to work.

The nature of his new duties entailed a significant increase in travel. The need to counsel frequently with bishops, whose supervision was his chief responsibility, required frequent visits throughout the scattered stake. He was thorough in assessing the condition of a ward and detailed in suggesting means of improvement. This was done in a kindly way, yet with enough persuasion to encourage compliance. Good performance was rewarded with genuine praise, while carelessness and lack of cooperation were met with pointed reminders. He was a consistent, caring, and convincing administrator.

The increase in church duties was matched by growing responsibilities in his business. Kimball-Greenhalgh was in a growth pattern coincident with the improving economy of the Gila Valley. Other business interests now included KGLU, organized only months after Spencer's call as stake president. The radio station, in turn, launched its partners— Spencer Kimball, Joseph Greenhalgh, Louis Long, and Jesse Udall—into a variety of other business associations. All this diminished the time Spencer spent with his family or in rest or relaxation. The pervasive demands on his time caused President Kimball to abandon any semblance of a regular, consistent work schedule. He simply worked until everything was done, regardless of the hour of the day or night. When he returned to Safford in the morning from an out-of-town trip, for instance, it was not uncommon for him to go directly to his office to handle paperwork that had accumulated in his absence. Or, if he went home first, it would usually be only to shower, shave, change his clothes, and grab a bite to eat, all on the run. It was this kind of fast-paced schedule that created in the Kimball children the perception their father was always coming or going or engaged in a church meeting or a business conference.

As the economy improved, Kimball-Greenhalgh turned more to real estate development. In 1938, a sixteen-acre tract was purchased from Lester Bingham for six thousand dollars. The next year, an adjoining tract of twenty-four acres was purchased. Pending subdivision and development, the forty acres were leased for farming. Out of this tract,

The Kimballs' dream home under construction in Safford, Arizona, 1940.

President Kimball carved a large site on which he and Camilla planned to build their dream home.

They had done preliminary planning on this project for several years. They had in mind a building whose architecture would reflect the influence of Indian and Mexican cultures on the Southwest. To that end, they had taken pictures of representative homes in Albuquerque, El Paso, Tucson, and other southwestern cities over a period of several years. From these they culled ideas out of which they developed a composite picture of the kind of building that would suit their tastes and needs. Through 1939, their plans solidified into a six-room, pueblo-style home with a bath and a half and a utility space. By early 1940, the drawings had been completed, estimates were invited, and the successful bidder commenced construction in March. Three months later, the Kimballs moved in. During construction, the progress of which they watched daily with avid interest, they completed the planning and purchase of the home's new furnishings. Most of the furniture was Monterrey style, purchased from Barker Brothers in Los Angeles. Indian pictures adorned the walls. There was an Indian design in the bedspreads, with matching curtains embroidered by

Camilla. Beyond the house was a barn and corral for the cows, a pigpen, and a chicken coop. In between was a garden plot and an orchard.

But the yards were for beauty as well as utility. A row of colorful oleanders marked the north boundary of the lot and, in time, grew taller than the house. And a variety of flowers added splashes of color around the yard. A final touch, which accentuated the desert motif they sought to portray, was a cactus garden that bordered either side of the long driveway leading to the house. Here were found many specimens of indigenous cactus plants obtained from the nearby desert. Most striking among them was a night-blooming cereus, which bloomed for only one night and whose delicate fragrance permeated the whole neighborhood.

It was in this charming place, the creation of their own artistry, skill, and industry, that Spencer and Camilla Kimball planned to spend their remaining days. Here was their little niche, surrounded by family and friends, with every resource and facility needed to make life full and rewarding. No wonder Spencer had expressed the hope that he might be released as stake president after two years or so. That would have left him free of the burden of care as stake president and free to pursue his own objectives while practicing his religion and serving in subordinate, less demanding positions in the Church. It was not to be, however. While superficially that may have seemed alluring, there was more to Spencer Kimball's future than settling down contentedly to milk his cows and tend his garden and his orchard.

The Kimballs purchased a register for their new home in which guests wrote their names. During the first week in January 1941, Elder John A. Widtsoe of the Quorum of the Twelve signed the Kimballs' register. He had arrived by train on assignment to attend the quarterly conference of the Mount Graham Stake. Two of the apostle's associates, Harold B. Lee and Orville Stott of the Welfare Department, arrived later by automobile.

Following the stake conference, which featured the call of Harold Mitchell to the stake presidency succeeding Bert Hatch, who had requested a release, Brother Lee remained in the valley to hold a series of welfare meetings. On Monday, January 6, he accompanied President Kimball to Duncan for this purpose. The next day a similar meeting was held in Thatcher, following which, at the insistence of President Kimball, the visitor addressed the Safford Rotary Club about Church welfare. The next day, a lengthy regional welfare meeting was held, during which, at President Kimball's request, Elder Lee broke away long enough to speak to the students at the academy. And on Thursday, President Kimball drove Elder Lee to Phoenix, which afforded them the opportunity to become better acquainted on a personal basis. It was an acquaintance that would take on a new meaning sooner than either of them realized.

Two days after driving Elder Lee to Phoenix, President Kimball reported he had a "very painful" boil on his right leg. During the next two years, he was afflicted with over sixty boils, or carbuncles, which appeared on different parts of his body—on his ribs, his hip, his left leg, his right temple, his finger, and elsewhere. Sometimes they came in bunches, as on May 4, 1942, when he reported he had slept very little the night before because of ten boils on different parts of his body. Consistent with his practice of numbering and cataloging things, he kept track of them. So, on January 19, 1942, he reported that "boil #33" had appeared. He never dwelled unduly on the pain or the inconvenience of these eruptions. He would merely note their presence, sometimes reporting that they were painful or caused sleeplessness. Occasionally, he dismissed his afflictions with humor. "My carbuncle is better," he noted on January 23, 1942. "I think I will likely live—Ha—"

President Kimball had been troubled with boils intermittently for many years before this heavy siege began in the early 1940s. The first one had appeared on his neck in April 1915 while he served as a missionary in Hannibal,

Missouri. After 1942, he continued to be troubled with them off and on until years later when the doctors controlled them with drugs. Perhaps more significant than the boils themselves is that they did not deter his work. Neither pain nor embarrassment caused him to stay home to nurse them.

By now, Kimball-Greenhalgh had a branch office in Duncan where Spencer spent some of his time. He tried to schedule his visits to coincide with church assignments so as to save travel expense to the Church. Spencer also began to use the radio station for business or civic purposes, as when he talked on the radio in support of the infantile paralysis fund drive, or to promote Boy Scout Week, or when he sang with the Conquistadores to honor the alumni of the academy. The radio also was used to announce Church events, as when announcement was made of a stake quarterly conference featuring Presiding Bishop LeGrand Richards.

Shortly after Bishop Richards returned to Salt Lake City, President Kimball finalized plans to go there for the April general conference. His plans also included a trip to Flint, Michigan, afterward to pick up a new Buick. The local car dealer made the necessary arrangements.

Spencer and Camilla traveled to general conference with Jesse and Lela Udall, going by way of Snowflake and Jacob Lake. In Salt Lake on April 6, Spencer was pleased when his friend Harold B. Lee was sustained as a member of the Quorum of the Twelve, filling the vacancy caused by the death of Reed Smoot, who had passed away the previous February while in St. Petersburg, Florida. And he was surprised when five men were called to serve as Assistants to the Twelve, an action he referred to as "a new departure." The first of these five, Marion G. Romney, was Camilla's cousin.

After conference, the Kimballs traveled east by Greyhound bus. Relieved of driving duties, they enjoyed the scenery. When that, reading, or visiting became tiresome and he couldn't sleep, Spencer turned to his diary. When he had uninterrupted time and no deadlines, his writing reflected a poetic, contemplative quality. "Pioneer trail to Omaha," he wrote while crossing Nebraska. "Open plains, gently rolling, grassy hills, wide expanse, smaller homes, larger barns, wet, mucky corrals." Beyond Omaha, as their route bent northward: "Still wintery with ice on the water and with trees and shrubs still hibernating in their nakedness." On the approach to Chicago: "Land oozing like a saturated sponge." And of the city itself: "What a dirty, black, noisy and busy city."

This negative impression was softened after visiting some of Chicago's parks and Lakeshore Drive, after shopping in its well-stocked stores, and after enjoying the new movie *Life with Father.* Any residual negatives disappeared when they attended impressive Easter services at Soldier Field.

On schedule on April 14, the travelers arrived in Flint, Michigan, where the factory reportedly turned out a new Buick every minute. They watched their 1941 white Buick Special come off the assembly line, and after signing the papers, they were on their way to Detroit, Michigan, where they picked up a new Chrysler for Harold Mitchell. Originally it was planned to tow one of the cars, but when that was found to be impractical, Spencer and Camilla each drove one of them.

Their five-day trip home took them across Indiana, Illinois, Missouri, Oklahoma, Texas, and New Mexico, exposing them for the first time to vast areas of the United States. Near Claremore, Oklahoma, they encountered a deluge unlike anything they had ever experienced. "The sky crowded down on us so stifling and blackening we turned our lights on full force and inched along through the floods."

What they experienced in Oklahoma seemed to foreshadow the abnormal weather in the Gila Valley during the following months.

A freak storm struck not long after they returned to

Safford, with hailstones the size of golf balls. Other similar storms followed over a period of weeks, wreaking havoc on the crops, rooftops, and automobiles. They also produced an unexpected bonanza for Kimball-Greenhalgh, and Spencer was "very busy writing hail insurance." He also was busy outfitting his estate. He purchased a cow and her calf, naming the mother Frances Perkins in honor of the United States secretary of labor. He also purchased a 1936 Dodge pickup truck for hauling things. This saved the new Buick for family use. During the summer, the Kimball family traveled to San Francisco, California, to visit LeVan and his family. While in California they also visited Yosemite National Park and spent a few days on the beach near Los Angeles, returning home in time to register Olive Beth at the University of Arizona at Tucson.

Prior to the quarterly stake conference in late September, Spencer "developed a hoarseness" that was quite serious. "What is wrong with my voice?" he wondered. It was a question that would arise more ominously in the future. Soon after, a painful boil appeared on the side of his head. It was in this condition that he welcomed the conference visitor, Elder Alma Sonne, one of the new Assistants to the Twelve.

Throughout the conference, which ended on Sunday, September 28, there were heavy rains. The next morning, President Kimball received the disquieting news that a heavy crest on the Gila River was moving toward the narrows near Duncan, threatening an overflow.

He left immediately in the pickup. He found that Duncan's main street had been converted into a fast-flowing river and that the surrounding farms had been inundated. After ascertaining that everyone was out of danger, he moved promptly to arrange emergency relief. He counseled with the ward bishop to see that everyone had a place to sleep and food to eat. He asked his counselor, J. Vernon McGrath, to make a complete inventory of needs. He also telegraphed the First Presidency to report what had happened and the remedial actions he had taken and wired his congressman for government assistance in controlling the floodwaters. Soon after, a truck rolled from the bishops' storehouse in Safford carrying food, clothing, and bedding to fill the needs ascertained by President McGrath and those who had assisted him.

Once the welfare machinery had been set in motion, President Kimball rendered personal assistance wherever needed. He used the pickup to haul food, clothing, and bedding to the stricken area, returning with muddy clothing and bedding to be cleaned in Safford.

He also gave consolation and blessings to stricken members, helped move their belongings, and assisted in shoring up barricades. Meanwhile, he worked with the Red Cross and government agencies, coordinating the overall relief effort.

When the emergency needs had been satisfied, President Kimball began to counsel about the long-range goals of cleaning up and restoring the damaged homes and rehabilitating the farms whose topsoil had been eroded by the floodwaters. He was busy "from 8 A.M. to 9 P.M. without five minutes of relaxation or rest" the Sunday after the flood, laying plans for the future. Many similar planning meetings were held in the weeks ahead as the leaders sought to restore normalcy to the stricken area.

The flood complicated but did not eliminate personal life. On October 6, the Kimballs received word from San Francisco of the birth of their first grandchild, the daughter of LeVan and his wife, Kathryn. To celebrate, they dressed up like an aged couple and, knocking on the doors of their neighbors, announced the news in quavering voices.

The leaders in Salt Lake City had watched the drama of the Gila River flood with avid interest. It was the first real test of the Church welfare plan in a disaster situation. To see that the system worked as planned, with outlying units efficiently satisfying local needs with local resources, was reassuring. In order to appraise precisely what had happened, so the system could be fine-tuned for future use, and to help other local leaders understand how welfare should function in an emergency, Elders Harold B. Lee and Marion G. Romney went to Safford. Arriving on October 13, they held a meeting with President Kimball and his counselors and the presidents of several other neighboring stakes. After a briefing by President Kimball and instructions from the Brethren in Salt Lake City, everyone went to Duncan to inspect the flood damage. Then, over several days, special meetings were held with bishops and other priesthood leaders, followed by a general meeting with members of the Mount Graham and St. Joseph stakes.

President Kimball's handling of the flood disaster brought him to the favorable attention of all the leading brethren and, indeed, of the entire Church. Several articles about it appeared in the Church publications, including one he had written. These reflected favorably on the skillful way the emergency had been handled by the young stake president, whose name evoked memories of another Kimball and another stressful time in Church history. People, including those with decision-making authority, were beginning to look at Spencer W. Kimball in a new light.

With pressures from the flood easing, the Kimballs traveled to San Francisco to participate in the blessing of their first grandchild. At LeVan's request, the grandfather conferred the blessing, giving the little girl the name Barbara Jean Kimball. They also had a relaxing outing with their friends Jesse and Lela Udall when the four of them drove to Tucson on December 6 to see the football game between the University of Arizona and the University of Utah. It was shirtsleeve weather in the desert. After a pleasant afternoon in the sun, they had a bite to eat in Tucson, returning home after dark in a peaceful mood.

That mood was shattered the next day when the Japanese bombed Pearl Harbor. Suddenly the Kimballs' focus shifted from a local flood to a worldwide disaster. Ten days later, President Kimball became involved in the war effort when, at a meeting for civil defense, he was appointed chairman of housing arrangements for Graham County. Soon after came an assignment to chair the United War Fund Campaign for the county, working with his friend Delbert L. Stapley of Phoenix, the state chairman. Then he began to direct the thinking of the members of the stake toward a war economy. "I urged my people to buy defense bonds, to conserve tires, etc., and to help in civil defense in every way," he wrote following a stake meeting on December 28. Leading by example, he began to ride his bicycle around town whenever it was feasible to do so. In early March 1942, he went to Phoenix at the invitation of Governor Osborne to confer with a committee of prominent leaders about creating USO facilities near military bases to accommodate service personnel. Whatever had to be done to help the cause along and whatever he was capable of doing, Spencer Kimball did it willingly.

Occasionally he became weary of the constant drumbeat of duties that filled his days. "When can I ever get a few minutes to work for Kimball-Greenhalgh Insurance and Realty Company and myself, and to read and to see my family?" he asked plaintively. "Maybe some day when I am no good for them or anyone else." He savored rare moments alone. He noted a rare instance when "I read magazines all evening. What a joy to have a full evening to relax." Socializing provided an occasional escape valve, as when he and Camilla spent an evening with friends playing Rook, eating enchiladas, and enjoying good conversation. They left the party at 1:30 A.M. and had returned home and were preparing for bed when the whole crowd appeared at their house. Camilla raided her refrigerator and fed them again while they visited for another hour before the party finally ended.

It was a surprise when President David O. McKay, second counselor in the First Presidency, came as the official visitor to the stake conference in March 1942. Rarely did members of the First Presidency fill these assignments.

Presumably President McKay, who played a major role in developing the welfare program, wanted to see firsthand how the plan had worked in an emergency. A few days after President McKay's visit, President Kimball mailed a final report of the flood and its aftermath.

Rigid travel restrictions imposed by the war caused Spencer, Camilla, Andrew, and Eddie to ride the bus to Salt Lake City for the April general conference. Incredibly, they found the city blacked out at night from fear of Japanese bombing raids. Pearl Harbor had created a national paranoia that only time could erase. Its repercussions also had scrambled the orderly rhythms of American life, including the procedures of general conference. Only the General Authorities and selected local priesthood leaders had been invited to attend. Meetings were held in the Assembly Hall, except on Sunday when they convened in the temple. "A marvelous spirit was manifested" at the testimony meeting President Kimball attended there Sunday afternoon. The instructions at earlier meetings focused mainly on problems created by the war, the dislocation of families, immorality, and the needs of servicemen.

The Kimballs' new granddaughter lured them to San Francisco after the conference. They took a bus to Reno, Nevada, then flew from there to the coast. It was their first flight. President Kimball's excitement was reflected in his poetic descriptions of the rugged Sierra Nevadas, the lush farm lands around Sacramento, and the gleaming city by the bay. After visiting Barbara Jean, and, incidentally, her parents, they traveled home by bus.

Though they had been gone eleven days, the following week the Kimballs traveled to Phoenix, where Spencer had responsibility for a three-day convention attended by four hundred Rotarians. The details in planning it had occupied much of his time after the return from general conference. Only his ownership interest in Kimball-Greenhalgh gave Spencer Kimball the freedom to pursue these time-consuming activities.

A Kimball family portrait, 1942. Seated, left to right: Spencer, Camilla, Kathryn (holding the Kimballs' first granddaughter, Barbara), and Spencer LeVan. Standing: Olive Beth, Andrew, and Edward.

President Kimball went to the October 1942 general conference alone, traveling again by bus. He was surprised to receive an invitation to stay at the home of President J. Reuben Clark, first counselor in the First Presidency and also one of Spencer's many Woolley cousins. This had never happened before. Obviously President Clark, a pillar in welfare work, wanted to discuss the Gila River flood. "We spent the evening in visiting and discussion," wrote Spencer. Earlier, President Clark had asked Elder Harold B. Lee of the Quorum of the Twelve about President Kimball and his qualifications. An evening alone in relaxed conversation would enable a wise man like J. Reuben Clark to make his own appraisal.

The burden of President Clark's thinking at the time is suggested by his main conference address. There he differentiated between the united order and communism and explained the relationship between the united order and the welfare plan. As to the latter, he said: "Now, brethren, the

131

Church has made tremendous advances in the Welfare Plan. We shall have to make still greater advances. As the Message of the First Presidency said this morning, we are being told by Government officials that we face what we used to call 'hard times.' If the Welfare Plan is fully operative, we shall be able to care for every destitute Latter-day Saint wherever he may be." (In Conference Report, Oct. 1942, p. 58.)

Sunday afternoon, President Kimball was one of the few men called on to bear his testimony. If he had the feeling he was being scrutinized, it was intensified two weeks later, when President Clark and Elder Lee appeared in the Gila Valley to attend the St. Joseph stake conference and to hold other meetings. On Sunday night, a special meeting was held in Safford, where President Clark dedicated a new chapel. Elder Lee and President Kimball also were called on to speak. After lauding President Kimball for the work he had done in handling the flood emergency, President Clark commended Elder Lee, described the almost father-son relationship that existed between them, and suggested Elder Lee would one day be the president of the Church, given his youth compared to the other apostles. He remained silent about President Kimball's future. It seems apparent, however, that he and the other presiding brethren had Spencer Kimball in their sights as a future General Authority.

The next day President Kimball drove the visitors to Duncan to inspect the flood area and the reclamation work being done. That night was spent visiting. The visitors left the next day. "I picked cotton in the evening," wrote Spencer. He had a lot to think about as he picked.

One thing on his mind was the plan to celebrate his and Camilla's twenty-fifth wedding anniversary. They had decided on an open house. Six hundred invitations were sent to family and friends to come to their new home on November 16, 1942, to celebrate with them. The invitations were staggered from 2:00 P.M. on, to avoid a heavy crush at one time. The concept was good but it broke down in practice, as few wanted to leave. At the crest, hundreds of people crowded into and around the house to share their hosts' happiness.

Among those who came from out of town for the celebration were LeVan and his family, who arrived on the fourteenth. LeVan left on December 2 for San Francisco, where he planned to enlist in the navy. Kathryn and the baby joined him there a few days before Christmas. Later, LeVan was assigned to a naval language training unit at the University of Colorado at Boulder, where he studied Japanese. With the war heating up in the Pacific, LeVan's safety was a major concern of his parents as 1942 drew to a close.

President Kimball prepared his usual summary at the end of the year, concluding on a positive note. "It was a good year and we prospered and worked hard and tried . . . to do the right thing."

Chapter 12

Call to the Twelve

A t the April general conference in 1943, the special attention President Kimball had received after the flood was continued, even accelerated. He was invited again to stay at the home of President J. Reuben Clark, was called on to offer the invocation at the opening session of the conference, had dinner at the home of Elder Stephen L Richards of the Twelve, and because of conflicts had to decline invitations to dine at the homes of President David O. McKay and Elder Antoine R. Ivins.

Following the last session of the conference, Spencer met with some of his Woolley relatives in a social hour. Afterward, his cousin Preston Parkinson drove him to his hotel, where he stayed the last night of his stay in Salt Lake City. As they visited, Preston told Spencer that if he lived in Salt Lake City, he would surely be called to the Twelve, but that the Brethren "would never find him down in Arizona," to which Spencer responded: "Preston, that's silly. They would never pick me, with all the great men in the Church." Both cousins were wrong.

At the time, there were no vacancies in the Quorum of the Twelve. That changed on May 29, 1943, when Elder Sylvester Q. Cannon passed away. Less than a month later, a second vacancy was created when, on June 21, 1943, Rudger Clawson, president of the Quorum of the Twelve, died. During the process of selecting replacements, President Clark told Elder Harold B. Lee that the prophet seemed inclined to call Spencer W. Kimball. Once President Heber J. Grant had received the spiritual confirmation that Spencer Kimball was the man, he brought President Kimball's name before a meeting of the Council of the First Presidency and the Quorum of the Twelve on July 8, 1943. At that time, unanimous approval was given to call Spencer W. Kimball to the Twelve to fill the vacancy created by the death of Elder Sylvester Q. Cannon. Also at this meeting, George Albert Smith was approved and set apart as the president of the Quorum of the Twelve Apostles, replacing Rudger Clawson. The action to fill the vacancy in the Twelve created by President Clawson's death was not taken until two weeks later, when Elder Ezra Taft Benson was approved. Immediately following the council meeting on July 8, President J. Reuben Clark was authorized to extend the call to Elder Kimball by telephone. President Grant doubtless elected not to do it because he had previously suffered a stroke that had caused some impairment of speech. Under these circumstances, he deferred to his first counselor, President Clark.

It had been a routine morning at the Kimball-Greenhalgh agency that hot summer day. Spencer had been busy, as usual, handling the regular flow of business that had burgeoned in recent years, especially since the onset of the war. What had started sixteen years before as a struggling operation in which he had invested $150 had grown into the major insurance and real estate business in the Gila Valley and surrounding areas. The years of uncertainty, depression, and hard work had paid off so that now the business ran smoothly, producing regular, comfortable profits while increasing President Kimball's equity interest in the business—a business that now approximated a hundred thousand dollars in value. The agency stood as a testimonial to his skill, discipline, and enterprise and was a justifiable source of personal pride.

As President Kimball left the agency to go home for lunch that day, there was no objective circumstance to differentiate it from hundreds of others like it. Except when he met with the Rotarians or had a luncheon appointment, he usually went home at noon to eat with the family and to take a brief nap. Shortly after he got on his bicycle to pump home, the secretary in the agency received a call from President Clark in Salt Lake City, asking to speak to Spencer Kimball. He was told Mr. Kimball had gone home for lunch and should be there momentarily. As Spencer opened the door to his home, he heard Eddie say his daddy was not there. Then, as he saw his father enter the house, the son said, "Daddy, Salt Lake City is calling."

It was not uncommon for President Kimball to receive calls from Salt Lake. His role as stake president made regular contact with Church headquarters necessary, and these calls had become more frequent after the flood. Yet there was something about this call that was different. "An overpowering feeling came over me that instant," he wrote later, "that I was to be called to a high position in the Church." Until now, he had stifled any thought he was destined for high Church office. He had jocularly brushed aside the comments of his cousin, Preston Parkinson, as he seems to have closed his eyes to the significance of the many special contacts the presiding officers of the Church had made recently.

"If ever that thought had entered my mind in times past," he later explained, "I had quickly thrust it from me as being most unworthy." And in the few seconds it took him to walk across the room to pick up the phone, he also sought to thrust this "overpowering feeling" from him. "There was

no reason in the world why I should be called. I instanta-
neously convinced myself that it was impossible, that I was
not capable or prepared or worthy, that no one would be
called away from the headquarters of the Church and that
there was no reason whatever for the feeling."

President Clark greeted Spencer warmly and, without
preliminaries, suggested that he take a chair. Then, matter-
of-factly, he said he had just come from a meeting of the
Council of the First Presidency and the Quorum of the
Twelve, where it had been decided that Spencer W. Kimball
was to fill one of the vacancies in the Twelve. "Oh, Brother
Clark," said Spencer, as he slid from the chair to the floor,
"not me, you don't mean me. There must be some mistake. I
surely couldn't have heard you right." Affirming what he
had said, President Clark asked Spencer how he felt about
it. Assuring President Clark he accepted the call without
qualification, Spencer expressed feelings of incredulity: "I
am so weak and small and limited and incapable," said he.
Then he was assailed with self-doubt. He asked himself,
How could you be an apostle of the Lord? You are not worthy. You are insignificant. You shouldn't accept this calling.
You *can't* do it. As President Kimball had fallen silent during these reveries, President Clark spoke up to ask, "Are
you there?" Spencer then asked a series of questions about
the effect of the call on his family and business. Finally,
seeming overwhelmed by the magnitude of what the call
entailed, he asked if he could have a little time "to think this
thing through." In the discussion that followed, President
Kimball explained that he and Camilla had planned to leave
for Boulder, Colorado, the following Saturday to visit LeVan
and his family, and he asked if it would be permissible to fly
to Salt Lake from there so the matter could be discussed in
person. President Clark agreed but said he would be out of
town and Spencer should confer with President David O.
McKay instead.

President Kimball hung up the phone, turned to Camilla
and the boys, Andrew and Eddie, who had stood transfixed

during the conversation, and said quietly, "They have called me to become an apostle." When the impact of that struck home, Camilla asked if he were sure it was a call to the Twelve instead of a call as an Assistant. "Spencer assured me [President Clark] had said one of the Twelve," she reported later.

Since lunch was cooling on the table, the family went through the motions of eating it, saying little while deep in reflection. Afterward, the boys went outside while their father lay on the living room carpet to rest. Camilla sat beside him as they talked. While there was no doubt he would accept the call, there were nagging questions to consider. The dream home and the farm would have to be abandoned; the business he had labored so hard to build would have to be sold; and the family would have to leave their relatives and friends behind. Uppermost in his mind, however, was an overwhelming feeling of inadequacy. All this breached the wall of stoic self-control he had built up over the years by reining in his feelings at the innumerable funerals he had attended. "The tears came then, an inexhaustible flood. . . . I wept and wept. It seemed that all the conflicting thoughts of my mind were trying to wash themselves clean with tears. I was in convulsions of sobbing." Throughout this emotional purging, Camilla sat nearby, consoling her husband and stroking his hair while assuring him of his worthiness and his ability to fulfill the call.

He was distracted at his work Thursday afternoon and Friday, hardly capable of concentrating on it. The nights were filled with fitful, intermittent sleep, but mostly with fervent prayers. "How I prayed through those long, dark hours," he remembered, "prayers for forgiveness of my weaknesses and imperfections, prayers for strength to do the right, prayers that the family would all make the necessary adjustments in their feelings, but, above all, prayers that I might feel that I was called by the Lord through His servants and an assurance of acceptance."

President Kimball had a ward conference to conduct in

El Paso, Texas, en route to Boulder. He and Camilla, with their two boys, drove there Saturday morning. During the several hours on the road, they discussed the impact of the call on the family—"what to do, how it would affect us, the changes that would come to the boys and girl, their schooling, their friends, our life."

A pleasant dinner Saturday evening at the El Cortes Hotel, hosted by two couples from El Paso, proved to be a stressful experience. About the only topic they wanted to discuss was the one Spencer most wanted to avoid—filling the vacancies in the Twelve. The dreaded moment arrived when one of them asked him directly, "Brother Kimball, do you have any idea who will be called?" Startled, he gave a devious answer, for which he later hoped he would be forgiven, that preserved his duty of confidentiality while skirting the fact. "No," he answered, "I can't tell you."

After the conference, the boys were sent home on the train while Spencer and Camilla took the train north toward Colorado. The car was left in El Paso, and they planned to pick it up on the return trip. LeVan met them in Denver and was mystified when his father made a plane reservation for Salt Lake City before they went on to Boulder. He did not learn about the call until later.

Early the next morning in Boulder, Spencer arose after another night of restless turning, punctuated by fervent prayers for a spiritual confirmation of his call and an assurance that he was acceptable to the Lord. Without a specific destination in mind, he headed for the rugged hills to the west that had given the quiet university town its name. Passing through the campus and the slumbering neighborhoods around it, he climbed steadily toward the summit of a ridge above him, picking his way carefully around and over the boulders that obstructed his path. Reaching the summit of the ridge, he was startled by a snake that lay coiled on the ground. The adrenaline rush produced when he saw the snake gave him "an unexplainable sudden strength" that caused him to jump high over the snake's head. When the panic subsided, he fell into a reverie: "Could this be symbolic of my other worries and problems?" After reflecting on the incident and resting for a while, he looked further west to see a mountain that "rose rapidly and farther up almost precipitously to a high peak far above." Between the ridge and the base of the high mountain was a sloping little valley carpeted with ankle-high grass. As he crossed it and began to ascend the mountain, he started to pray aloud with an intensity he had not felt before. "Hot tears came flooding down my cheeks. I was praying . . . for special blessings from the Lord. I was telling Him that I had not asked for this position, that I was incapable of doing the work, that I was imperfect and weak and human, that I was unworthy of such a calling, though I had tried hard and my heart had been right."

After reflecting on "offenses and misunderstandings that a few people fancied they had" against him, he came to the crux of the thing for which he sought spiritual enlightenment: "Was I called by revelation?" he asked, "or, had the Brethren been impressed by the recent contacts in my home and stake when they had visited us, or by the accounts of my work in the flood rehabilitation, which reports I knew had been greatly exaggerated in my favor, or had I been called because of my relationship to one of the First Presidency?" In essence, he wanted to know whether he had been called because of the influence of men rather than by revelation from God.

As he continued his climb, the mountain became progressively steeper and more rugged. In climbing over a slide area where "it was almost impossible to make the grade," he stumbled over an old oak stick. Breaking off one end, it was "exactly the right length for a cane." Using the cane, which became another physical symbol of his search for enlightenment, he continued his upward climb while alternately praying and weeping. As he rounded a promontory, President Kimball was startled to see what appeared to be a cross on the peak above, silhouetted against the sky. It had been formed naturally by the angular alignment of two large limbs of a tree. However, the object of his climb and the unexpected appearance of the cross, symbolic of the One whom he had been called to serve, caused Spencer to regard it as "a sacred omen." It suggested to his mind that there on the peak above, near the tree with the cross, he would find what he sought. But before completing his ascent, he "threw" himself on the ground, where he "wept and prayed and pleaded with the Lord" to let him know where he stood. During this interlude, he thought about his parents; his grandfather, Heber C. Kimball; and other relatives, wondering how they felt about him and what role, if any, they had played in his selection. These reflections caused him to feel very near to them, "nearer than ever in my life." Spencer also engaged in extraordinary self-condemnation. "I mentally beat myself," he reported, "and chastised myself and accused myself."

At length he stirred, completed the climb, and, at the summit, sat on a ledge of the cliff to rest and reflect. As he gazed at the tortuous route of his climb and at the broad and fruitful valley spread below, he was reminded of the wealth he had accumulated and the greater share of the earth's riches he might yet gain were his call rescinded. This in turn reminded him of the Savior's ordeal in the wilderness when Lucifer tempted him with the wealth of the world. However, no sooner did these thoughts come than Spencer berated himself for having them. "I am filled with remorse. I had permitted myself to place myself . . . in a position comparable, in a small degree, to the position the Savior found Himself in when He was tempted; and I was filled with remorse because I felt I had cheapened the experiences of the Lord, having compared mine with His." With that, he lay down on the mountaintop, striving again for enlightenment. "How I prayed!" he wrote. "How I suffered! How I wept! How I struggled!" He then explained again specifically what he sought through these strivings: "There was one great desire—to get a testimony of my calling, to know that it was not human and inspired by ulterior motives, kindly as they might be."

During this interval, President Kimball drifted into slumber. "It seemed that in a dream I saw my grandfather and became conscious of the great work he had done. I cannot say it was a vision, but I do know that with this new experience came a calm like the dying wind, the quieting wave after the storm is passed." Rising from the ground, he walked to the ledge where he again sat down. "My tears were dry," wrote he, and "my soul was at peace. A calm feeling of assurance came over me, doubt and questionings subdued. It was as though a great burden had lifted. I sat in tranquil silence surveying the beautiful valley, thanking the Lord for the satisfaction and the reassuring answer to my prayers. Long I meditated here in peaceful quietude, apart, and felt nearer my Lord than ever at any time in my life." With that, Spencer W. Kimball was prepared to undertake his apostolic ministry without question or hesitancy. He descended from the mountain down the back side by a less precipitous route, using his cane, which, he said, "now seemed an important part of my spiritual experience."

Without making explanations about his long absence, Spencer changed his clothes and caught a flight to Salt Lake City. Taking a cab to 47 East South Temple, he was graciously received by President David O. McKay, who assured him the call had been dictated by spiritual means and not by personal considerations. Spencer already knew that from his experience on the mountain, but it was reassuring to hear it from President McKay. In this private setting, the new apostle was moved to bear his testimony about the reality and divinity of the Savior and about his commitment to serve Him always.

Through prior arrangement, the news of Elder Spencer W. Kimball's call to the Quorum of the Twelve was published soon after his interview with President McKay. It created a sensation. Few, if any, of the ardent Church watchers had focused on him as a viable candidate. Like Camilla, most thought vacancies in the Twelve would be filled from among the Assistants.

If the public was unprepared for his call, Spencer was even less prepared for the new response of others toward him. He had always admired and honored the members of the Twelve, had deferred to them, and had sought to emulate them. But it was a shock to feel such adulation and deference directed toward him. This change was illustrated in the conduct of his cousin, Preston Parkinson. As Preston accompanied Spencer to the train station to return to Boulder, he insisted on making stops along the way to introduce friends to his cousin, the new apostle. The sense of love and pride Spencer saw in his cousin's actions and the response of those to whom he was introduced was at once pleasing and humbling. In Boulder, Elder Kimball also was pleased with LeVan's favorable reaction to his call. And Camilla shared her husband's relief that the news was out so the embarrassing incident at the hotel in El Paso would not be repeated.

Back in Safford, Elder Kimball was flooded with letters, cards, and calls of congratulation. Of all these, one of the most significant to Spencer was a letter from John F. Nash, his former associate in the stake presidency, now a patriarch in Mesa, Arizona. "Surely the Lord is managing this work on earth," wrote the patriarch. "He knows where his servants are, even in the out of the way places, even in far off Arizona. Your father and grandfather have had something to do with it, for they have been close to you all of the time and they have interceded in councils in heaven for you, knowing that you were worthy of the place." The significance of the letter lay in its coincidence with some of the spiritual insights Elder Kimball had received on the mountain.

Spencer knew the supportive feelings expressed by so many were not shared by everyone. There were a few who harbored resentment or animosity toward him because of misunderstandings. It was on these he now focused his attention, realizing he could not serve effectively if there were unresolved conflicts. Two people believed they had been shortchanged in business dealings. Ignoring facts that contradicted their contentions, Elder Kimball wrote checks to reimburse what they felt was owed them. A woman who had long avoided him told Spencer she believed he had intervened with the governor to deprive her husband of employment. After Elder Kimball assured her he did not do that and, indeed, lacked such influence with the governor, she was mollified. And a co-worker in the Church whom Spencer had once criticized sternly was contacted so Spencer could apologize for any offense given. In this way, resolving problems one by one, he tried to wipe the slate clean of any irritant that could mar his ministry.

Meanwhile, he was busy making arrangements for the move to Salt Lake City. He sold his interest in the business for sixty-five thousand dollars, sold the house and its furnishings, and sold other real and personal property. He also severed his connection with the canal companies on whose boards of directors he had served, resigned from the positions he had held with the United War Fund and the USO, and ended his association with the local Rotary Club, the Boy Scouts, the Gila Junior College Board of Trustees, the Teachers Retirement Board, and the Arizona Association of Insurance Agents. It was not easy to sever these connections that had been such an integral part of his life for so long.

The void was filled partly by a round of farewell gatherings. Church, business and civic groups vied with each other to honor the new apostle. These gatherings usually turned into testimonials about Spencer's character and achievements. While he appreciated the sentiments, he was sometimes embarrassed by them and at a loss to know how to respond to them.

With all this going on, Elder Kimball found time to help Camilla pack their personal things. These were stowed in ninety-four sealed boxes, ready for shipping once they had a Salt Lake City address to which they could be sent. This was a mournful time for Camilla as she contemplated leaving her dream home, her friends, and especially her parents, who had assumed she would always be near. Besides, she had experienced some bleeding for which her doctor had recommended corrective treatment. On this account, they advanced their departure date so there would be time to remedy her problem in Salt Lake before school started.

Conflicting emotions tugged at the Kimballs as they left Safford in the Buick on August 26, 1943. It was a wrenching, sad experience to leave their home, while excitement and uncertainty lay ahead. How would the family fare in a large city where they were unknown, except through the new prominence of the father? Of special concern was the readjustment of their sons, especially Andrew, who as an athlete, a scholar, and the elected senior class president would have been at the center of things at the Safford high school the next year. Conscious of their mixed feelings, Elder Kimball attempted to focus attention positively on their new home. "We have left Arizona," he told them. "From now on, Utah is the best place in the world, the finest people, the best climate, the most wonderful schools." In time, this psychology worked. At first, however, there was doubt.

Despite a crush on housing caused by the war, the Kimballs were able to rent accommodations at the Temple Square Hotel for a few days while they looked for something permanent. Through the Church, Elder Kimball arranged to rent the home of Graham Doxey, who had been called on a mission. As it would not be available for two months, they were fortunate to be invited by Spencer's cousin, Vi Woolley, to live with her temporarily in the old Woolley family home. Camilla then entered the hospital for twenty-four hours of radium treatment that checked the bleeding but left her weak.

With the family settled as comfortably as the circumstances allowed, Elder Kimball returned to Safford by train to wind up his affairs and participate in the reorganization of the Mount Graham stake presidency, which Elder Harold B.

Lee had been assigned to oversee. As the conference approached, Elder Kimball received disquieting news from Salt Lake. Soon after the boys were enrolled in school, Andrew at East High School and Eddie at Roosevelt Junior High School, a polio scare had forced the closure of all the city schools. Cooped up in the house, the boys, reported Camilla, were like caged lions. So discontented was Andrew that he said he wanted to return to Safford to complete his senior year. To aggravate matters, a friend had invited Andrew to stay at his home. And to cap it all, Camilla, who was still weak from the radium treatments, wrote to Spencer despairing over the finality of the move to Salt Lake. Anxious about the members of his family, Elder Kimball arose early the morning of the stake reorganization and wrote a long letter to them that he shared with Elder Lee. He first sought to stiffen their resolve by a challenge. "It will not be easy for you," he wrote, "but who wants an easy job?" Then, after reminding them of their heritage, he strengthened his message: "None of them," he wrote, referring to the Eyrings, the Romneys, the Woolleys, and the Kimballs, "would squirm or whine or hesitate as a difficult situation presented itself." Then, moderating the tone, he pleaded for their understanding and support. "This is such a great responsibility for such a little man. You can help me so much. I promise you I will do my best to qualify and bring you honor. I am relying on you to help me and I am pleading that you will live for me, pray for me, help me." In conclusion, the father parted the curtain to provide insight into the inner struggles he suffered as he sought divine confirmation of his call. "The spirit of the evil one has tempted me a thousand times to not accept the work because I am weak and unworthy and incapable."

The letter and favorable developments in Salt Lake restored peace to the Kimball household. The polio scare ended and the boys returned to school. At East High School, Andrew formed a close friendship with two athletes—Mitt Smith, the youngest son of Elder Joseph Fielding Smith, and Oscar W. McConkie Jr., younger brother of Bruce R.

McConkie—and soon was caught up in the athletic, academic, and social life of the school. Eddie adjusted well at Roosevelt, and when the family moved into the gracious Doxey home, Camilla's trauma began to ease.

Meanwhile, in Safford, Elder Kimball's counselor, J. Harold Mitchell, was called as the new stake president. Once the new leaders had been instructed and set apart, Elder Lee left for other duties and Spencer completed final arrangements for his departure. A few days later, when he boarded the Gila Monster, there was not a soul in sight to bid him good-bye. Given the numerous events previously held in his honor, it was not realistic to think another one would be organized to see him off. He did not expect that. But he did wish *someone* would have been there to wish him godspeed as he left the valley. Although he berated himself for the sentiment, he shared his disappointment in a tender note to Camilla. "I tried to explain to myself, but it still hurt just a little. I think I am not so indispensable as I had imagined—life seems to go on nicely in Safford in spite of my going. . . . I had no reason to expect it, but just thought maybe one or two would chance by as the train came in to say goodbye."

In Salt Lake, Elder Kimball found that an office had been prepared for him in the Administration Building at 47 East South Temple. In the days before the general conference, he became acquainted with his new surroundings, received visitors, and called on some of the Brethren. As he entered the office of President Heber J. Grant, the eighty-six-year-old prophet did not rise to his feet because of the partial paralysis he had suffered. When Elder Kimball walked to his chair, President Grant took his hand and, drawing him down, gave him a fatherly kiss on the cheek. This unexpected gesture of friendship from the prophet impressed Elder Kimball deeply. It seems apparent President Grant had had his eye on this young man for many years as he watched him develop under the rigors of a remote desert community. Spencer also visited President J. Reuben Clark, who briefed him about his duties as a member of the Twelve and about the procedures of the conference.

Elder Kimball took his place in the audience as the conference began Friday morning, October 1, 1943. He was not presented for sustaining vote until the afternoon session, along with the other General Authorities. Although their calls had been announced long before, when the names of Spencer W. Kimball and Ezra Taft Benson were read, a thrill ran through the audience. And later, when all hands were raised to sustain them, Elder Kimball experienced an electric shock through his body. After the sustaining, the two new apostles were invited to take their places on the stand. Because he had been called first, Elder Kimball took his seat beside Elder Harold B. Lee, and Elder Benson sat at the end of the row to the left of Elder Kimball.

It was intimidating to sit facing the Tabernacle audience. "Thousands of eyes were upon us," Elder Kimball wrote later, "appraising, weighing, honoring us." The sense of being closely watched was intensified when he was called on to speak. "How I reached the pulpit I hardly know. What a moment—a sea of upturned, wondering, expectant faces met my gaze." He spoke for fifteen minutes in a sweet, straightforward way, expressing gratitude, pledging support for his leaders, and bearing fervent testimony. The impact of the talk was powerful and positive. Yet he was dissatisfied with it. "I felt I had failed and continued to tell myself that I had failed as Brother Benson gave his . . . testimony."

This reaction suggests one reason why so many people were so attracted to President Spencer W. Kimball. His words and conduct created a sense he was "one of us," an ordinary man who, by some anomaly, had been elevated to a high position. His words describing his reaction to the sustaining affirm this: "I seemed to be swimming in a daze. It seemed so unreal and impossible that I—just poor, weak Spencer Kimball—could be being sustained as an Apostle of the Lord Jesus Christ and tears welled in my eyes."

*Spencer W. Kimball
in the 1940s.*

The culminating act occurred the following Thursday, October 7, 1943, when he was ordained and set apart. Ordinarily, this would have taken place in the upper room of the Salt Lake Temple, where the First Presidency and the Twelve hold their weekly council meetings. However, because of President Grant's infirmities, it took place in the First Presidency's council room in the north end of the main floor of the Administration Building. After an opening prayer, President Grant called on President David O. McKay to give the apostolic charge to the two new brethren. After they had accepted the charge, committing themselves to put their callings and the interests of the Church ahead of everything else, they were ordained and set apart. Because of the difficulty President Grant had in standing, Elder Kimball knelt before him. With the hands of all members of the council placed on Spencer's head, the prophet ordained him an apostle and set him apart as a member of the Quorum of the Twelve. In doing so, he conferred on Elder Kimball all the authority necessary to lead the Church, which authority was to be held in suspension pending the happening of two events: that he survive to become the senior living apostle and that he then be ordained and set apart as the president of the Church by the other living apostles. The same procedure was then followed for Elder Benson.

With that, Elder Spencer W. Kimball, the sixty-second apostle to be ordained and set apart as a member of the Twelve in this dispensation, was officially prepared to begin his apostolic ministry. It was a ministry that would span forty-two years and a month; would see him travel as extensively through the world as any of his apostolic brethren, ancient or modern; would see him endure physical ailments and difficulties more extensive and persistent than any of his prophetic predecessors, Job excepted; would see him elevated to the prophetic office; would see him undertake prophetic initiatives that would exert a lasting, global influence on the Church; would see him stimulate, through his example and exhortations, the entire Church to an extraordinary level of activity and commitment; and would see him, through his empathy and understanding, arouse special feelings of love from the rank and file of the Church, especially from the underprivileged and the scorned.

Chapter 13

First Apostolic Years

The Council of the First Presidency and the Quorum of the Twelve, which Elder Kimball now joined, was an unusual body whose distinguished members gave him feelings of inadequacy. The backgrounds of the Brethren were diverse: of the fifteen members, five were educators (President David O. McKay and Elders Richard R. Lyman, John A. Widtsoe, Joseph F. Merrill, and Harold B. Lee); four were attorneys (President J. Reuben Clark and Elders Stephen L Richards, Charles A. Callis, and Albert E. Bowen); three were businessmen (President Heber J. Grant and Elders George Albert Smith and Spencer W. Kimball); one was a farmer (Elder George F. Richards); one was a historian and author (Elder Joseph Fielding Smith); and one was an agricultural expert (Elder Ezra Taft Benson). More significantly, the thirteen members of the council, excluding Elders Kimball and Benson, had rendered a combined 310 years of apostolic service, an average of almost 24 years each. Considering what that service represented in terms of meetings attended, sermons delivered, counseling provided, blessings given, ordinations and settings apart performed, and miles traveled, the aggregate was overwhelming. It is not surprising, then, that Elder Kimball, whose natural tendency was to minimize, if not to belittle, his own achievements, approached his new duties with feelings of inadequacy and some anxiety. It is possible that the unusual dedication he showed in his assignment derived in part from a determination to measure up to the members of the council and to carve a niche for himself through diligent work.

Church membership at the time was less than a million, divided into 146 stakes and 38 missions. Even though stake conferences were held quarterly and the First Presidency ordinarily did not attend them, there still were enough General Authorities, even traveling in pairs, to cover most of them. The opportunity to travel with a companion was especially helpful to Elder Kimball as he began his apostolic career. It provided effective training as the senior companion demonstrated how the work should be done. And long hours of traveling together with other leaders gave him insight into the policies and procedures of the Church and enabled him to share testimonies and learn about Church problems and personalities.

A conference with Elder Harold B. Lee in Parowan, Utah, only a few weeks after Elder Kimball's ordination was especially helpful. The week before, the Quorum of the Twelve, and indeed the entire Church, had been shaken by the excommunication of Elder Richard R. Lyman of the Twelve. It had been most difficult for Elder Kimball to sit in judgment on one whom he so recently had sustained as an apostle. Because Elder Lee, together with Elder Joseph Fielding Smith, had been assigned to investigate the rumors about Elder Lyman and had learned the facts, he was able to clarify Elder Kimball's understanding and bring the tragedy into proper perspective.

During the next four years, Elder Kimball became well trained in his field duties through regular stake conference and mission tour assignments. Conversely, the members of the Church became acquainted with him and his distinctive leadership style. It was a style like the one he used in supervising wards as a stake president. Recommendations were made only after careful analysis of the reports and the local conditions and leaders. The care he gave to his analysis and his supportive attitude encouraged others' acceptance of his suggestions. "The brethren seemed to be warming up to me," he wrote after visiting a stake in California, "and seemed happy at my careful analysis of the work." Such care was intensified when a stake reorganization was involved. Aware that the choice of a new leader would profoundly affect the stake and its members for years, he devoted "mighty prayer and deliberation" to the process of selection, as he did in reorganizing a stake presidency in Colorado.

His public addresses in stake conferences bore marks of qualities in his character. They were never trivial. To him, this was "serious business" whose purpose was not to be obscured by light-minded joking or irrelevant storytelling. Still, he was not morose at the pulpit but generally reflected an uplifting, genial attitude. And occasionally his remarks were enlivened by an impromptu song to illustrate a point. At a conference in Rigby, Idaho, as he urged the members to write regularly to their servicemen, he interrupted his remarks to sing "Where Is My Soldier Boy Tonight?" without accompaniment. However, if circumstances required it, Elder Kimball was pointed in suggesting changes in attitudes or practices. He spoke strongly against laxness in performing missionary service. "I have borne down hard on this thought in several of the talks because I am convinced that they have settled down in their lethargic state, receiving all the time and giving little. They need to give and to sacrifice to build their faith."

His relations with stake members who hosted him were cordial. He immediately put them at ease, accepting graciously what was offered, demanding nothing, and expressing profuse thanks for even the most commonplace things. If there were children in the home, he always befriended them, learning their names and sensitively inquiring about their goals. He never failed to suggest a mission as a main goal, especially for boys, and later he began to give them each a dollar, and sometimes more, for their mission funds. Often he sang and played the piano for them and their parents. And if his hosts lived on a farm, he invariably helped milk the cows, often over strong objections. These qualities endeared him to the members of the Church everywhere. They always looked forward to his coming.

The frequency of these assignments and the rigors that often attended them were wearing, even for one as young and vigorous as Elder Kimball. Still, he would ask to be excused from an assignment only under the most extreme conditions. The limit of what he thought extreme is suggested by an assignment he had to the Lost River Stake in Idaho in the dead of winter. He had a bad cold, a boil in his left ear, and a carbuncle on his neck. "But, I felt I could go as I have always tried to be one hundred percent dependable." On the bus, he gave up his seat to an old man who was sick, and he "sat on a jump seat all the way to Arco in considerable agony." At his destination, he felt better after helping with the chores around the farm and "enjoying another of Sister Anderson's excellent meals."

Occasionally Camilla accompanied her husband on his assignments. He insisted she go with him to Delta, Utah, where, as a young woman, she had taught home economics at the Millard Stake Academy. A nostalgic talk she gave brought many to the stand afterwards to reacquaint themselves and to reminisce about her earlier experiences at the academy. Before returning home, the Kimballs were reminded of the dislocations of war when they inspected Topaz, where sixteen hundred Japanese Americans were housed in rough barracks on a dusty, barren compound surrounded by wire fences. The confinement of the internees at Topaz was also a bleak reminder that LeVan was now aboard a ship somewhere in the Pacific, at war with the Japanese. His ship was later attacked and badly damaged. LeVan was thrown into the sea but was rescued.

Camilla also accompanied Elder Kimball on his first lengthy trip as a General Authority. They traveled east by train in February 1944 to attend stake conferences in Chicago, New York, and Washington, D.C. The trip also was distinguished by the trail of relatives they found along the way. In Chicago was Jasmine Edmunds, a Romney cousin and the wife of stake president John K. Edmunds. In New York was Camilla's sister Catherine, wife of financier William F. Edwards, whose children Caroline, Weston, and Robert entertained Uncle Spencer with games. Their little sister, Catherine, was too young to join in the fun. "A wholesome, healthy family," Elder Kimball wrote of them. The day before the New York stake conference, the Kimballs drove out of the city to visit another cousin, Mary Bennion, daughter of Uncle George Woolley. And the day after the conference, they traveled to New Jersey to visit Camilla's brother, Dr. Henry Eyring, a professor at Princeton University, whose sons, Ted and Hal, Elder Kimball described as "splendid boys, well trained." Hal, whose full name was Henry B. Eyring, would later become a General Authority of the Church. The father, Dr. Eyring, who was then associated with Dr. Albert Einstein, took the Kimballs through the laboratory, introducing them to several of the professors.

In Washington, D.C., Elder Kimball participated in reorganizing the stake presidency from which Elder Ezra Taft Benson was released. He was replaced by Edgar B. Brossard, a member of the U.S. Tariff Commission. The Kimballs spent a pleasant evening at the home of Elder and Sister Benson, visiting with their family and playing games. Later, Elder Benson showed Spencer through the offices of the farm cooperative where he had been working and introduced him to several prominent government officials.

Here in the nation's capital, the travelers also found

more relatives and a special friend. Kathleen Carpenter, wife of Sam Carpenter of the stake presidency, was Camilla's cousin, and Nicholas Udall was the son of Elder Kimball's deceased sister, Ruth. With Nicholas was his uncle, Jesse Udall, President Kimball's good friend from Safford. Jesse had an army desk job in Washington.

The effort Spencer and Camilla made on this trip to renew acquaintance with relatives was one of their salient traits. They loved their families and took special interest in them. Reflecting that interest, Elder Kimball became the president of the Heber C. Kimball family association shortly after returning from the East. He injected new life into the organization. A major achievement was spearheading the update and reprinting of President Heber C. Kimball's biography.

Also, a significant change in their immediate family had occurred a few months earlier when Olive Beth married Grant Mack, a returned missionary from New England, who soon after entered the navy.

Elder Kimball toured several missions during this period. The procedure was always the same: he interviewed each missionary personally, held missionary training sessions, and spoke to members and investigators at public meetings. One of his first tours, the tour of the Spanish American Mission with President Loren Jones, had a major impact on Elder Kimball. It was his first in-depth exposure to Mexican members. Meetings were held with them in California, Arizona, New Mexico, Texas, and Colorado. When possible, Elder Kimball ate and slept in the homes of Spanish-speaking members. This gave him an understanding of their culture and their problems. The insights he received began a lifelong advocacy for their rights and privileges in the Church. "It has been glorious," he wrote after completing the tour, "and we have really learned to think a great deal of the people. They have been so kind and considerate. They have been so appreciative of our eating with them and sleeping in their beds and our interest in them."

It did not take long for the word to seep out, through the efficient grapevine of the Spanish-speaking members of the Church in the United States, that Elder Kimball was genuinely interested in them and wanted to understand their problems and help them. In time, that same perception would find its way into the minds of so-called minority and underprivileged groups everywhere.

In the spring of 1945, Elder Kimball toured the Eastern States Mission. Aside from the usual enjoyment of meeting with the missionaries and members, he enjoyed visiting early Church history sites within the mission, including the Joseph Smith and Whitmer farms, the Hill Cumorah, the Sacred Grove, the Martin Harris home, and Palmyra, where the Book of Mormon was first published. Of special personal interest was a visit to Mendon, New York, where his Kimball ancestors had lived for many years and where they had formed a close relationship with the Young family. It was here that Heber C. Kimball and Brigham Young first became acquainted as young men; their acquaintance grew through the years as their influence grew among the Latter-day Saints. Ironically, the past came alive for Elder Kimball when he visited the place of the dead, Mendon's old cemetery. As Elder Kimball picked his way among the headstones, whose inscriptions had been dimmed by wind and storm, he found the grave of his great-grandfather, Solomon Farnham Kimball. He also found the headstone of Miriam Works Young, Brigham Young's first wife, who was a good friend of Vilate Kimball, Heber C. Kimball's first wife. The ancestral trail that led from this verdant village to arid Arizona was fascinating to contemplate.

During this tour, Elder Kimball received word that President Heber J. Grant had passed away on May 14, 1945, exactly a week after the German surrender was signed at Reims. His death was not unexpected, as his vitality had slowly subsided following the stroke he had suffered several years before. Elder Kimball returned to Salt Lake City immediately. There he joined with his brethren in paying respects to their deceased leader. Following a private devotional, the Brethren accompanied the family to the Tabernacle, where a capacity crowd awaited. After appropriate eulogies, interspersed with some of President Grant's favorite hymns, Elder Kimball and Camilla joined the long cortege that accompanied the hearse to the cemetery, high on Salt Lake City's north bench. They were struck by manifestations of respect from both members of the Church and those who were not members who lined the route of the procession. Most notable were members of the Catholic clergy, who stood quietly near Third East and South Temple while the bells of the Cathedral of the Madeleine tolled their condolences, and the nurses in training at the Catholic-owned Holy Cross Hospital, who stood at respectful attention at Tenth East.

The global interests of the Church dictated the need for a prompt reorganization of the First Presidency. It took place in the upper room of the Salt Lake Temple on May 21, 1945. Elder Kimball was impressed by the symbolism when President Grant's counselors took their places in the semicircle according to seniority, with President Clark seated between Elders Charles A. Callis and Albert E. Bowen and President McKay between Elders George F. Richards and Joseph Fielding Smith. When each member of the council had spoken, it was decided that reorganization of the First Presidency should not be delayed. Then, on motion of Elder George F. Richards, duly seconded, Elder George Albert Smith was unanimously approved as the eighth President of the Church. He, in turn, named J. Reuben Clark and David O. McKay as his counselors. Also, Elder George F. Richards was chosen to serve as the president of the Twelve. In due course, President Smith was ordained and set apart and the other three were approved and set apart to their respective positions.

Ten days later, President George Albert Smith set Elder Kimball on a path that would define a major element of his apostolic career. "Today President George Albert Smith asked me to assist in supervising the Navajo-Zuni Mission," he wrote. "This is a fulfillment of my patriarchal blessing." Here he referred to statements in the patriarchal blessing given to him by the patriarch Samuel Claridge when Spencer was nine years old: "You will preach the gospel to many people, but more especially to the Lamanites. . . . You will see them organized and be prepared to stand as a bulwark around the people." Such were the expectations aroused by these promises that Elder Kimball was troubled when, during his mission to the central states, he did not so much as meet an Indian, let alone teach one. The assignment from President Smith relieved Elder Kimball of anxieties about the patriarch's promises and seemed to imbue him with a new burst of energy.

Since his role was merely to "assist" with this one mission, Elder Kimball was limited in what he could do. He occasionally met with President Smith and others to discuss the administration of the mission, as he did on June 11, 1945, when he, Elder Antoine R. Ivins, and Ralph Evans were closeted with the Prophet. Later, after his call to the Twelve in October 1945, Elder Matthew Cowley was added to this group. Elder Kimball served in this subordinate role until September 1946, when his responsibilities with the Lamanites were greatly expanded. Meanwhile, three important incidents occurred that helped prepare him for this expanded role.

The first took place a few weeks after he was appointed to assist with the Navajo-Zuni Mission. At a stake conference in Denver, Colorado, he emphasized the need for Latter-day Saints to use prayer as a tool in handling the responsibilities and challenges of life. Apparently moved by his own words, he decided to return to the mountain near Boulder to reinforce through prayer the impact of the spiritual experience he had had there in the summer of 1943 and to gain strength and insights for his future work. "Up at 5 A.M.," he wrote on June 26, 1945, "I began to relive my unusual experience at this place July 14, 1943. As in 1943, I followed my footsteps of that early morning, up to the hill, past the sanitarium south and west, up over the little back- bone." When he came in sight of the summit, Elder Kimball found that the cross he saw before had been broken. "I found a cross beam," he explained, "and carried it up the hill . . . and fixed it the best I could." Finding a suitable place, he then engaged in lengthy, fervent prayer, after which he "lay down in the same spot and slept for a while." Awakening, he admired the beautiful scenery, then returned by the back side as he did before. He had been gone for six hours.

The second incident occurred in the summer of 1946, when President Smith assigned Elder Kimball and Elder Matthew Cowley to conduct a six-week tour of the Hawaiian Islands. Their wives accompanied them. Since both apostles served on the Navajo-Zuni Mission commit- tee and the Polynesians are considered to be of the same extraction as the American Indians, it is possible that President Smith made this assignment as a preliminary to the action he would take a few weeks later. During this tour, Elder Kimball gained many insights into the character and motivations of the Polynesians, insights that would be important when his role with the Lamanites was later enlarged.

The third incident consisted of a vivid dream Elder Kimball had in mid-August about people in different cul- tures, especially the Lamanites. In the dream, which he thought may have been induced by frequent thoughts he had had about the Lamanites during his waking hours, he saw himself among American Indians in Arizona and New Mexico.

On September 13, 1946, President George Albert Smith invited Elder Kimball to his office, where he extended to him a call with global responsibilities. "Now, I want you to look after the Indians," Elder Kimball quoted President Smith as saying. "They have been neglected. You watch all the Indians. I want you to have charge and look after all the

Indians in all the world; and this includes those in the islands, also." Elder Kimball assured the prophet he would do his best. Later in the day, in a meeting of the Council of the First Presidency and the Quorum of the Twelve, President Smith elaborated on the responsibilities the Brethren had toward the Lamanites. Elder Kimball quoted him as saying: "It is our duty to see that this work is carried to the world. I was talking with one of the Brethren this morning in regard to the Indians; and I feel that the work of disseminating the gospel among the Indians is one of the most important things we have to do, not only the Indians close to us, but all over the world, in the islands of the sea, and elsewhere."

Although Elder Kimball's duties were clearly defined as to scope, they were nebulous as to the means of fulfilling them. With the call, President Smith had merely handed him some files that contained miscellaneous correspondence and reports about the Lamanites, names and addresses of key people, and information about several American Indian organizations. It also was affirmed that Elders Matthew Cowley and Antoine Ivins would work with him and that Ralph Evans, president of the Navajo-Zuni Mission, would be available to help. This was all. He received nothing else.

Given the magnitude of the task and the minimal resources then available to perform it, Elder Kimball, understandably, was assailed with feelings of inadequacy and self-doubt. Was he a big enough man to do the job? How could he presume to undertake a mammoth job of this kind? It was during this period of self-doubt, a month after President Smith had extended the global call, that Elder Kimball experienced a terrifying ordeal. It occurred on October 19, 1946, in Pleasant Grove, Utah, during a weekend visit to a stake conference. He had gone to bed and had fallen asleep when he awoke with a start. He detected a depressing, ominous presence in the room, "bleak and black and fearsome." Turning on the light, he tried to read to dispel the feeling. It didn't work. The feeling persisted and became even more oppressive. "I felt almost as if I were being enveloped and taken over." He defined his apprehension as being "a deep fear of the unknown, something or somebody one could not wrestle with." Unable to grapple with this unseen presence, Elder Kimball began to struggle inwardly for dominance over it. "I sweat and fought and fought and sweat," he explained later, during the course of which he remembered the "temple program." For the first time in his life, he "invoked the power of the priesthood in that particular way." This produced the relief he sought, and the loathsome presence and influence were dispelled.

For days afterward, he reflected on this singular experience. What did it mean or portend? Did it mean he was marked for destruction by the adversary? Or was it merely Satan's reaction to Elder Kimball "getting into a program" that would upset his plans? A key to the answer seemed to be his recollection of the satanic assault made on his grandfather, Heber C. Kimball, and his associates at the threshold of the Church's proselyting effort in Great Britain. Now at the threshold of another major Church initiative, Elder Kimball believed the powers of darkness had been aroused to try to thwart this new "program."

A week after the ordeal in Pleasant Grove, President Smith gave Elders Kimball and Cowley some on-the-job training. The three of them traveled south to visit the Navajo Indian Reservation, which covers a vast tract in the Four Corners area of Utah, Arizona, New Mexico, and Colorado. They stopped first in Blanding, Utah, to visit a group of Navajos who lived nearby. "My sympathy was stirred," wrote Elder Kimball, "to see these people defrauded and downtrodden." His concern was directed toward the United States government, which had defaulted on its obligations under the 1868 treaty with the Navajos to provide adequate schools for Navajo children. Elder Kimball believed education was the key to unlock the door to opportunity and development for the Navajos and for all Lamanites. As we shall see, this was the basic objective that underlay his many efforts to lift the Lamanites, including the novel Indian Children Placement Program.

The three Church leaders went from Blanding to the Navajo tribal headquarters at Window Rock, Arizona, to attend meetings of the tribal council scheduled October 28 and 29, 1946. Their purpose was to seek official recognition for the Church on the reservation so that Church facilities could be built or rented—facilities in which to teach members of the tribe or conduct worship services. Previous efforts to obtain recognition had been blocked by the determined efforts of other religious groups who were already operating on the reservation and who were fearful of allowing the Latter-day Saints to enter. The Brethren expected opposition from these groups again.

The first day was occupied entirely with other items on the tribal council's agenda, which enabled the visitors to study the participants and their surroundings. Elder Kimball, who had never seen anything like this meeting before, was intensely fascinated. The octagonal council room had been constructed according to Navajo design to resemble a tent. Most Navajo men present were dressed in blue jeans and colorful flannel shirts, jackets, and boots, with their long black hair rolled into neat knots at the back of their necks. The Navajo women wore long, colorful pleated skirts, bright blouses, and moccasins and were adorned with beautiful Indian jewelry. Present also in the council room, whose atmosphere was tinged with the combined odors of tobacco smoke and desert sage, were government officials and visitors like the apostles and representatives of other churches.

On the second day, the question of recognition of the Latter-day Saints came before the council. In his initial presentation, President Smith, speaking through an interpreter, emphasized that the purpose of the Church in seeking recognition was to bless and uplift the Navajo people. Several spoke in opposition to the request. Most of the reasons given in opposition were nebulous. In essence, they came down to the idea that some Navajos just didn't want the Mormons around. One opponent, however, was specific. He was offended that two Mormon elders had blessed one of his tribe members who was in the hospital. President Smith's mild response seemed to turn the tide of sentiment in favor of the Latter-day Saints. He stressed the common kinship all people have to God; expressed surprise at the complaint, noting that he would be happy, if he were ill, to have any good Christian come "to visit me and bind up my wounds and pour on the sacred oil"; and reiterated that the only purpose of the Latter-day Saints was to help the members of the tribe. While the request was denied at this time, Elder Kimball believed the favorable impression made had laid the groundwork for success in the future. The Brethren completed their tour the next day, visiting Fort Defiance; Gallup, New Mexico; and Snowflake, Arizona, where meetings were held.

The month after these meetings with President Smith and Elder Cowley, Elder Kimball began his long odyssey in behalf of his Lamanite friends. In connection with a stake conference in the Young Stake at Farmington, New Mexico, he scheduled a special meeting with Native Americans living in the area. This began a practice he followed routinely through the years of holding special meetings for Lamanites in conjunction with stake conference assignments. In addition, he held numerous meetings with Lamanites other than those held in connection with stake conferences.

During the year 1947, Elder Kimball also launched a vigorous campaign to raise the public consciousness about the plight and needs of the Native Americans. This included correspondence with senators and other public officials; talks given at Rotary clubs; letters to mission presidents, urging them to assign missionaries to work with any Native Americans within their missions; sermons delivered at ward, stake, and general meetings, which included sermons about the Lamanites given at both the April and October general conferences; and extensive mailings of pamphlets about the

*Elder Kimball
visits with a
Native American
family. Helping
Lamanites discover
their heritage as
sons and daughters
of God was one of
Spencer W. Kimball's
continuing quests.*

Lamanites. Three days before the end of the year, he wrote about his publicity plans for the future: "I am preparing some articles for the *Era,* a series for the *[Deseret] News* and sermons . . . I am to give." He also gave this assessment of his public relations efforts during the year: "I have done everything I could to stimulate interest in the needs of the Indians, not only for food and clothing and bedding they need so desperately but for the economic, spiritual and educational needs which are even more desperate."

In addition to these public relations initiatives and his

numerous meetings with small American Indian groups, there were other significant events during the year that expanded his influence among the Lamanites. In May he completed a month-long mission tour in Mexico with President Arwell Pierce. Because Elder Kimball considered the Mexican people (as well as others in Central and South America and the islands of the Pacific) to be within the ambit of those whom President Smith had charged him to shepherd, he looked at them with new eyes as he traveled throughout the country during this tour. In early July, he traveled to Flagstaff, Arizona, where he supervised the installation of Eugene Flake as the president of the Navajo-Zuni Mission replacing Ralph Evans. Arrangements were made to effect the change there because on July 4, a gala Indian celebration was held in Flagstaff and attended by several thousand Native Americans representing many tribes. An all-Indian parade and a rodeo were special features of the celebration. President Evans introduced Elder Kimball to prominent Indian leaders whose acquaintance would be helpful in the future. Afterward, he traveled to Moenkopi, Tuba City, Oraibi, and Sand Hills, where meetings were held. At Sand Hills he witnessed the baptism of four Native American converts, a promising sign.

The most encouraging event of the year, reflecting progress in Elder Kimball's Indian program, was a Lamanite conference held in Mesa, Arizona, the first week in November. Several hundred Lamanites from all over the Southwest and from northern Mexico across the border gathered in Mesa for instruction and motivation and for special sessions in the Arizona Temple. "We tried to hear from and recognize as many of the prominent Mexicans as possible," wrote Elder Kimball. And what especially pleased him was the temple session: "There were sixty-nine who went through for the first time, and twenty marriages. It was glorious to see the temple filled with the dark-skinned Lamanites, beginning to come into their own."

Elder Kimball's persistent promotion of Lamanite causes

effected a major change in the perception people had about them and the coverage given to them in the press. "The *Deseret News* came for pictures about Indians," he wrote on December 8, 1947. "It is pleasing to note the great volume of publicity that we are getting now in this program."

Chapter 14

An Unwanted Pause

W hile the Indian program was Elder Kimball's main focus during 1947, other important things claimed his attention. At a personal level, the family's move to the new home on Laird Drive was significant. The Doxeys had returned from their mission in the autumn of 1946, making it imperative that the Kimballs find other housing. The postwar crush on builders delayed the completion of their new home until the spring of 1947. During the interval, the Kimballs lived in the cramped quarters of an apartment in the Belvedere, a facility on South State Street, only a block from the Church Administration Building. While this was convenient for Spencer, it was burdensome for the family, who had been accustomed to the comforts of a spacious home. They moved into the basement of the Laird Drive home the first week in March 1947, even though artisans were still at work on it. It was a charming but unpretentious place that compared favorably with their dream home in Safford.

At this time, the at-home Kimball family included only

the parents and Eddie. LeVan and Olive Beth were married, and Andrew had left on his mission the previous autumn. The extended family was augmented by the birth of Olive Beth's daughter the week following the Kimballs' move to Laird Drive. And in August, LeVan, now regularly called Spence, left with his family for England, where he began his studies as a Rhodes Scholar at Oxford.

At the institutional level also, 1947 was a significant year. Two deaths—the death in October 1946 of Bishop Marvin O. Ashton, first counselor in the Presiding Bishopric, and the death in January 1947 of Elder Charles A. Callis of the Quorum of the Twelve—created vacancies in the ranks of the General Authorities that were filled at the April general conference. Henry D. Moyle was called to the Twelve at that time, while Thorpe B. Isaacson was called to the Presiding Bishopric. Both new General Authorities would in the years ahead serve as members of the First Presidency.

The most dramatic Church event of the year was the centennial celebration of the arrival of the Latter-day Saints in the Salt Lake Valley. It was fraught with personal significance for Elder Kimball, given the key role his grandfather had played in Church history. To commemorate the event, Spencer joined a reenactment of the pioneer trek. Instead of traveling in wagons, the modern trekkers rode in automobiles, following the route of the pioneer company as near as practicable. Elder Kimball joined the caravan at Nauvoo, Illinois, on July 13. For the next nine days, he vicariously lived the experiences of the pioneers as the modern caravan passed places so well known in Mormon history—Garden Grove, Mt. Pisgah, Grand Island, Fort Laramie, Casper, Independence Rock, Devil's Gate, and Fort Bridger. Two days after arriving in Salt Lake on July 22, he attended the unveiling and dedication of the "This Is the Place" Monument. He was pleased that a figure representing his grandfather, Heber C. Kimball, was atop the main tower of the monument and that Heber and his wife were also represented in bas relief on one of its lower wings.

Less than a year after these historic events, Elder Kimball entered one of the most stressful and depressing periods of his life. It was precipitated by a minor accident while touring the Navajo-Zuni Mission in May 1948. His traveling companion was Golden Buchanan, who had joined Elder Kimball on the train at Milford, Utah, as the apostle was traveling to Los Angeles. While waiting in Los Angeles to obtain an automobile, Elder Kimball was introduced to Chief Tahachee of the Kawie tribe and his wife, both of whom had joined the Church. The Indian chief was an actor who had appeared in numerous pictures and was well known in the Hollywood movie industry. Elder Kimball foresaw that this convert could be helpful in his work with the Lamanites. "Brother Tahachee seemed to be very humble and willing to fit into the program," he recorded.

En route to Phoenix, Arizona, Elder Kimball asked Brother Buchanan to take a detour so he could visit some Indians in a remote area of the desert. It was a fateful decision. Off the surfaced highway, the car became stuck in the sand. Isolated from all help, the two felt their only remedy was to push. They alternated, with one pushing while the other gunned the motor. Again and again they repeated the procedure, inching the car along until at last it reached more solid ground and eventually the highway. In this process, Elder Kimball's heart was under great stress. The normal strain of lifting and pushing to the utmost of his strength was aggravated by the heat of the desert.

While he was perspiring heavily and breathing hard, with his heart racing from these exertions, Elder Kimball felt no immediate ill effects. He was only fifty-three years old and in excellent health. Years of work on the farm had toughened his body, which from infancy had been healthy. And after moving to Salt Lake City, he had sought to maintain his health by swimming and working out at the Deseret Gymnasium. On this account, Elder Kimball quickly put the incident out of his mind. And on this account, he minimized the seriousness of the ordeal he experienced that night.

It occurred in the home of Glen Stapley in Phoenix, where Elder Kimball was a guest. He had just finished a warm bath when he experienced a massive pain that seemed to fill his whole chest area. It was so intense that all else was forgotten as he struggled to fight it off. Gradually the pain subsided. He did not know how long it had lasted. Nor did he know how heavily he had perspired during the incident until afterward when he found himself drenched. Because of his previous robust health, Elder Kimball could not believe this one episode was life-threatening or even very serious. And because it had not persisted long, he decided to ignore it and go on with the tour. He did, however, mention it to Brother Buchanan, although he seems to have minimized the intensity of what was certainly a heart attack.

During the next eleven days, Elder Kimball and his companion crisscrossed several Indian reservations in Arizona and New Mexico. Much of their travel was on rough, unsurfaced roads. Along the way they held meetings with Indians and Indian missionaries and also with tribal leaders, as they did at Sacaton, where they met with the tribal council. Here Elder Kimball also met with a bishop, "instructing him to make the Church program fit into the needs of the Indians." Near Globe, Arizona, he visited the Tenijieth family; here he was surprised and quite pleased to meet five-year-old Spencer Kimball Tenijieth. He was not surprised, however, to see the squalid conditions in which most of the Lamanites lived, with little food, flimsy housing, poor sanitation, and nothing to ward off disease except their faith. So, along the way, he administered to the sick, invoking God's blessings on them. "I do hope the Lord will find it in his providence to heal her," he wrote after blessing an aged woman in the Tenijieth home, "or at least to stop her pain."

While much he saw was discouraging, there were positive signs. "The attitudes of the Indians and the officials on the reservation are changing in our way," he wrote optimistically after visiting an Apache tribe near Whiteriver, Arizona.

Golden Buchanan seems to have sensed that Elder Kimball's attack in Phoenix was more serious than the apostle would have had him believe. He felt compelled, therefore, to share his concern with someone. The opportunity came when they visited the San Carlos Reservation in southeastern Arizona. Here they met Jesse Udall, president of the St. Joseph Stake, to whom Golden Buchanan confided his concerns. In turn, President Udall mentioned it to Elder Mark E. Petersen during a stake conference visit. Elder Petersen then raised the matter with the Brethren in Salt Lake City. The result was that on May 15, Elder Petersen called Spencer Kimball at the request of the Brethren to say they were concerned about his health and to suggest that he curtail the tour. "I was embarrassed," wrote Elder Kimball, "to have brought concern to the brethren." Yet it gave him "quite a lift" to know about their feelings. "I am so small and weak in this great work of the Lord that it had hardly occurred to me that I would ever be missed from it should anything happen to me." When Elder Petersen called, Spencer was in Snowflake, Arizona, for a stake conference. Obedient to the Brethren, he suspended the tour and returned home immediately after the conference.

While Elder Kimball was amenable to the wishes of the Brethren, he was not yet prepared to yield to the counsel of his doctor. Two days after returning from Snowflake, he went to his cousin Doctor J. LeRoy Kimball for a physical checkup. The doctor was concerned about the changes that had occurred since the last exam and told the patient his heart had been damaged. He recommended that the apostle quit work for a month and take it easy. Elder Kimball was incredulous. "It seemed so impossible, so silly." He could not visualize himself, one of the youngest and healthiest members of the Twelve, lolling around while his older and less vigorous brethren did the work. Yet he did not want to ignore the doctor completely. So he made a concession. He began to walk more slowly and ride the elevator.

With this self-prescribed therapy in place, he caught the bus a few days later for Rigby, Idaho, to conduct a stake conference. Any thought that his wisdom surpassed the doctor's evaporated at a meeting Saturday afternoon. "I had a pain in my chest and thought I had done wrong." The next day he had a "heaviness" in his chest and wished he had followed the doctor's instructions.

An event five days later finally convinced Elder Kimball he was a sick man and should yield to the advice of his doctor. During the night of May 28, 1948, after four days of bed rest, he awakened with severe chest pains like those he had suffered in Phoenix. It was unmistakable. He was having another major heart attack. He awakened Camilla and, overcome with the depression that usually accompanies these episodes, began to talk about things his wife did not want to hear—about funeral arrangements, about winding up their business affairs in Safford, and about important personal and family matters.

The doctor who was summoned examined Spencer again and advised him that he would recover if he followed directions. The doctor's remedy was clear. "He said that with *determined inactivity*, I should get along alright." The doctor knew his patient well. If he could convince him to be determined and disciplined about inactivity, there was hope he would obey.

For five weeks Spencer followed the doctor's orders exactly. He seldom stirred from bed. Only occasional reading or visits from family and friends interrupted his restful routine. He suffered occasional bouts of pain, but he did not report them to others. To do so, he feared, might bring further restrictions. On June 30, he went to the doctor for another examination. The results were inconclusive. Most signs were positive, but one was negative. However, since the good outweighed the bad, the doctor loosened the reins and allowed the patient to go outside the house but not to work. Elder Kimball began to go to the library to study books about the Lamanites. This triggered a yearning to visit the reservation again. After exacting a promise that Elder Kimball would rest there and not work, the doctor approved.

Elder Kimball and his friend Golden Buchanan headed south for New Mexico on July 8, 1948. The day had historical significance for the apostle. It was five years to the day since he had received the electrifying call from President Clark. He relived the event in his diary, as he did other related events in succeeding days. He also lamented how little he had achieved since then. This sense of failure and the restrictions imposed by his heart problems created the most stressful aspect of his convalescence.

Having borrowed a trailer-tent, Elder Kimball camped in a beautiful stand of pines near the hogan of his friend Howela Polacca. Here in this remote part of Navajo land called Pleasant Valley, near the people whom he loved, Spencer Kimball sought both physical and spiritual renewal.

He remained there for two weeks, sharing his camp first with Golden Buchanan, who left after a few days, and then with Elder Ellsworth, a missionary who was recuperating from an injury. The camp routine was relaxed and unstructured. Shared cooking and cleanup duties occupied little time, leaving most of the days free for reading, writing, and reflection or for leisurely reconnoitering of the area. Because Elder Ellsworth had a bad knee, Elder Kimball fashioned him a cane; then, to be fashionable, he made one for himself. Thus equipped, the unlikely pair slowly ranged over the area, inspecting points of interest, marveling at the quiet seclusion of the place, and cementing friendly relations with their Indian neighbors. During one outing they found names of the Polacca family chiseled into the red cliffs north of camp. Armed with tools their next visit, they sought to create a visual linkage with the family when Elder Ellsworth chiseled a large E close to their names and the apostle commenced to etch a human head nearby. Later, Elder Kimball sculpted a rough bust of himself from a piece of white sandstone, much to the enjoyment of the Indians, who were fascinated by his work.

The apostle's main point of interest there was the Indians themselves, their personality and their lifestyle. He found a wry sense of humor hidden beneath their quiet, stoic manner. He also learned about other cultural distinctions, such as their habit of avoiding direct eye contact as a mark of respect and a recognition of one's privacy and their habit of pointing with pursed lips and a toss of the head since to point with the finger was considered a mark of disrespect or even aggression. He was impressed with the simplicity and sincerity of their faith as he worshipped with them. And he was touched when he and Elder Ellsworth came upon young Frances Polacca, during one of their meanderings, who was loudly singing "Come, Come, Ye Saints" as she herded the family sheep. Her reticence melted when she consented to teach the two visitors how to count in Navajo and sing a Navajo song. Elder Kimball later endeared himself to the family when he sang the song with a colored band around his head.

Golden Buchanan and his wife picked up Elder Kimball on July 23 and delivered him home the next day. In assessing the effects of the trip, Spencer had to admit that while enjoyable, his trip had helped his health little, if at all. The next day, after attending services in his ward, he was "jittery and nervous." And an effort to work at his desk during the next few days proved futile. "My heart pains were so severe that I did not need a physician to send me back to bed."

The need to avoid unscheduled visits, telephone calls, and the temptation to work dictated the decision to go to Long Beach, California, for a lengthy rest. It was felt too that the lower altitude would help. Elder Kimball, accompanied by Camilla, left for the coast on August 7, 1948. They found a small, comfortable apartment in view of the ocean to call home for six weeks. Here they lived by the sun, with no schedules, no meetings, no appointments, and no visitors except those invited to call. Camilla did all the shopping, cooking, laundering, and housecleaning, leaving her husband free to concentrate on his convalescence. It was hard duty for him. It was like jacking up the rear wheels of a race car, then gunning the motor. It was comparatively easy to slow Elder Kimball down physically, but that did not slow down his mind, which continued to race ahead. And with no work on which his thoughts could focus, he often turned to self-criticism. "Thousands of people in the church are measuring the church, their church, by me. They look at me with my smallness, my ineptitude, my weaknesses, my narrow limitations and say 'What a weak church to have such weak leadership.'" He added this comment, providing insight into the motivations that impelled him to work so hard and with such persistence: "I have tried by double expenditure of energy to measure up."

During this Long Beach interlude, regular contact was maintained with Salt Lake City, chiefly through the reports Camilla made of her husband's condition. "Spencer is impatient to get back to his work [but] every unusual physical or emotional strain seems to end in distress and a sleepless night," she wrote in one letter. The Brethren responded, urging that he continue the mending process without concern about his church duties.

In addition to letters from the Brethren, many other letters of a purely personal nature came from Salt Lake and elsewhere to brighten and lift the patient. A special one came from President George Albert Smith, filled with words of love and encouragement. It mentioned the long siege of ill health President Smith had passed through during the early years of his apostleship, noting particularly the many weeks of convalescence he had spent at nearby Ocean Park.

By mid-September, Elder Kimball began to show signs of improvement. "It is now past noon and I have had no distress for two full days," he wrote on September 14. This and other favorable signs signified the end of the Long Beach interlude. He returned to Salt Lake City ten days later and immediately went to see Doctor Kimball. Pleased with his progress, the doctor told Spencer he could begin to work "a little," but that he should "take it easy for three months." In order to obtain clearance from the authorities, Elder Kimball went to see President Smith the next day, where he reported the doctor's findings. The prophet concurred with the doctor and authorized Spencer to return to work on a reduced schedule, but cautioned him "not to overdo."

Elder Kimball lost no time advising Elder George F. Richards, president of the Quorum of the Twelve, that the doctor and President Smith had lifted the work restrictions that had been imposed on him. President Richards promptly assigned him to attend the conference of the Wells stake on Sunday, September 26. However, Elder Kimball did not speak during the conference, nor did he speak at the general conference the following weekend, although he attended some of the sessions.

During the next six months, Elder Kimball began to ease back into his customary work routines, although he continued to suffer periodic bouts of pain. In addition to his headquarters and field assignments, he performed special priesthood functions for members of his family. On December 8, he performed the temple marriage of his son Andrew and Mildred Phyllis Jones; two weeks later, he spoke at funeral services for his sister Helen, who died after a long, agonizing battle with cancer of the face. The emotional turmoil caused by watching his sister waste away haunted Elder Kimball and created a special terror for him when he was later stricken with cancer of the throat.

In mid-January 1949, he and Elder Mark E. Petersen reorganized the presidency of the Los Angeles Stake and afterward, at the request of President George Albert Smith, stayed over a day for a meeting with the presidents of eight stakes in southern California to discuss plans for the construction of a temple in Los Angeles. At this time, Salt Lake was experiencing one of its most severe winters. The heavy snows had driven herds of deer into the city, where they survived by feeding on neighborhood shrubberies. During the month of January, there were only eighteen hours when the temperature rose above freezing. This prompted Elder Kimball to seek a winter break in the Gila Valley. He took the bus there from Los Angeles and spent five pleasant days in the sun, visiting the folks at Pima and riding horses.

There were few breaks for Elder Kimball during the next seven months. In addition to stake conferences and the general conference, he traveled into Mexico for a series of meetings and conducted two lengthy tours into the Navajo-Zuni Mission. On returning to Salt Lake City on August 17 following the last tour, he suffered severe chest pains, and "most of the symptoms of last year returned." He told no one about this. He was afraid if word of it got back to the Brethren, they would ground him again. He wanted none of that. It seems at this time that he decided he would rather die working than waste away as an invalid. During the October general conference, he suffered another severe attack but told no one. Shortly afterward, he left for the East to divide the Northern States Mission, which, with the numerous meetings held, the acquisition of new mission homes, and the training of a new mission president, occupied almost three weeks. After completing these heavy duties, he could have gone home for a little rest before attending a stake conference in Lovell, Wyoming, on November 19 and 20. Instead, he decided to spend the intervening ten days working with Indians or Indian missionaries in Minnesota, Wisconsin, North Dakota, and Montana. Included were meetings in such out-of-the-way places as the Berthold Indian Reservation in North Dakota and Wolf Point, Chicken Hill, and Lame Deer, Montana.

Throughout this entire month, Elder Kimball suffered occasional chest pains that he mentioned to no one. He worked through them stoically so the Brethren would not find out. He continued to work until December 19, when he finally faced up to the need to see the doctor again. He expected but did not like the results: "He recommended a long rest. He also recommended two weeks in the hospital, but I talked him out of that."

He was unable, however, to talk the First Presidency out of their instruction that he take another long rest. It was decided that he should go to the Gila Valley for this purpose. Because several locations were on the way there, Spencer did not consider it a violation of the First Presidency's instructions when he stopped in Gallup to hold a meeting with the Indian missionaries and in Bylas to inspect a new meetinghouse being constructed for the Indians.

Elder Kimball spent a month in the Gila Valley resting, visiting with family and friends, reading, and writing. He felt better and pleaded with the Brethren to let him go back to work. They urged him to take at least another month. He spent several weeks in California in Los Angeles and in Berkeley, where he and Camilla stayed with Camilla's brother Joe Eyring and his wife. Returning home on February 18, he announced, "I am ready to go back to work." He qualified the statement by adding, "The only thing is that my voice is very bad."

Elder Kimball had suffered with hoarseness for several months. At first he ignored it. Later he tried over-the-counter remedies that did not help. Then he became worried. Fearful of a malignancy, he consulted Dr. Leland Cowan, a cancer specialist. "He seemed worried," the patient wrote after the examination on March 8, 1950. "I came home much worried myself. Cancer would render me useless from now on for the church."

Dr. Cowan brought Dr. LeRoy Smith, a throat specialist, onto the case. Following an examination two days later, Dr. Smith "thought it was not too bad" but wanted to examine him again. On April 3, Elder Kimball was examined jointly by both doctors. "It looks ominous. If they let it run unchecked it may be cancer and so beyond control." He was terrified by the prospect of enduring the agonies his sister

Helen had suffered. "I think death would be welcome by heart trouble rather than the grim spectre of cancer." He also felt depressed that his ministry would be shortened or hindered, and he lamented that perhaps he had served less effectively than he might have. "How can I face inactivity because of physical handicaps?" he wrote.

The next day the two doctors recommended a specimen be taken from his vocal cords for analysis. Only in this way could they be sure whether there was a malignancy. They also recommended another specialist, Dr. Ralph Rigby, for the job. While he abhorred the prospect, Elder Kimball had no viable option but to agree. To decline would be a risky gamble, one he could not take.

The following week was spent in nervous anticipation. Even the sessions of general conference could not entirely divert his attention from the pending surgery. Intermittently he was reminded of the prospect that his voice might be stilled permanently and that he might suffer an agonizing death like his sister Helen, slowly wasting away with cancer. Perhaps the only time these grim thoughts were entirely absent was while he struggled through an eight-minute talk delivered the first day of the conference. Was it possible the Saints had heard his voice for the last time?

Fortified by priesthood blessings and the prayers of his family, Elder Kimball entered the hospital the morning of April 11, 1950. The medicinal odors that permeated the building were a powerful reminder of why he was there. And the elaborate preliminaries, when he was robed in hospital gear, given pills and painkilling shots, and wheeled to the operating room, confirmed the reality of the coming unwanted event. There, while he was under anesthesia, the surgery was performed.

Afterward the patient was placed on a gurney for return to his private room. Only groggily aware of what went on about him, Elder Kimball suddenly aroused on hearing one of the orderlies profane the name of the Savior. "Please don't say that," he whispered. "He is the one I love above everybody in this world. Please." After a moment of silence, the orderly quietly said, "I shouldn't have said that. I am sorry."

Two days later, the doctor called to say the specimen was not cancerous. Unaccountably the news did not cheer him up. "I am still depressed," he admitted in his diary. "I seem to have forebodings that all is not well and that I might never get back my voice which is so precious and indispensable in my work." Yet he was prepared for that eventuality should the Lord decree it. "I have prayed 'Thy will be done.'"

The following weekend, Elder Kimball accompanied Elder Harold B. Lee to a stake conference in the Cache Valley. Unable to speak, he sat silent during the sessions, still depressed. Three days later, the despondency lifted when President J. Reuben Clark and Elders Harold B. Lee and Henry D. Moyle gave him a blessing. "After the administration I went home much relieved. I felt a calm assurance come over me which has remained." That feeling caused him to resist the doctors' recommendation that his throat be cauterized. "My voice seems nearly natural this morning," he wrote on April 23. And it continued to improve until within a few months he was back to normal. For more than six years afterward, Elder Kimball was able to perform his work with good voice and only occasional, minimal difficulties. He always viewed his recovery as a miracle.

Chapter 15

The Work Continues

I t was so good to be holding a conference again," wrote Elder Kimball a month after the surgery. He was in Glendale, Arizona, at the time, enjoying both the conference and the balmy, spring weather of the Salt River Valley. It was good to be alive. And his recent inactivity had brought a new appreciation for the work and its interesting variety.

He and Elder Richard L. Evans soon had an unusual experience at a stake reorganization in northern Utah, where they called the second counselor as the new stake president. The first counselor was shattered. He had assumed his role as first counselor gave him precedence. When he absented himself from a meeting, the visitors went to his home, where, with some effort, they were able to mollify him. Later, when assigned to reorganize a stake in Colorado, Elder Kimball was impressed that the stake president should not be released. After checking with Salt Lake, he left the president in office but gave him two new counselors. And at a Salt Lake stake known for its high statistical performance, he surprised the members by calling them to repentance for failure to perform at the level of which they were capable. Translated, this meant they should lengthen their stride and quicken their pace.

Meanwhile, there were major changes at Church headquarters. In early August, Elder George F. Richards, President of the Quorum of the Twelve, passed away at age eighty-nine. Earlier the same day, Elder Kimball had administered to this guileless man. On September 30, David O. McKay was set apart as the president of the Quorum of the Twelve, replacing Elder Richards while retaining his position as the second counselor in the First Presidency. Elder Kimball was pleased when, at the same time, his friend and fellow Arizonan, Delbert L. Stapley, was approved to fill the vacancy in the Twelve caused by President Richards's death.

The most significant change in the general leadership occurred on April 4, 1951, when President George Albert Smith passed away. It was his eighty-first birthday. Because the prophet's death occurred during general conference, last-minute changes were necessary to accommodate the funeral. Afterward, a special council meeting was held to consider the reorganization of the First Presidency. All agreed there should be no delay. After the Brethren counseled together, David O. McKay was approved and ordained as the ninth President of the Church. Unexpectedly, he nominated Stephen L Richards as his first counselor and J. Reuben Clark as the second. Elder Kimball seemed to express the feelings of the other members of the council about this action and the response of President Clark, who had been the first counselor in the First Presidency for almost twenty years. "I was shocked. What fortitude and self-control, what self-mastery. How could any mortal take a blow like that and stand?" Still, there was no criticism of President McKay, and all acknowledged that he was entitled to select his counselors and assign them as he wished. The situation was not unlike Elder Kimball's decision in Cache Valley to select the second counselor as the new stake president instead of selecting the first

*Elder Kimball admiring
a piece of Indian pottery.*

counselor. The best interest of the work was paramount over any personal consideration.

The change in leadership effected no change in Elder Kimball's assignments or status. Soon after being ordained, President McKay counseled with Spencer about his responsibilities. As to the work with the Lamanites, the prophet was quoted as saying, "This work must go on. If we permit this work to lag or lapse or permit it to be abandoned, the Lord will surely hold us accountable for it."

Imbued with that idea, Elder Kimball left to tour the North Central States Mission. Before their departure, he and Camilla arranged for their Lamanite foster daughter, Helen John, to stay with Woolley relatives. The concern they had for this girl was no less anxious than their concern for their natural daughter, Olive Beth.

During the tour Elder Kimball, as usual, sandwiched special meetings with Indians between missionary and general meetings. Near Emo in Manitoba he met with his "old friend, Chief Horton," who arranged a meeting with fifteen Indians in an old schoolhouse on the reservation. Here the apostle developed a familiar theme, that the Lamanites are a favored people, conditionally entitled to special blessings as promised in the Book of Mormon. From that place he went on to Fort Francis for a similar meeting. His efforts to elevate the status of Indians and their feelings of self-worth were unflagging. He seemed driven by the special charge President George Albert Smith had given him, which now had been affirmed by President McKay.

Intermittently during the tour, Elder Kimball experienced "slight heart pains" that were worrisome. He had no way of knowing whether they warned of another major attack and, if so, whether another attack would end it all. It was life on the edge, a condition that added a sense of urgency to everything he did. It also added a spur to a personality already inured to the idea that work was intended to be perpetual. So he continued to ignore these episodes, working through them as he did the first of July, when, oblivious of his health, he held meetings on the Barona, Pala, and Paiuma Indian reservations in connection with a stake conference in southern California.

On returning home, however, Elder Kimball decided to take a break in his routine. He and Camilla accepted the offer of the Graham Doxey family to use their cabin in the mountains east of Salt Lake City for a retreat. Spencer took along materials to work on for his father's and grandfather's biographies, so as to negate any idea he was loafing. He was merely changing his workplace to a spot where, incidentally, he could enjoy the beauty and solitude of the mountains.

Soon after arriving at the cabin, he experienced more heart pains. They continued off and on for three days, after which he finally acknowledged, "I have had endless pain since very early in the morning. It has hardly ceased. I wonder what to do. I perhaps should go down out of the elevation. I dare not let anyone know of my feelings, even the Brethren or my family. They would put me on the sick list and give me no activity. It would take months or years to get back to activity again." He then was assailed with morbid fears of death and expressed the hope that his family would complete the biographies he was working on. To this wish he added: "I might hope my children [also] will take from my many journals and write a simple little story or biography of me. I would like for my posterity to remember me and to know that I have tried so very hard to measure up."

Soon after he returned to the lower elevation, the pains left. "That was a scare," he admitted. And to confirm his diagnosis that the pains were caused by the altitude, he went to Doctor Kimball for another checkup. It was encouraging to be told his heart was "almost well," although the doctor seemed concerned about the duration and intensity of the pains suffered in the mountains.

The Kimballs decided to complete their vacation on the coast, where Spencer would not be troubled by the altitude. They drove to Santa Cruz, California, south of San Francisco, where, a few miles south of the city, they found a comfortable cottage near the beach where they holed up. Writing, reading, meditating, swimming, beachcombing, and some sculpting filled their days. They attended Sunday meetings in the little branch at Santa Cruz, and to maintain his personal involvement in the work, Elder Kimball held a testimony meeting with twenty-nine missionaries of the Northern California Mission. The change of scene accomplished its purpose. "All in all it has been a delightful two weeks plus and I hope I have stored up a reservoir of strength and vigor to last me now for another year so that I may better serve my Maker and my people."

The October general conference that year was distinguished by the call of Elder Marion G. Romney to the Twelve and by the call of four new Assistants to the Twelve: George Q. Morris, Stayner Richards, ElRay L. Christiansen, and John Longden. These seasoned men added new strength to the leading councils and provided much needed help in administering the affairs of the rapidly growing Church. During the eight years since Elder Kimball's call to the Twelve, forty-five new stakes and four new missions had been created, with an increase of over two hundred thousand new members. While the Church was poised for even more significant growth in the future, there were deterring factors which troubled Elder Kimball and his brethren. Chief among these was the restriction imposed on calling new missionaries because of the Korean War.

At first, approval was given to call married seventies to compensate for the loss of the younger missionaries and to allow priesthood quorums to bear the full cost of keeping them in the field, if necessary. This idea was abandoned at the October 1951 general conference, when it was announced that married seventies would not be called unless they or their families provided the financing. The concern was the implication of a paid clergy. This caused a marked decrease in the number of missionaries in the field, as those being released were not replaced.

Elder Kimball became acutely aware of this dwindling when, shortly after general conference, he toured the Central States Mission. It was the first time he had toured his old mission field since his call to the Twelve. On every hand were nostalgic reminders of the past. The Ozarks recalled his first hesitant tracting experiences; a missionary meeting in the chapel at Independence, Missouri, brought to mind his labors in preparing it for dedication; in Hannibal he met one of the members whom he was instrumental in converting thirty-six years before; and certain intersections in St. Louis summoned up memories of street meetings held there long ago and of the missionary companions who shared the preaching duties and the communal living arrangements in the old conference house.

But the tour also held some hints of the future. Here Elder Kimball met two local leaders who in the future would provide significant leadership as mission presidents in England: T. Bowring Woodbury, who lived in Kansas, and James A. Cullimore, who lived in Oklahoma. Elder Cullimore later became a General Authority, first as an Assistant to the Twelve and then as a member of the First Quorum of the Seventy.

Several years later Elder Kimball was able to evaluate the work in England during a five-month tour abroad. He and Sister Kimball left Salt Lake City in April 1955 and flew to New York, where they boarded the *Queen Mary*. The ship docked at Southampton, England, after a smooth Atlantic crossing. After traveling to London, the Kimballs flew to Frankfurt, Germany, where they were accommodated in the mission home. Elder Kimball was unprepared for the scars of the war still evident in Frankfurt after ten years. Entire blocks of rubble, stark and depressing, stood out like ugly blemishes on the face of the city. This was his shocking introduction to the wreckage he found in major cities throughout Germany—in Munich, Hannover, Berlin, Hamburg, Kiel, Cologne, Herne, Stuttgart, and Saarbrücken. "Oh the devastation!" he wrote. "Devastation on every hand. Jagged walls, piles of rubble, empty windows." He wept at the sight. He also reflected on the causes and the consequences of the destruction: "Piles of rubbish to mark the place of proud, haughty buildings. Buildings levelled, pride levelled; innocence suffered; haughtiness silenced and humbled."

From Frankfurt the Kimballs were driven to Berchtesgaden in Bavaria, where they participated in a four-day conference for servicemen and their wives. They were housed in the Evergreen Lodge, a luxurious retreat built at the direction of Adolf Hitler. The meetings included worship services, instruction sessions, road shows, banquets, and, in conclusion, a testimony meeting where "they vied with each other to get the floor." There were 650 at one banquet, including a hundred missionaries from the West German Mission. "There were 650 glasses of milk, perhaps the most milk Europe has seen, or ever served, in one banquet." The next day, Elder Kimball held an all-day training and testimony meeting with the missionaries.

En route to Frankfurt, he had stopped in Munich to hold a meeting with the local Saints and to dedicate the site for a new chapel. From Frankfurt he and Sister Kimball flew to Oslo, Norway, to begin a tour of the first of ten missions in Europe and Great Britain. Traveling by automobile, except in the far north near Narvik where seaplanes were used, the apostle visited most of the branches and districts in the scattered mission. Among other cities visited was Trondheim, the birthplace of Elder John A. Widtsoe. At Bodo he was interested in a sign that showed the mileage to various places on the globe—Cairo, Egypt; South Africa; the Aleutians; etc. And in flying to Narvik, he was fascinated by the deep fjords over which they flew, low enough to see "the beautiful water, and the shallows, and the depths, the shadows and the light, the fishing villages and the acres of racks with cod drying." In Narvik, within the Arctic Circle, they spent a night without darkness and were able to read the newspaper indoors at 1:30 in the morning without electric lights.

He traveled throughout the country of Sweden, mostly by automobile, holding forty-five meetings in less than three weeks, dedicating eight meetinghouses, and interviewing and instructing the missionaries. In Sweden, as elsewhere, the Saints were admonished to put their lives in order and to prepare to go to the temple then nearing completion in Switzerland. The missionaries were urged to spend more time in "pure proselyting" and to discontinue working too much on Church buildings and in the branches. He was astonished at "the language power" of the missionaries. "When I see over and over the many people who have been in America for years and some a lifetime and still struggling with the language, then see these young missionaries handling the language fast and fluently in several months, it amazes me."

There followed tours in Finland, where there were only five hundred members of the Church; Denmark, whose neat, well-groomed countryside reminded Elder Kimball of a "continuous park"; Great Britain; and the Netherlands, his son Ed's old mission field. Here the apostle walked from the mission home over the sand dunes to the North Sea, whose waters were kept from the land by an ingenious diking system. "The farms are beautiful with flowers and flowering crops. Everybody seems to be busy and work hard," he wrote.

Elder Kimball spent more than three weeks in Great Britain, holding meetings throughout England and in Wales, Ireland, and Scotland. Of the numerous meetings held there, none was more important and meaningful to him than the one held in Preston, England, on July 3, where he dedicated a small chapel on Ribbleton Avenue. He also visited places of historic interest to the Church: the chapel of the Reverend James Fielding, the brother of Joseph Fielding, where Heber C. Kimball and his brethren first preached in Preston; the Marketplace, where Camilla's ancestor Miles Romney was first exposed to the teachings of Mormonism; the apartment where the Mormon missionaries were assaulted by evil spirits; and the River Ribble where the first baptisms into the Church in England were performed.

After the tours in Great Britain had been completed, one of the local leaders summarized Elder Kimball's "prophetic vision" of how the Church would grow there: total activity and full-hearted devotion of all; an aggressive program of reactivation; an accelerated emphasis on missionary work, with full-time British missionaries supplying all missionaries for Great Britain and some missionaries for Europe; the British Saints remaining in their homes to build up the Church locally; the British Saints seeking more prominence in business and government affairs; proper teaching of children by parents; proper preparation by officers and teachers in performing Church duties; obedience to the law of tithing and all other commandments of God; and members of the

Church having large families. We see in this key elements of the prophetic vision for the entire Church that President Kimball later shared with the regional representatives.

Before leaving England, Elder Kimball, weary from the strain of his crowded schedule and feeling the need for divine guidance, offered a special prayer: "I asked the Lord to help me in my work that I might impress the missionaries and the people and increase the effectiveness of the work which I feel needs some stimulating. I asked him to take care of my family."

In Paris, Camilla parted with her husband to fly to Cairo, where she joined her sister Caroline and brother Joe, who were members of a BYU touring group. After accompanying the group through Egypt, Palestine, Turkey, and Greece, she rejoined Spencer at Vienna, Austria. In her absence, Elder Kimball completed a two-week tour of France. Her arrival in Vienna was cause for celebration: "How sweet she looked. How glad I was to have her back at my side. She is so strong and splendid. How I love her. How I have missed her."

The following month was spent touring Switzerland and Germany. The contrast between the two countries was striking. The peaceful, picturesque villages of Switzerland, untouched by the war, were like jewels in their Alpine setting. Life here had run its untroubled, customary course. The homes, the office buildings, and the shops were intact. At Zurich, during a rare shopping spree, they purchased Swiss watches for the four children and their spouses. In Germany, however, was the devastation. And at Dachau was the evidence of depravity. The ghastly ovens where the victims died and the mounds marking where their bodies were dumped in common graves sickened the apostle. "It was good to get away from this horrible atmosphere and back into the green of the countryside." He could never equate that degenerate period of history with the upright character of the German people. He always ascribed it to the ghoulish character of the Nazi leaders, chiefly Hitler.

As he worked his way through the mission districts in Germany, holding numerous meetings with members and missionaries, he was struck again with a condition he had found elsewhere: "Too much labor on chapels—too little labor from the people. We must train them to make sacrifices as do some of our people in the wards and stakes." He persistently urged the missionaries to increase the time of "pure proselyting," avoiding the nonessentials and the things the members could easily do. He learned at Kiel how the efficient missionary grapevine had complicated his work. "They had heard from other missionaries that I was coming to greatly increase their efforts and devotion and seemed to resist it." It was difficult to overcome this resistance. And the negative attitudes of the missionaries carried over into the general meetings: "I was much upset, very low and feeling bad. I had difficulty in stirring myself to a satisfactory effort not to disappoint the people who came. I was so weary and nervous and I wondered if I was about to break." After a good night's rest, he was ready to try again.

In Berlin he felt the oppressive influence of communism, reflected in the distracted and solemn attitude of the thirty-four missionaries from the Soviet zone. He interviewed each one separately. Once their wall of reticence had been breached, he found that many of them were basically happy and jovial like the other missionaries. It was reported that one of them was heard to say of Elder Kimball, "He looks like such a simple man." His reaction was typical: "I hardly knew how to take that, Ha."

The mission tours ended at Stuttgart on September 9, 1955. The next day, he and Camilla flew to Bern, Switzerland. The first session dedicating the temple was held the morning of the eleventh. He spent the noon hour alone in the temple that day, "preparing mind and heart for the afternoon, unhurried, quiet, respectful and reverential." He was the first speaker in the afternoon session. The sessions the following day were conducted in German for the benefit of the Swiss-Austrian and West German Saints. Something

said at one of the sessions troubled Elder Kimball. "I wondered at what was said, . . . if they thought I had pushed too
hard, was too exacting, asked too much of them; but many
missionaries expressed appreciation for the lift and vision
given them." The negative reactions did not deter him from
saying what he thought needed to be said. The positive reactions encouraged him to stay the course.

The Kimballs left Switzerland on September 17 and took
a train to Paris, where they spent several days holding meetings with the missionaries and the Saints, attending the
opera, visiting historic sites, and taking a short cruise on the
Seine. They boarded the *Queen Elizabeth* at Cherbourg on the
twenty-second and arrived home six days later.

This lengthy tour gave Elder Kimball precise insights
into the work throughout Europe and Great Britain, as an
earlier tour of Central America in company with Elder
Bruce R. McConkie, then of the Seventy, had expanded his
knowledge of the seven countries in that area. It was during
his tour with Elder McConkie in October and November
1952 that Elder Kimball had dedicated Central America for
the preaching of the gospel. The Central American Mission
was then established, with headquarters in Guatemala.
Gordon M. Romney was the first mission president.

Later, in June 1956, Elder Kimball and Elder Harold B.
Lee traveled to Mexico to divide the Mexican Mission, crea-
ting the Northern Mexican Mission. The formal division
occurred at a historic meeting held in Mexico City, following which Elder Lee toured the Mexican Mission with
President Claudius Bowman and Elder Kimball toured the
Northern Mexican Mission with its new president, Joseph T.
Bentley. Establishing the headquarters of the new mission in
Monterrey, Elder Kimball supervised the acquisition and
furnishing of the new mission home, assisted by President
Bentley and by Bishop Gordon Affleck, who had been sent
from Salt Lake City to help acquire the furnishings. The
apostle then spent two busy weeks traveling throughout the
new mission, visiting the scattered districts and branches,

instructing the missionaries, holding meetings with the Saints, eating in their humble homes, and scouting for possible building sites in the areas where the membership of the Church was more populous. While in Europe he wept at the devastation; here he wept at the poverty of the people. He was touched by their humility and their sweetness and by their desires to improve. He foresaw a bright future for them and for the Church in Mexico.

These experiences, along with visits to Canada and Hawaii, had begun to flesh out in Elder Kimball's mind a clearer conception of the opportunities and challenges of a global church. That conception would be broadened and intensified in the years ahead as his travels took him to other parts of the world. All this would be vital to his understanding of the needs and potentials of the Church and its members everywhere when he became the President of the Church.

Wherever he taught around the world, Elder Kimball always oriented his sermons to the perceived needs of his audience. In Escalante, for instance, a remote community in southern Utah, he urged the members to build another impounding dam. He also encouraged them to use their land more efficiently, to rotate their crops, and to plant crops that would produce a greater yield. He also counseled them to plant fruit trees and shade trees, to paint their houses and barns, to repair their fences, and to tidy up their yards. A congregation in Idaho was admonished to build up the local economy by buying at home. And at a conference in Nevada, Elder Kimball came down hard on laxness and misconduct, exhorting the people to obedience and good works. Audiences at general conferences were treated to powerful sermons denouncing profanity, idleness, immorality, and the love of filthy lucre. Seminary and institute teachers were told to be orthodox in their instructions and to be role models to their students, living lives worthy of emulation. Students were urged to be morally clean, to excel in their studies, to prepare for missions and temple marriage, and to develop their native talents. His zealousness in building up the Church and its members sometimes made it difficult to craft a talk intended for a large, diverse audience. So a *Church of the Air* talk delivered on NBC radio had to be "toned down" at the request of the network.

During this period of extensive travel, while Elder Kimball's knowledge of the Church and the world was growing and his leadership style was being honed, significant changes occurred at Church headquarters and in his personal life. In less than two years, during 1952 and 1953, four members of the Twelve passed on—Elders Joseph F. Merrill, John A. Widtsoe, Albert E. Bowen, and Matthew Cowley. Elder Kimball wished that when the time came he could pass on in the same way Elders Merrill and Cowley had died—quietly in their sleep. He and Camilla occupied a room adjacent to the Cowleys in a Los Angeles, California, hotel the night Matthew died. It was December 13, 1953. The Kimballs and the Cowleys were part of a group of General Authorities and their wives who had traveled to Los Angeles for the cornerstone laying of the Los Angeles Temple. During the night, Sister Cowley knocked on the Kimballs' door to say, "I think Matthew is dead." They rushed in in their nightclothes "and found him lying peacefully in his bed." He was gone. It was incredible. They had seen him alive and well the night before, jovial and friendly as usual. His passing doubly affected Elder Kimball. Not only had they shared the apostleship, but they had shared the same love and empathy for the Lamanites. And Elder Cowley had been an important member of the Indian Committee, which Elder Kimball chaired.

The replacements for these four deceased apostles were Elders LeGrand Richards, Adam S. Bennion, Richard L. Evans, and George Q. Morris. Because Elder Richards had been the Presiding Bishop, Joseph L. Wirthlin, his first counselor, was called to replace him. At the same time, Carl W. Beuhner was called to fill the vacancy in the Presiding Bishopric. And because Elder Evans had been a member of the First Council of Seventy, Elder Marion D. Hanks was called to replace him at the October general conference in 1953. At this same general conference, Elder Hugh B. Brown was called as an Assistant to the Twelve, replacing Stayner Richards, who had passed away.

Elder Kimball was assigned to help train these new General Authorities in their duties. He accompanied them on stake conference assignments as he did on the weekend of October 24 and 25, 1953, when he and Elder Hanks attended a stake conference together in Provo, Utah. Here the new Seventy not only saw how a conference should be conducted, but he was shown an effective teaching technique as Elder Kimball personally demonstrated to stake missionaries how they should do their work. The thirty-two-year-old General Authority was also given an astonishing insight into Elder Kimball's conception of work as he followed him through a seemingly endless series of meetings from the time of their arrival in Provo until they left for home.

Meanwhile, the circumstances at home were stressful. Four days before the Provo conference, Camilla broke her arm while shopping at ZCMI. She was taken to the hospital, where the arm was put in a cast. Her condition was serious enough that the doctor insisted she remain in the hospital overnight. The following day, the day before Elder Kimball left for the Provo conference, he stayed home from the office to nurse his wife and to tidy up around the house. Because Camilla had suffered considerable trauma from the accident, Spencer was anxious to return home from Provo promptly after the conference. He found her in good spirits, though somewhat distressed by the awkward cast on her arm.

In addition, the Kimball family mourned two deaths in early 1954. Andrew's infant daughter, Carol Jean, died in February, and Camilla's mother, Caroline Romney Eyring, passed away in April. The death of Mother Eyring required that arrangements be made for the care of her adult daughter Mary, who was deaf. Later that year, Mary came to Salt

Lake to live with the Kimballs. This became her home until she passed away years afterward. Physical handicaps, illnesses, injuries, and death were accepted stoically in this family, and the difficulties and sadness they brought were managed without complaint.

On the bright side, the Kimballs welcomed a new member into the family in June when Ed was married in the temple to Bee Madsen. It was a source of gratitude to Spencer and Camilla that all of their children had been sealed in the temple to good companions. And each grandchild, in turn, was welcomed to the clan with the same enthusiasm accorded to Barbara Jean, grandchild number one, when the grandparents, dressed as a tottering, old couple, masqueraded before their friends.

In December 1956, Elder Kimball was assigned to preside at the St. Joseph stake conference on the eighth and ninth of the month. He and Camilla decided to drive to Thatcher, taking advantage of the assignment to enjoy a few days in the desert sun. They left on December 5, driving only as far as Marysvale, Utah. There was no hurry. Moreover, early winter storms and low temperatures made driving hazardous, dictating the need for moderate speed.

As he drove, Elder Kimball was distracted by an incident which had occurred at a council meeting three days earlier. The report of an Assistant to the Twelve had been read, outlining his tour of the Southwest Indian Mission. It "infuriated" Elder Kimball "because it was so extremely negative." Conceding that the report honestly reflected the assistant's findings, Spencer nevertheless flatly rejected it: "On such a brief tour, he could not know the circumstances." Elder Kimball had been so careful always to portray the Indians in a positive, sympathetic light. He feared this negative report could undermine some of his efforts. Absorbed in his thoughts, he slowly became aware that the road was icy and snow-packed in spots as they drove upward into the Kaibab Forest in northern Arizona. Upon reaching the summit near Jacob Lake, he shifted into low gear and began the treacherous descent. Several miles below the summit, he came upon a stalled truck whose driver was shoveling gravel beneath the wheels for traction. Spencer slowed the car to a crawl. As he approached, however, his car slid out of control, gently colliding with the truck. The impact veered the car toward the shoulder of the highway. Still out of control, it went over the embankment, careening and bumping downhill over boulders and underbrush until it jolted to a stop against a tree fifty feet below the highway. With the wheel in his hands, Elder Kimball maintained an upright position in the car seat throughout the ordeal. Camilla, however, was thrown against the door handles and then onto the floor, suffering painful bruises and, as it appeared later, several fractured ribs. Thinking Camilla's cries were from fear, Spencer said, "Well, Mama, I guess we are all right." "No," she answered, "I am dying." Because of Camilla's intense pain, Spencer made no effort to move her from the floor at that time. Soon the truck driver and several other motorists scrambled down the embankment to help. Through strenuous effort, they were able to dislodge the car and push it onto an old road nearby. Later, with the aid of a road grader, it was pulled up to the highway. Meanwhile, with help from one of the men, Spencer carefully lifted Camilla onto the seat of the car, where she was more comfortable but was still in pain, unable to breathe without great discomfort.

Elder Kimball asked one of the motorists to summon an ambulance and a doctor from Kanab when he reached a telephone. No one came. While they waited, he and a member of the Church who had come upon the scene gave Camilla a blessing. He also gave her aspirin tablets from his bag and a handful of snow to quench her thirst. Eventually a highway patrolman arrived to make a record of the accident, but he offered no help. They decided self-help was their only remedy. Partially prying a bent fender off the tire and ignoring a defect in the brakes, Elder Kimball drove the car cautiously into the service station at Jacob Lake. No one there could or would help either. So they crawled the thirty miles back to Kanab, where Camilla was admitted to the hospital and the local stake president joined Elder Kimball in administering to her. At Camilla's insistence, Spencer boarded a bus for Thatcher at 2:15 A.M. to fulfill his conference assignment. He returned on the eleventh by bus to find Camilla in better spirits, but aching from cracked ribs, fluid in her lungs, and abrasions on her back. The next day their son-in-law Grant Mack arrived from Salt Lake City with his station wagon, which was fitted with a soft bed. It took nine hours to drive Camilla back to Salt Lake City. Although the road was surfaced all the way, she felt every crack and crevice.

Chapter 16

The Worst-Case Scenario

Except for occasional hoarseness when he had a cold, Elder Kimball's voice had been remarkably strong for several years, ever since the special administration he received in 1950. However, following general conference in 1956, it began to trouble him again. He was concerned. He seemed to know instinctively that something drastic was wrong. This caused him to restrict the use of his voice. "I know I must, so I am beginning to write more of my letters and journal etc. so that I can save my voice from the dictation. I shall try to reduce my conversation with people and to limit my speaking in the pulpit." Two days later, he received a health blessing from Elder Delbert L. Stapley, after which he reported, "I have felt much better since." Indeed, he felt so much better that two weeks after receiving the blessing, while at a stake conference in Grantsville, Utah, he spoke for almost nine hours, either from the pulpit or while counseling. He paid the price. On January 11, 1957, he awakened to find dry blood in his throat. He immediately consulted both Doctor

Kimball and Doctor Cowan. Their diagnosis was troubling: "It is possible there might be low-grade cancer." A month later, after numerous examinations, Dr. Cowan recommended another biopsy to test for cancer. This time he referred Elder Kimball to Dr. Hayes Martin, a specialist in New York City reputed to be one of the best in the world. After consulting with Camilla and others in the family, Spencer decided to have the biopsy done. He did not consult with the First Presidency or the other Brethren. He was afraid he would be restricted in his activity again, something he wanted to avoid at all costs. Because he had stake conference assignments in Washington, D.C., and New York the end of February and the first of March, Elder Kimball believed that he could have the biopsy performed afterward and, as had happened with the first biopsy, that he would be able to continue his work with little or no interruption. At the time, therefore, he saw no need to consult the Brethren about his plans. It was a decision he would regret.

Meanwhile, he continued with his work as if he were in good health. He conducted conferences in the Holladay, East Jordan, and Logan, Utah, stakes. He also toured part of the California Mission and held some meetings in Phoenix, Arizona. While so close, he traveled to Safford, where he checked on his remaining properties and other interests. Back in Salt Lake City, he conferred with LeVan "regarding the estate and matters pertaining to family problems, looking toward my absence and the possible difficulties facing us." He also visited the trust department of the bank to check on deeds, insurance policies, and other documents.

In the midst of these preparations, Elder Harold B. Lee came to visit. "Brother Lee asked me if I had some other motive in going to New York; and I told him of my troubles and problems; and I am sure he already knew about it." Even though Elder Kimball suspected others also knew about his plans for the biopsy in New York, perhaps even the members of the First Presidency, he still did not go to them because of the inordinate fear he would be restricted in his assignments.

Elder and Sister Kimball boarded the train for New York City on February 21. During the following two days, he engaged in lengthy conversations with Camilla and in deep reflections about what lay ahead. At first he was uncertain and uncomposed. He "saw all the horrors and deprivations." Then, as he considered his abundant lifestyle, his family, and the many privileges and opportunities he had enjoyed, "a calm tranquility" began to settle on him. This feeling was induced in large part by his recollection of a vivid dream he had had of his father a year before. Seeing Andrew vibrant and smiling in the dream, Spencer was overjoyed, reaching out to touch him and calling loudly and happily, "Father, Father, I am so glad to see you." When he awakened from the dream, the son "was smiling and happy." Now his recollection of the dream filled him again with joy and with an assurance that all was well, regardless of the outcome of the impending surgery.

They were met at the depot in New York by their son Andrew, who then lived in the New York suburbs. Elder Kimball had a satisfying experience during the stake conference held over the weekend. "It was pleasing to set apart my own beloved son Andrew as the second counselor in the Westchester Ward bishopric. This brought a great deal of joy to have our own son in the bishopric."

The Kimballs spent the next few days with Andrew and his family before going to Washington, D.C., for the other stake conference. Elder Kimball, understandably nervous about the surgery, had difficulty sleeping. A persistent cough aggravated the condition. For diversion they visited the United Nations, where they heard a spirited debate about the withdrawal of Israel from the Gaza Strip; played mah-jongg, a favorite family game; visited and blessed a Woolley cousin who was in a nearby sanitarium; and had dinner at the home of stake president George Mortimer. One evening, while the other adults went to the theater in the city, Spencer stayed with the grandchildren.

At the Washington, D.C., stake conference, Elder Kimball invited Elder Ezra Taft Benson, who was at the time serving as the U.S. secretary of agriculture, to join him on the stand at the general sessions and to share the pulpit. Following the last session, Spencer and Camilla went to the Benson home for refreshments. They were driven there in a chauffeured black Cadillac limousine. Unaccustomed to the wealthy ways of Washington, Elder Kimball found this "a little rich for our blood." During a leisurely visit, Elder Kimball briefed his colleague about the goings-on at Church headquarters but remained silent about his rendezvous with Doctor Martin.

That rendezvous occurred two days later in Doctor Martin's Manhattan office, where Elder Kimball was shocked to be told he would have to maintain "absolute silence" for thirty days after the surgery. This news upset his plans for a quick return to service and elevated his level of apprehension. He regretted that he hadn't discussed his upcoming surgery with the prophet, and he feared that his prolonged forced silence after surgery might indefinitely prolong the period of his inactivity. The doctor tried to lower the patient's concerns by saying he assumed there was no malignancy until it was proven otherwise. Yet the doctor's demeanor and tone seemed to imply he thought it was malignant, rendering his assumption meaningless to Spencer. Moreover, the doctor's detached, impersonal, and clinical approach, so unlike the warm and concerned attitude of Elder Kimball's Salt Lake doctors, caused Spencer to feel more like a statistic or a medical problem than a human being whose apostolic career seemed to hang in the balance. This perception was reinforced by his later contacts with medical associates of Doctor Martin and with support personnel at the Memorial Hospital, which he entered the next day.

That evening Elder Kimball again engaged in deep reflection about the impending surgery and its implications, confiding these thoughts to his diary: "The possibility of cancer, the possibility of removal of the vocal cords, the possibility of death, have not seemed to terrify me as they could have done earlier and did, in reality, when I had the first scare several years ago. Then I was agitated and frantic. This time I am as calm as a summer morning. I have no fear of death. I feel sure I can meet any situation without a voice if that comes. I pray constantly to my Heavenly Father, but I have made no demands upon Him. I pray only 'Thy will be done.' If my work justifies my continuation of it, I pray my life and my voice be extended and strengthened. If my work is done and others can fill in now to better advantage, then I am resigned to whatever He wills; 'Thy will be done.' This is my request in every prayer. I have not been able to press too hard and insist on healing. That I want very much if the Lord wants to continue my work. I am calm and unruffled."

The next day was gray and dismal. Elder Kimball and Camilla went alone by cab to the Memorial Hospital, arriving at 2:00 P.M., according to Doctor Martin's instructions. Reporting to the information desk, they were airily told to go to the admissions office. There they were "shooed out like flies" and told to return to the information desk. Here the attendant, now preoccupied in visiting with a friend, bluntly told them to sit down and wait until their names were called. Camilla, who acted as spokesman since Spencer was already under the doctor's decree of silence, asked how that would be possible as no one had even asked their names. It took an hour to breach the hospital's wall of inertia and red tape. Finally the patient was taken to room 1037, overlooking the East River. After visiting a while, Camilla had to leave in order to meet Andrew in time to catch the train.

With Camilla gone, Elder Kimball had great difficulty communicating with the stream of nurses, interns, and doctors who now came to help prepare him for the surgery the next day. They gave him a writing pad and pencil for this purpose. He soon found, however, that these instruments were useless as he could get no answers. To one doctor he scribbled the question: "How does it look?" The curt answer was "Let's not ask too many questions." Another who was asked how long he would be under anesthesia answered, "Just long enough."

Camilla and Andrew came the following day in time to have another family prayer before the surgery. By then Elder Kimball was so under the influence of the shots that had been administered that he was only vaguely aware of what went on about him. He later had a dim recollection of being wheeled to the brightly lighted operating room, with its array of gleaming equipment and instruments, and of the robed and masked doctors and nurses who surrounded him. Then came sixteen hours of darkness during which the doctors removed a specimen from his throat for the lab test and the patient lay unconscious in recovery.

His first recollection afterward was of a nurse attempting to roll him over in order to change the sheets on the bed. Still groggy and uncertain what was going on or what was expected of him, Elder Kimball was surprised at her angry tone and the rough way she treated him. "Don't be so cross," he pleaded. "I don't know just what you want." He was more than surprised and not a little hurt when she retorted in anger, "You're talking to the wrong nurse. Just because you lord it over everybody in your own home, you are not going to lord it over me."

His brief comments, spoken unthinkingly in violation of the doctor's orders, were difficult to utter because his tongue was so bruised, cut, and swollen it almost filled his mouth. To his question as to what happened to his tongue, the doctor responded sharply, "We did what we had to do."

During the next two days as he lay in the hospital, unable to speak, hurting from the surgery as the drugs wore off, and in a strange and what to him was a hostile environment, the calm and poised attitude with which he had faced the surgery was now put to the test. "I begin now to realize what I have tried to anticipate and visualize. My voice is gone. I can say no word above a little, light whisper. My tongue will likely get well. The soreness in my throat will likely be gone soon and my voice—. To face a future without a voice is terrifying. I thought I was prepared for it, but when reality strikes, it comes with a bang. . . . I am treading deep water. I see a dark cloud and the silver lining is not yet perceptible. It will probably clear up. I must meet the issue, and I will."

Two days later, he was released from the hospital and taken to Andrew's home. Here he read, ruminated, wrote in his diary, and watched television. Conversation was almost an impossibility. His inability to speak seemed to inhibit the adults and baffle the children. Any questions he scribbled usually were answered with a yes or no, or if one word would not suffice, with the briefest kind of response, as if his inability to speak had also impeded his ability to understand. He was cheered by thoughtful letters from Elder Lee and Elder Stapley, telling of the concern of the Brethren and of their prayers and pleadings for him in the temple meetings.

On Sunday, Elder Kimball accompanied Andrew to priesthood meeting. His presence was acknowledged, but he could say nothing. Some things said in the class needed refutation, he felt, but he was "powerless" to do anything about it.

Three days later he received the lab report. It was inconclusive. While technically it concluded the specimen was benign, it was "borderline." Doctor Martin suggested he return home where Doctor Cowan could monitor his condition, and then come back later for a "look-see."

En route home Spencer and Camilla stopped to visit LeVan and his family. The reaction of the grandchildren was troubling. On finding their grandfather could not speak, they froze up, looking at him "curiously." In Salt Lake City, the Mack children reacted the same way. It created a strained alienation and caused Spencer to wonder whether he ought to forget about doctors and "just let nature take its course." The prospects seemed "dismal," especially after Doctor Cowan emphasized strongly that he should not even try to whisper. "It is oppressive. People make a friendly gesture to speak and as soon as they find I cannot speak, they lapse into silence. I write a message and people reach for a pencil and pad. I move my lips and they follow suit."

These annoyances were only a minor part of the pressures imposed by Elder Kimball's month of silence. The greatest anxiety came from his inability to function in his apostolic calling. He attended a council meeting in the temple a few days after returning from the East. There Elder Harold B. Lee read four reports Spencer had typed out covering his last assignments, including the stake conferences in New York and Washington, D.C. Beyond that, he had no part to play whatever, except to listen to the discussions and to indicate his approval or disapproval by hand vote of matters before the council. At the April general conference, President McKay acknowledged his presence but announced he would not speak because of illness. "Many wondered why I was present and yet ill." Anyone who asked later about his condition was answered with a shrug or a brief explanation scribbled on a pad he carried around. This usually created a conspiratorial atmosphere as the questioner, not knowing what to say in response, lapsed into silence or asked to use the pencil and pad to scribble a comment. The conditions were better in his office, where he could type his comments. While this expedited the interchanges, it did not eliminate the awkwardness his silence inevitably created.

Unable to function in any meaningful way, Elder Kimball decided the best thing to do was to get out of town. He and Camilla traveled to Missoula, Montana, where they spent several days visiting with Ed and his family. The son, who was on the faculty at the university's law school, was able to provide good counsel about his father's estate. Later, learning that Camilla's father was ill in Arizona, they decided to drive there to visit with him. However, he passed away before they arrived in Mesa, where he was living at the time of his death. Following funeral services in the Mesa Fifth Ward, they traveled to Pima for memorial services.

When they returned to Salt Lake City on April 18, it had been six weeks since the surgery. Anxious to have the restriction of silence lifted, Elder Kimball went immediately to Doctor Cowan, who found one vocal cord had healed completely although the other one had not. The improvement caused the doctor to loosen the reins. "He released me slightly, saying I could now whisper a little." This enabled him to perform two marriages in the temple. "I waited until all was totally quiet and whispered lightly the ceremony. Camilla said it could be heard satisfactorily." This success prompted him to go to Joseph Fielding Smith, the president of the Quorum of the Twelve, to request he be permitted to attend stake conferences again. President Smith put him off, saying he wanted to confer with the doctor first. As Spencer left, President Smith embraced him, a gesture which made him "so happy."

Meanwhile, Elder Kimball began to use his voice a little during his daily work. At a meeting with the Indian Placement committee on May 14, he used his "soft whispering voice." And five days later he announced exultantly: "After pressing President Smith considerably for weeks, and the doctor also, I finally got my first assignment in about three months. I am to do some investigating in the Los Angeles and Redondo stakes as to some divisions, etc. I am so happy to be coming back to activity, even though I shall not be able to preach for some time." Not long afterward, he received a regular stake conference assignment to direct the organization of the Missoula, Montana, stake in company with one of the junior brethren. President Smith jokingly said the assignment was being made on condition that Elder Kimball keep his mouth shut. He "listened and prompted" but did not speak at the conference, although he did set apart the president of the stake and several others, using his "still, small voice."

The following weekend, which was the last round of stake conference assignments before the summer break, Elder Kimball was assigned to the Hyrum, Utah, stake. On returning home, he was "shocked" to hear President McKay ask about the effect of his whispering on others. The prophet also expressed concern that Elder Kimball's "enthusiasm and devotion could cause him to go beyond the point of wisdom." Elder Kimball was at a loss to know how to interpret these comments. That they might have been intended as a personal criticism was a devastating thought. This possibility made more onerous a distinct weakening of his voice. And when Doctor Cowan found that one of his vocal cords still had not healed, causing him to recommend further surgery, Elder Kimball was understandably distraught.

Realizing that his failure to seek the counsel of President McKay before Doctor Martin performed the biopsy was a serious error, Elder Kimball now sought to make amends. He wrote a lengthy letter to President McKay, outlining in detail what had happened. He expressed regret that he had not conferred with the prophet about it. He acknowledged that all his energies and indeed his very life were dedicated to the Lord and were therefore subject to the prophet's direction. He also explained that the doctors had now recommended that he undergo surgery to remove the vocal cord that had not healed and, perhaps, to do some "trimming" on the other one, and he sought President McKay's counsel as to what he should do. "He said he had wondered why I had gone ahead with a serious operation without consulting the brethren, but my letter cleared it up." He also told Elder Kimball he wanted time to consider prayerfully how to advise him and suggested he return the next day. When they met again, President McKay told Elder Kimball to follow the recommendations of his doctors. He consoled him, saying that even should he lose his voice entirely, he could still serve effectively in other ways, such as by writing. The prophet cited the example of Helen Keller, who, though blind, deaf, and mute, had rendered significant service through her example of persistence in the face of over-whelming obstacles. The surgery had been scheduled for the last of July, and President McKay said Elder Harold B. Lee would be in New York at that time and that Elder Kimball should take him to the consultations with Doctor Martin.

Elder Kimball and Camilla left Salt Lake City on July 23, "destination known, but destiny unknown." En route they spent a day in Ann Arbor to visit LeVan and his family, who had moved there after LeVan had been recruited to fill a prestigious position on the faculty of the University of Michigan law school. Elder and Sister Lee met them in New York. At the interview with Doctor Martin, Elder Lee led in the conversation due to the condition of Elder Kimball's throat. He explained how reliant the patient was on his voice and how dependent his responsibilities were on the ability to speak. Also he emphasized that Elder Kimball was "no ordinary man" and admonished the doctor to wield his skill in a way to prevent voicelessness. Elder Kimball was pleased that the doctor seemed to understand his apostolic role for the first time and the critical importance of his voice in fulfilling it. "This was a time when I was everlastingly grateful for the presence and strength of Brother Lee."

The surgery was set for Monday, July 29, three days hence. Friday night, Elder Kimball and Camilla had dinner with friends. Since the doctor had not restricted him in speaking as he had done following the biopsy, Spencer abandoned whispering and spoke normally. "How good it seemed! I had saved my voice as a miser saves his coins; but knowing that the voice would be gone, and with no opposition from the doctor, I used it." On Saturday, Andrew came to the city to join his parents in a "celebration." They circled the island of Manhattan in a boat, had dinner together, and "saw some good shows." But all the while, Elder Kimball was "fighting a mighty battle inside." Surgery to remove one vocal cord and trim the other one was far different from a biopsy, so his initial attitude was much different this time. "The idea was stifling, terror ridden," and created an uncharacteristic rebellion in him. Camilla and Andrew detected his attitude and sought to coax him out of it. "They took me to task, arguing with me, pleading with me and finally I capitulated. I gave up and quit fighting. My mind had been made up; now my spirit yielded and I was ready."

Elder Lee and Roy Fugal came to the hospital Monday morning to give the patient a special blessing. Later, before the drugs took effect, Elder Kimball said to Doctor Hayes Martin, "There are thousands of people praying for you this morning that you will be blessed in your decisions." Following the lengthy and delicate operation, Elder Kimball was in recovery for five hours. On regaining consciousness he found the tube in his throat made him "wheeze like an old worn-out horse." He later wrote, "I still had a little fringe of a voice way down in the lower register, and I had great hope that I could take of that little and make something of it; but the next day it was gone totally."

There followed six hectic days in the hospital with almost no sleep, much pain in the neck and chest, and a constant dull headache. These days were hardly distinguishable, merging together into a vague mass like a troubled dream. "It was the never-ending nights that tried my soul. . . . I have been through some deep water." In an effort to minimize the pain and discomfort, he spent many hours ransacking his memory, reliving events of long ago, reaching back to his childhood. This made the ordeal bearable.

At the end of six days, he left the hospital and moved to the Eastern States Mission home across the street from Central Park, where he continued his convalescence. Gradually he began to use the voice that was left, being careful not to overdo. "I am using my gruff voice a little every day," he wrote to Doctor Cowan on August 17. "I don't let it get weary. I am not whispering much any more. I think I am being very careful but I am using the voice and feel it enlarging and increasing in quality." The letter also mentioned voice culture lessons he was taking to help control breathing and improve voice projection. Later he tried

211

mechanical devices to help amplify his voice, but they proved to be ineffective.

During this difficult period, he was built up and comforted by the constant attentions of Camilla. Also he was heartened by the numerous letters and get-well cards he received. One in particular, a letter dated August 21, 1957, from the Twelve, had special meaning. It read in part: "We were touched by Elder Harold's affectionate account of your heroic encounter with catastrophe. We reached out toward you in fasting and faith and love. In a unity which was moving we implored our Heavenly Father to touch you by the power of his holy spirit that you may go forward with us with all the devotion, effectiveness, and spiritual power which have endeared you to all of us. Just know we are pulling for you with all the energy of our souls."

Elder Kimball returned to Salt Lake City the first week in September. On the fifth he attended the council meeting in the temple, where he spoke briefly, expressing gratitude for the prayers and faith of the Brethren in his behalf. He was moved by comments made by President David O. McKay: "There is no doubt in our minds that He has blessed you beyond even the doctors' fondest expectations. The Lord be praised. It is glorious to hear your voice, just glorious. Here in this upper room we express not only vocally, as we did this morning, but in our hearts, thanksgiving for the blessings of the Lord."

During the next three months, Elder Kimball used his voice sparingly as the healing process continued. He spent much time with the family, especially the grandchildren, whom he tended for their parents, playing games, cutting their hair, and acting as their chauffeur. He conducted interviews in his office, providing counsel for priesthood leaders and for individuals with serious personal problems. He had been urged to refer those with personal problems to their local leaders. However, he found it impossible to refuse anyone who came for counsel. And as word got out that he was willing to help, people flocked to him like children clamoring for candy. It was his experience counseling thousands in trouble that formed the core of his widely quoted book *The Miracle of Forgiveness*. That he had helped so many in trouble confirmed a personal sense that his ministry had meaning. This feeling compounded his hurt when a woman accused him of breaking up her marriage because of counsel he had given. "It was very distressing because of my throat condition; and now to feel that I was not helping people was very difficult to take." That she later acknowledged her feelings were really directed toward the doctrines and policies of the Church, not Elder Kimball personally, did not appreciably alter the sense of failure her accusation had aroused.

Elder Kimball had no formal assignments during this period, although he personally arranged a meeting with the presidencies of four stakes in the Uintah Basin of eastern Utah, where the Indian work had been declining. "We hope they are now tuned up to go to work," he wrote afterward.

As his voice grew stronger, he became more anxious to receive conference assignments. On December 5 he wrote a pleading letter to the First Presidency: "I am not asking you to give me assignments to satisfy me but I am confident that even in my condition I can still render a small service." That was followed five days later by a letter from Doctor Cowan to the Brethren advising that Elder Kimball could now use his voice and return to his normal activities, provided that he did not "go beyond reason." Soon after, he delivered his first sermon since the surgery. He spoke for twenty-five minutes at a stake conference in Safford, where his fellow Arizonan, Delbert L. Stapley, was the assigned visitor. "I could have spoken longer," he wrote, being buoyed up by the loving support of his old friends. He told them of his experiences in New York, where he fell among thieves who cut his throat and stole his voice. The experience boosted his self-confidence, assuring him that with amplifying equipment he could be heard and understood by a large audience.

His pleading letter to the First Presidency, the confirmation of Doctor Cowan that his voice was sufficiently healed, and the experience in Safford caused the Brethren to grant Elder Kimball's request for conference assignments. On January 12, 1958, he attended and spoke successfully at the conference of the Riverside Stake in Salt Lake City. He then received assignments for the two succeeding weekends to accompany Elder Harold B. Lee to divide the Houston Texas Stake, creating the San Antonio Texas Stake, and to organize a new stake at Shreveport, Louisiana. In Houston the two apostles completed lengthy interviews to select the leaders of the two stakes and retired late, occupying the same hotel room. Elder Kimball handled his part of the interviewing all right, although it was difficult. Although he had not divulged the fact to Elder Lee, he had boils in his nostrils which were painful and which caused some bleeding. After they retired, Elder Kimball couldn't sleep, tossing and turning as he attempted to find a comfortable position. This kept Elder Lee awake also. "He kept asking if there was anything he could do for me and I tried to cover up. I was sure it was serious and that I might be sent to the hospital with all the publicity that would bring and the consequent loss of service and long-delayed assignments again. He came and kneeled by my bed and gave me a wonderful blessing, and in moments, I was relieved."

Having gotten over this hurdle successfully, Elder Kimball faced a more difficult one the next day. After presenting the officers for sustaining vote, Elder Lee called on him to speak. Elder Kimball was equipped with a special microphone to amplify his voice so he could be heard by the large audience. Apparently because of anxiety, his voice was so weak when he started that he could not be heard, or at least, he could not be understood, even with the special equipment. Embarrassed, he paused to compose himself, then started again, slowly, quietly. As he got into the talk, he began to speak more positively and with self-confidence. Seemingly he was aided by the rapt attention the audience gave to him. His listeners leaned forward, concentrating on his sermon so as not to miss a word. This was one of the few side benefits of his throat surgeries. Another was the quality of the voice that emerged from them. It was not a rasping, unpleasant voice as some had feared it would be. Rather, it was a mellow, engaging voice whose tone and timbre conveyed a sense of deep sincerity, spirituality, and urgency. It was a distinctive voice that became recognizable around the world. And it was a voice that inevitably reminded those who heard it of the trials, traumas, and testings to which its owner had been subjected.

Had his own feelings been consulted, Elder Kimball would not have spoken at the afternoon session of the Houston conference, because he felt he had failed earlier. But Elder Lee insisted that he do so because he felt it was important for Elder Kimball to build self-confidence and for the Saints to hear his testimony. His summary of the two general sessions was typical: "The Sunday meetings were excellent and the speaking excellent, except for my poor efforts."

En route to Shreveport during the week, the brethren stopped in Huntsville, Texas, where a special meeting was held to dedicate a new chapel. Elder Kimball tried to "beg off" from speaking, but Elder Lee would have none of it. He insisted, and Elder Kimball complied. "I was glad he insisted, for I realize I cannot quit." By the time of the conference at Shreveport over the weekend of January 26 and 27, the pattern had been set. Elder Kimball did his share of the interviewing to select the leaders of the new stake and spoke at both of the general sessions, while Elder Lee conducted and handled the business of the conference. There was no resistance on the part of Elder Kimball as there had been in Houston and Huntsville. He had done well, had carried his end of the load effectively, and had demonstrated to himself and to his companion that he was prepared to continue his ministry with his new voice. But one hurdle still remained, unknown to both of them.

After the meetings at Shreveport, it was intended originally that Elder Kimball would return home while Elder Lee traveled to New York to attend corporate board meetings. After discussion, however, it was decided Elder Kimball would go to New York also, and that once there he would get therapy training from specialists to help in his public speaking. They left Shreveport by train and, finding they had a long layover at Texarkana, decided to hold an impromptu meeting. They contacted the branch president and a hurried meeting was arranged, using a Methodist chapel that had no sound system. Almost two hundred members and friends crowded into the long and narrow chapel to hear the two apostles. This was the acid test for Elder Kimball, who until now had always had an amplifying system. Though he approached the task with some trepidation, he spoke for a half hour and was easily heard by the attentive congregation.

Arriving in New York the morning of January 29, the two apostles checked into the Waldorf Astoria and then went together to the National Hospital, where arrangements were made for Elder Kimball to receive therapy training about diet, exercise, and voice use to help in his public speaking. That evening they had dinner with the religious editor of the United Press. In addition to the therapy training he took during the following several days, Elder Kimball visited the offices of Dr. Hayes Martin, where, in the absence of Doctor Martin, who was out of the city, two associate doctors examined his throat and found it to be healed completely.

On the way home, Elder Kimball stopped in Ann Arbor, where he witnessed the baptism of his grandson David, performed by the father, LeVan, following which Elder Kimball confirmed him. He arrived home February 4, 1958, now fully prepared to take up his apostolic labors again.

Chapter 17

Making Up
for Lost Time

For the next twelve years, Elder Kimball had no serious problems with his throat. Through trial and error, he learned how to accommodate his disability to changing conditions. Usually good amplifying equipment was available, which simplified his task. If not, he would alter his normal mode of speaking to increase the volume, being careful not to strain his voice. He soon learned when he had reached the limit of his vocal capacity and would not attempt to exceed it except in rare cases of emergency. If the conditions were too extreme, he simply would not speak. He did not wish to put at risk this priceless tool of communication, which he valued now more than ever.

With his voice problems solved and his heart free from pain, he was in a position to render service in a way he had not known for a long time. "It was a glorious day to feel back in service at normal [capacity], or nearly so, and to be so regarded and accepted. When President Smith gave to me and Brother Richards the reorganization of the Lost

River Stake as an additional assignment, it made me very happy."

With the restrictions lifted, Elder Kimball went to work with a vengeance. In the seven weeks before the April general conference, he conducted stake conferences in the Ogden, Parowan, Lost River, Butte, Oakland, and Houston stakes, in addition to touring the West Spanish-American Mission with President Leland M. Perry. He was amused by the reaction of some people who were not aware of the reason for his husky voice. "You sure have a bad cold," one said, admonishing him to nurse it, perhaps with a favorite home remedy. Later a chiropractor "came to offer his services, saying he had seen laryngitis healed by treatment." On the part of those who knew the reasons for his changed voice, he detected a greater deference toward him and a more intense interest in what he said.

At Church headquarters, Elder Kimball's workload was increased by his appointment to the board of directors of the Beneficial Life Insurance Company. At the same time, Howard W. Hunter, a prominent stake president in southern California, also was appointed as a new board member. The following year, Elder Hunter would be called to the Twelve.

The April general conference was distinguished by the call of Elder Hugh B. Brown to the Twelve, replacing Elder Adam S. Bennion, who had died. At the same time, Elders Gordon B. Hinckley and Henry D. Taylor were called as Assistants to the Twelve and Elder A. Theodore Tuttle was called as a member of the First Quorum of the Seventy, replacing Elder Oscar Kirkham, who had died.

For two successive weekends following general conference, Elder Kimball took Elder Tuttle with him on stake conference assignments. "I brought him to break him in, and he did well in everything. He received the mantle all right. He was eloquent and impressive." At the last of these two conferences, which was a stake division, Elder Kimball gathered all the new officers together to give them his customary

*Elder Kimball on
the front porch of
the Kimballs' home
on Laird Drive
in Salt Lake City.*

instructions. They were admonished to pay a full tithing, to keep the Word of Wisdom, to sustain the General Authorities, to be modest in their dress and speech, to avoid playing cards and gambling, to not entertain sympathy for cult groups, to attend all scheduled church meetings, to hold family prayer, and to maintain strict chastity. Leaders and members throughout the Church were treated to these and sometimes other more extensive instructions, all designed to help them toward the elusive goal of perfection. He was amused by the comments of a young boy who came to shake hands after a stake conference session, who said, "Brother Kimball, you gave us good words. I will always remember them."

219

The remainder of 1958 was taken up with a continual round of stake conferences, with their attendant travel; special speaking assignments, as when he addressed the students at Utah State University in Logan, Utah; and his headquarters assignments, which included counseling a constant stream of people, young and old, who came seeking guidance regarding their personal problems. Seeing how his cousin seemed to be overdoing it again, President Clark sent a cautionary letter to Elder Kimball.

"There is a great doctrine of relativity in the Church," wrote he. "There are things that are important, of prime importance; there are things that are secondary and some even tertiary. I think the Lord has preserved and healed you for the primary things; and how much I wish that you would try to distinguish them and the secondary and tertiary and keep your strength for the first." It is apparent that Elder Kimball was never able to make this distinction with any success and that all things pertaining to his ministry seemed to him to be of primary importance. The result was that he continued to plow ahead, working hard every day until everything was finished, without reference to President Clark's careful distinctions.

In December 1958, Elder Kimball was pleased to receive the assignment to make an extensive tour of missions in South America. Only four other General Authorities had traveled there. Presidents David O. McKay and Stephen L Richards of the First Presidency and Elders Mark E. Petersen and Henry D. Moyle of the Twelve each had spent a short time there, but none of them had made the kind of lengthy, in-depth tour and study Elder Kimball would now undertake.

It would occupy ten weeks, taking him into Brazil, Uruguay, Paraguay, Argentina, Chile, Peru, and Bolivia, and would entail thirty-five thousand miles of travel during which he would hold over a hundred meetings with missionaries and members, dedicate five new chapels, and meet with high government officials. In retrospect, this tour represented the first significant step taken by a General Authority to establish the Church firmly in South America. And the recommendations he made afterward provided a blueprint for the future development of the Church in those countries.

Elder Kimball and Camilla began their great adventure on January 16, 1959, when they boarded the SS *Argentina* in New York City, bound for Rio de Janeiro, Brazil. It was a rough passage marked by turbulence so violent that at times passengers had to cling to stationary objects to prevent being thrown to the deck. When the weather allowed it, Spencer and Camilla brushed up on their Spanish (the language of every country they would visit except Brazil), studied the scriptures, pored over reports and maps, walked the decks for exercise, and enjoyed the shipboard activities, especially the visit of King Neptune when their ship crossed the equator. Each passenger was given a certificate signed by Neptune, attesting to induction into his kingdom.

At Rio they were met by W. Grant Bangerter, president of the Brazilian Mission, and an enthusiastic group of missionaries and members, all vying to give the visitors a welcoming *brazo*. This was the Kimballs' introduction to the warm and affectionate nature of the South American people. It was an outpouring that would be repeated over and over during the coming weeks.

President Bangerter, a future General Authority, was an early missionary in Brazil who had served as a young man when Brazilian missionaries spoke German and worked chiefly among German-speaking people in southern Brazil. Later Elder Bangerter led the first Portuguese-speaking missionaries into Portugal, fulfilling Elder Kimball's vision that Brazilian or other South American missionaries, the descendants of immigrants, could be the bridge for carrying the gospel into European countries.

After holding meetings in Rió, Niteroi, São Paulo, and Santos, Brazil, the Kimballs flew to Montevideo, Uruguay. The mission president here was Arthur Jensen, who not only supervised the work in Uruguay but also in Paraguay, Bolivia, and Peru. After a brief meeting with President Jensen's missionaries working near Montevideo, the travelers flew to Buenos Aires, where a large group of Saints met them, headed by Loren Pace, president of the Argentine Mission. President Pace also supervised the work in Chile.

Having met the three mission presidents within two weeks after his arrival in South America, visiting with them and their families, inspecting their mission homes and offices, and holding a few meetings, Elder Kimball was prepared for the intensive work of the tour. For almost two months he traveled within these seven South American countries, by plane and by automobile, directing, interviewing, and motivating the missionaries; inspiring the members in general meetings; counseling and instructing the local leaders of branches and districts; and attending talent shows, dances, and other social events held along the way. He dedicated chapels at Rosario, Argentina; Isla Patrulla, Uruguay; Ipomeia and Juiz de Fora, Brazil; and Toquepala, Peru. He was especially interested in the native Indians on the Altiplano in Bolivia and Peru and considered them to be descendants of Lehi's colony.

The hectic nature of the tour is suggested by his diary entry of February 28, made while traveling in Uruguay: "We had a quick sandwich and the ubiquitous CRUSH (a bottled orange drink). Isla Patrulla is in the deep gaucho country. Our beautiful little chapel was as clean and neat as it could be and ready for dedication. After a terrific day in which we moved about like a cyclone and held meetings in different parts of the city and a TV and radio interview and to bed very late—1:30 or 2:00 A.M.—we had to get up and be ready for a 6:00 A.M. departure for the north and east."

At Buenos Aires, Argentina, Elder Kimball was reflective when he visited the park where, in December 1925, Elder Melvin J. Ballard had dedicated the land of South America for the preaching of the gospel. The apostle had said at that time that the work would grow slowly at first, like the acorn of an oak tree, but that in time it would flourish and spread throughout the continent. At the time of this tour, Elder Kimball could already see the verdant beginning of the fulfillment of that prophecy, with thriving branches of the Church in the seven countries he visited and with an extraordinary potential for future growth.

At Ipomeia, Brazil, where he dedicated a lovely new meetinghouse, Elder Kimball became aware of the curious way the Church had grown in South America. This, he learned, was the site of one of the first Latter-day Saint communities in all of Brazil, established not long after Elder Ballard's prayer of dedication by missionaries sent there by the mission president in Buenos Aires. The mission president, Reinhold Stoof, had sent the missionaries because of a pleading letter to President Heber J. Grant, forwarded to President Stoof, from a German immigrant woman, Augusta Lippelt, who had been converted in her native land and who wanted Church literature. From the nucleus of this woman and her children, and later her husband, Robert Lippelt, and other German immigrant converts, the Church had spread among the German-speaking people in southern Brazil, accounting for the fact that in the early days of Church proselyting there, the missionaries spoke German, not Portuguese.

When Elder Kimball returned to Salt Lake City from this tour a few days before April general conference in 1959, he was an unabashed promoter of Church development in South America, even as his father had become an unabashed promoter of the virtues of the Gila Valley after he moved there. Indeed, in his official report of the tour, he said the statement of Horace Greeley, "Go west, young man, go west," should be changed to "Go south, young man, go south." He wrote to the First Presidency, "We are but scratching the surface in our work in this land."

Undoubtedly this enthusiasm accounted in large part for the many assignments to South America he received during the years ahead and for the dominant role he played in the

Church's development there. And it is undoubtedly true, also, that the experiences he had there among people of different cultures and ethnic backgrounds helped prepare him for the revelation on priesthood he received in 1978.

Meanwhile, he recommended that three new missions be created in South America, one from a division of Brazil, one in Chile, and one in Peru-Bolivia. He also expressed the opinion that in the not-distant future, stakes could be created in São Paulo and Curitiba, Brazil; Montevideo, Uruguay; and Buenos Aires and Rosario, Argentina. He also mentioned the large number of members in the South American missions who traced their ancestry to Portugal, Spain, and Italy and confidently expected they would help provide the foundation for extending the work into those European countries. Because none of the Brethren who had visited South America previously had made recommendations of such far-reaching import, it would take a while for these ideas to be assimilated, confirmed by the Spirit, and acted on at Church headquarters. Elder Kimball would see to it they were not sidetracked.

Major changes in the Church leadership occurred not long after Elder Kimball returned from his South American tour. President Stephen L Richards died on May 19, 1959. President McKay was distraught. President Richards had been the prophet's closest friend since their school days at the University of Utah. It was that closeness that had prompted him to select President Richards as his first counselor in preference to President Clark. Although there was great need for the vacancy to be filled promptly, President McKay, mourning the loss of his friend, did not act for more than three weeks. Finally, on June 12, he presented to the council the names of J. Reuben Clark and Henry D. Moyle as his first and second counselors. And at the following October general conference, Elder Howard W. Hunter was sustained as a member of the Twelve, filling the vacancy caused by President Moyle's call as a counselor.

Returning from South America, Elder Kimball resumed

work on two important projects he had spearheaded, a new mission presidents' handbook and a color film about work with the Lamanites, *On Their Shoulders.* When the film was completed, he arranged to show it to the General Authorities and other leaders at Church headquarters. He was pleased with the results: "I believe it will open doors, both with the brethren and with the tribal authorities." He also used it at many other meetings to stimulate an interest in his program, especially as he attempted to stir up stake and mission presidents.

A tour of the New England Mission in May 1960 with President John E. Carr shifted Elder Kimball's focus temporarily from the Lamanites to his ancestry. During the tour they visited Sheldon, Franklin County, Vermont, where Heber C. Kimball was born on June 14, 1801. "We thought this the prettiest part of Vermont," wrote the apostle, approvingly and with unabashed bias. The visit inspired him with one of his few attempts at musical composition when afterward he wrote a song entitled "Great, Great Grandpa," which he taught to his grandchildren and which they sang at a Kimball family reunion the following month and also at the dedication of the restored Heber C. Kimball home in Nauvoo, Illinois, in July. "They made quite a hit," wrote the composer of his grandchildren's performances. At another stop on the tour, Elder Kimball was reminded again of family when at Cambridge, Massachusetts, he found that his nephew—Henry Eyring's son Hal, a student at Harvard—was a counselor in the district presidency. Elder Kimball would live to see this nephew, whose full name was Henry B. Eyring, called as a counselor in the Presiding Bishopric.

Ordinarily on these tours, Elder Kimball was positive and upbeat, reflecting the inherently optimistic quality of his character. Occasionally, however, when provoked, he could be outspokenly critical, even condemnatory. This occurred at one stop on the tour where he found a quarrelsome, bitter attitude among the members, even some of the leaders.

"We carried our call to repentance over nearly twenty minutes into the priesthood meeting time, and left it on a note of warning. I told them it was the first step to apostasy and bore down weightily." There was steel and fire in this man, a quality that usually was concealed behind a cloak of benign goodwill.

Chapter 18

Expanding Horizons

A t the 1960 October general conference, Elder Kimball delivered a significant talk which he entitled "The Day of the Lamanite Is Here." It reflected recent advances made in the status of Lamanites and painted a positive picture of their expanded future role. Two days later, he and Camilla left on a four-month tour that would take them around the world. With them were leaders of general Church auxiliaries and their companions, who were to participate in meetings scheduled in New Zealand and Australia. It was Elder Kimball's first venture into the South Pacific, where he would be exposed to other people considered to be of Lamanite descent. His assignments were to create four new stakes, two in Australia and two in New Zealand; to reorganize the Auckland, New Zealand, stake; to hold a stake conference in the Sydney, Australia, stake; and to tour four missions, two each in Australia and New Zealand. He had yearned and prayed for more assignments. Now his prayers had been answered to an extent unimaginable two years earlier.

Before leaving Salt Lake City, Elder Kimball received a special blessing from Presidents David O. McKay and Henry D. Moyle. President J. Reuben Clark, who had severe problems with his legs, was unable to be present. President Clark had attended and had spoken at general conference but now was indisposed. After listening to his conference talk, Elder Kimball had written, "He is still himself above the knees."

En route to Sydney, Australia, their first conference, the travelers paused in Hawaii, where, to prepare spiritually for the work ahead, they attended an endowment session in the Hawaii Temple and afterward held a testimony meeting. That night, Elder Kimball had a vivid dream about the Maoris in New Zealand. He seemed to be magnetically drawn to these people, perhaps because of his special commission to work with Lamanites around the world, or maybe because of the influence of his departed associate in the Lamanite work, Matthew Cowley, who had spent many years working among the Maoris.

The Sydney, Australia, stake, where Elder Kimball began his work in the South Pacific on October 16, 1960, had been organized only a few months before this visit. It was the first quarterly conference after the stake's organization. He thoroughly reviewed the progress of the stake during its short existence, counseled priesthood leaders, and motivated members during general meetings. Meanwhile, representatives of the Relief Society, Primary, YWMIA, YMMIA, and Sunday School general boards and of the Genealogical Society gave instructions to their stake counterparts. A similar procedure was followed at the other stake conferences held during the tour.

On the two succeeding weekends following the Sydney conference, Elder Kimball organized new stakes in Brisbane, Australia, and Melbourne, Australia. The party then flew to Auckland, New Zealand, where on November 6 he reorganized the Auckland stake. And on the two succeeding weekends following this reorganization, he organized new stakes in Hamilton, New Zealand, and Hawkes Bay, New Zealand. "It has been like a whirlwind of tornadic proportions as we have moved from place to place," he wrote after completing the work at Hawkes Bay. "I have [been conscious of] the awesome responsibility and through these days have prayed much and earnestly and have felt the presence of my Lord and His guidance and have relied completely on Him and feel that the work has been done about as it should be."

During this period, Elder Kimball received a telephone call from President Henry D. Moyle, who said President McKay was concerned they were "overdoing" Elder Kimball and excused him from the two mission tours in Australia. Apparently someone had called Salt Lake City to report the hectic pace Elder Kimball had been keeping.

After completing his stake conference assignments, Elder Kimball toured the New Zealand South Mission with President Alexander P. Anderson. Their wives accompanied them. As usual, missionary training and testimony meetings and general meetings with members and investigators were held throughout the South Island during the two-week tour. The Kimballs then traveled to the North Island, where they toured the New Zealand Mission with President Robert L. Simpson and his wife Jillaire. Feeling Elder Kimball needed a break from his strenuous schedule, President Simpson suggested they take off a day to visit the world-famous Waitomo Caves near Te Kuiti. At first Elder Kimball declined, saying he did not have the time. He relented only when Camilla spoke up to say her brother Henry Eyring had told her that this was one of the most extraordinary sights in the world and that she should not fail to see it. Elder Kimball yielded and agreed to go, though he remained skeptical. As they walked on an uneven path at the caves, Elder Kimball and President Simpson were behind their wives when they saw Camilla fall to the ground. Running forward, Elder Kimball anxiously kneeled down to comfort and help his wife, saying, "I knew we shouldn't have done anything extra." The party returned to

Wellington, where Sister Kimball remained in the mission home for four days with Jillaire Simpson, nursing a sprained knee, while their husbands completed the tour.

"This is the first time in two months I have been able to sit down to catch up on my diary," wrote Elder Kimball on December 18, 1960, after the tour was completed. There would have been ample time to return home for Christmas. However, the Kimballs decided against this. Because they were halfway around the world, they decided instead to travel west, completing a "trip around the world," something they might never have another chance to do. So three days later, after clearing with Salt Lake City, they left Wellington on the first leg of a seven-week journey that would expose them to some of the most fabled cities and exotic cultures of the civilized world.

Their first stop was in the island state of Singapore, situated at the southern extremity of the Malay Peninsula. Here they hired a young guide, Atah, to conduct them on a tour of the city. Everywhere, intermixed with the predominant Chinese influence, were signs of the island's former status as a British crown colony, including an imposing statue of Sir Thomas Stamford Raffles of the British East India Company, who, a hundred and forty years before, had negotiated an agreement with the Malay chief that gave the British control of this strategic location. That control had ended only two years before the Kimballs' visit, when Singapore became an independent state. The travelers spent Christmas Day in Kuala Lumpur, capital of Malaya, before going to what Elder Kimball called "Saigon the Fantastic" in Vietnam. The apostle was interested to see how the new independent government had sought to erase evidence of the French influence, which had predominated for almost a century, by changing street names and tearing down many French monuments. Next came Bangkok, capital of Thailand, where Elder Kimball was "amazed by the luxuries of the palace" and astonished by the glut of watercraft on the Chao Phraya River that ran the gamut "from small canoelike ships to battleships, motor boats, row boats, and junks used as living quarters, etc." The Kimballs greeted the new year in Burma, after visiting Rangoon and before arriving in Calcutta. They spent a week in India. In addition to Calcutta, their itinerary included Banaras, Agra, and Delhi. Outside Agra, they visited the Taj Mahal. "We go to bed dreaming of the beautiful, priceless Taj Mahal," wrote Elder Kimball. And as he traveled through the country, amazed at the masses of people, his mind turned to the possibility of undertaking missionary work there. This idea was intensified when in Delhi he met, converted, and baptized Mr. Mongoldan Dipty. After this experience, he contacted the United States ambassador to discuss whether permission could be obtained to proselyte in India. He was told the chances were practically nil. "The only possibility," he wrote after the interview, "is to send in a wise couple and let them work alone." Shortly after he returned to Salt Lake City, President David O. McKay asked Elder Kimball about this baptism. "Apparently he had heard about it from other sources and was concerned. But when he heard the full story, he said I was entitled to my inspiration and that the baptism was all right, even though there was no branch to which he could be attached." Later Mr. Dipty immigrated to the United States and Elder Kimball assisted in finding employment for him.

Leaving India, the travelers spent a weekend in Karachi, Pakistan, at the Hotel Metropole. They went to a Church of England cathedral on Sunday but, finding the services were not in English, spent the afternoon in their hotel room reading the scriptures and writing. Their flight from Karachi was scheduled to land in Tehran, but bad weather required it to continue to Beirut.

The Kimballs spent almost three weeks in the Middle East, visiting ancient sites that brought alive people and events they had heard about since childhood. Near Beirut was the place from which the sacred cedars of Lebanon were obtained for Solomon's Temple; in Tehran was the

231

Elder and Sister Kimball visit Egypt during their trip around the world, 1960.

shah's luxurious palace and the museum filled with ancient artifacts; and in Damascus, "the ancient home of the prophets," was the Street Called Straight, where Paul was befriended by Ananias following the apostle's astonishing vision.

As interesting as these places were, they could not compare with the compelling impact of what Spencer and Camilla found in Egypt and Palestine. From their luxurious room in the Nile Hilton, they could look out on the wide river, swarming with water traffic. They accompanied a tour to the desert, where, after mounting camels, they inspected the Great Sphinx and the pyramids, ancient symbols of Egyptian skill, dominance, and superstition. They visited the massive Mosque at the Citadel, whose floors were covered with opulent rugs and where the apostle was attracted by the "light from the waning sun, shining through the stained glass windows." Here they learned about the assault on this bastion by Napoleon, some of whose cannonballs were "still lodged in the walls." And they visited the teeming bazaars in the city, where they made selective purchases.

Boarding a train, they took an overnight upriver to inspect the wonders of ancient Luxor, Karnak, Thebes, and the Valley of the Kings. "The vocabulary runs out after colossal, stupendous, and unbelievable," wrote Elder Kimball afterward. This trip also opened his eyes to the wealth of the fertile Nile Valley and to the dilemma the Israelites faced as they weighed the options presented by Moses' proposal to leave. "As we saw the lush vegetation, the cabbages, the melons and the onions, the forage and the grain, we could understand a little their concern about leaving the known, however odious, for the unknown."

The week the Kimballs spent in the Holy Land only whetted their appetite for more; they would return the following December with Elder Howard W. Hunter and his wife, Claire, for a more thorough study. Meanwhile, they filled each day of this visit with a crowded schedule of sightseeing and travel. Within and near Jerusalem, they visited the Via Dolorosa, the route along which it is thought that the Savior carried his cross; the Church of the Holy Sepulchre; the Jaffa Gate; the Garden of Gethsemane; the Mount of Olives; and the Garden Tomb, about which Elder Kimball wrote: "There was [such] a holy influence here that we stayed and stayed. . . . We went inside and read about the burial and the resurrection, then knelt together and each had a solemn prayer, a prayer of gratitude that we know the Lord and know our Heavenly Father and KNOW that he lived, and died, and was resurrected and rose and ascended and lives." He returned a few days later: "I went to the Garden Tomb again and had a few moments alone there. It was too early for tourists. I feel sure each time that this could be the place where the Lord's body was resurrected." Elsewhere in the Holy Land, they visited Mount Hermon, the Jordan River, Jericho, the Dead Sea, Bethany, Capernaum, Nazareth, Mount Tabor, and the Sea of Galilee, places they could now readily relate in their minds to the ancient biblical stories.

During the ten days after leaving the Holy Land, the Kimballs made brief stops in Athens, Corinth, Rome, Madrid, Toledo, and Lisbon. At each of these cities, and elsewhere on the tour, they visited the places of major interest to travelers, storing in their minds images of what they had seen and heard; filling their diaries with descriptions of people, places, and events; and saving voluminous quantities of printed materials, brochures, maps, travel guides, and news articles that were later sorted and classified and inserted in the diaries. Since both of the Kimballs were avid diarists, their combined records provide a rich source of historical data, significant not only to themselves and their family but also to the Church. Spencer, especially, derived much enjoyment from reviewing these materials, reliving and savoring the events they recorded and using them as a resource in preparing talks and articles or in confirming his remembrance of past events. Convinced of the value of these personal records, he was enthusiastic in urging others to keep similar records of their own lives; when he became the President of the Church, he extended these admonitions to members everywhere, especially to the General Authorities, whose apostolic ministries, he taught, would be incomplete without the accurate written record of their labors that only they could provide.

Chapter 19

Missionaries, Minorities, and South America

Elder Kimball's status as the third most senior member of the Quorum of the Twelve, the global mandate to shepherd the Lamanites, and the enlarged perceptions of the work gained from his world travels and many mission tours combined at this time to give him a powerful voice on missionary matters in the Twelve, which is the missionary committee of the Church. Indeed, because of President Joseph Fielding Smith's responsibility for the overall supervision of the quorum and Elder Harold B. Lee's heavy involvement in welfare, the correlation committee, and many other matters, it is not unreasonable to say Elder Kimball's voice had become dominant in the area of missionary work. His role with missionary work was formalized in 1963 when he became the chairman of the Missionary Executive Committee.

A few months after Elder Kimball returned from his trip around the world, a missionary initiative he had strongly urged was put in place when stakes were grouped together for training in stake missionary work. On July 9, 1961, at a

After returning home from their trip around the world, Spencer and Camilla greet grandsons Stephen and Thomas Mack in 1961.

meeting of all General Authorities and general auxiliary leaders, regional supervisors of stake missionary work were set apart and charged to train and motivate stake mission leaders and missionaries within their regions. Elder Kimball and other members of the Twelve gave direction to these regional supervisors, as Elder Kimball did in May 1962, when he met with two of these regional leaders, Thomas S. Monson (who would be called to the Quorum of the Twelve the following year) and T. Bowring Woodbury, and the stake leaders and missionaries of nine stakes. In these meetings, Elder Kimball, assisted by the regional supervisors, gave instructions about finding, fellowshipping, teaching, baptizing, and integrating new members and about the relationship of stake missionaries to seventies quorums.

With these procedures in place within organized stakes, Elder Kimball and his brethren of the Twelve began to focus on restructuring missionary work outside the stakes as a means of giving it greater emphasis throughout the world.

At the quarterly meeting of the Twelve on April 10, 1963, for instance, they discussed the possibility of dividing the world into ten districts, with about eight missions in each district. The plan was that nine members of the Twelve would each be assigned to a district, with two members of the Twelve sharing a tenth district, leaving the president of the Quorum of the Twelve free of a district assignment. It would be two years before these proposals received the final approval of the Council of the First Presidency and the Quorum of the Twelve.

Meanwhile, Elder Kimball continued filling stake conference and mission tour assignments as before. In May 1964, he was again assigned to conduct mission tours in South America. This time he went by air, flying to New York and thence to Buenos Aires, with intermediate stops in Caracas, Venezuela, and Campinas, Brazil. He saw that some of the recommendations made after his first trip had been followed. There were now seven missions in South America rather than three. The mission in Brazil had been divided, and separate missions had been created in Chile and the Andean countries as he had recommended. The mission in Argentina also had been divided. In addition, Elder A. Theodore Tuttle of the First Council of Seventy was now stationed in Montevideo, Uruguay, with the responsibility to oversee the work in South America.

Elder Kimball commenced his work with a seminar in Buenos Aires for the seven mission presidents and their wives. Then during a period of five weeks, he crisscrossed the continent, holding missionary and general meetings in Argentina, Uruguay, Brazil, Chile, Bolivia, Peru, and Ecuador. He was impressed by the rapid growth that had taken place since his tour several years before and encouraged by the potential for future growth. Frequently as he conducted interviews, he heard stories of faith and integrity that rivaled those of the early Latter-day Saints in the United States. This gave him confidence that the Church would thrive there and would become a powerful force in the cultural life of South America, as it had already done in North America.

In Viña del Mar on the Chilean coast west of Santiago, he was impressed by the fertility of the land, and he wondered whether father Lehi and his family had landed there after their crossing, as some scholars had speculated. The special charge Elder Kimball had received to work with Lehi's descendants had created in him a more than academic interest in learning all he could about present-day Lamanites. During this tour, Elder Kimball avidly searched, as he did during many other South American tours he made in the years ahead, for evidence of a people whose ancestors had not intermingled with European immigrants. He ultimately found one in Otavalo, Ecuador, that he felt might be of pure Lamanite descent.

Across the continent in Brazil, Elder Kimball again encountered a serious problem that impeded the vigorous growth of the Church. In this country, where slavery had been allowed until 1888, there was a large percentage of the population that could not enjoy the full blessings of the Church because of its limiting policy on who could hold the priesthood. Elder Kimball and his brethren were acutely aware of this problem, not only as it related to Brazil, but to other countries as well. In the early 1960s, for instance, Church headquarters began receiving letters from people in West Africa, pleading for missionaries and for the opportunity to join the Church. The Brethren had responded by sending literature and equipment but had declined to send missionaries. Without priesthood holders, it would have been impossible to establish the Church there with any semblance of completeness. Only functions not requiring priesthood authority could have been performed. Elder Kimball and his brethren yearned for a change in that policy but knew it would not occur unless by revelation from God. Elder Kimball was made painfully aware of the heartache of black Church members when he attended a meeting in Curitiba, Brazil, where several young men of African ancestry bore their testimonies. "My heart was touched," he wrote later, "as [these] boys bore their testimonies, especially by one who seemed very humble." There can be little doubt that this and other similar experiences during the years he traveled in Brazil were significant factors prompting President Spencer W. Kimball to pray fervently for a solution to this dilemma. The result was the revelation on priesthood he received in 1978, fourteen years after this experience in Brazil.

When Elder Kimball returned from his 1964 trip to South America, he was convinced it was time to begin organizing stakes there. As he analyzed the various centers of strength, he decided the best place to start was Montevideo, Uruguay. The mission president, J. Thomas Fyans, had made a concerted effort to prepare the leaders for stakehood; there was a large body of devoted Church members who met in substantial church buildings; there was a complex in Montevideo that officed Church accounting, finance, and building personnel; and Elder A. Theodore Tuttle, the South American supervisor, lived there. During the summer break, Elder Kimball compiled the supporting data, and on September 3, 1964, he made a formal proposal in the weekly temple meeting that the Church create a stake in Montevideo, Uruguay. The Brethren declined to approve it. Elder Kimball was disappointed but not disheartened. "I felt that I presented a good case, almost an air tight case," he confided to his diary. "I fought pretty hard to put it over, but finally yielded; but I will try again. I am sure it is the right thing to do." He had to wait three years before this proposal was approved. Meanwhile, he obtained approval to organize stakes in São Paulo, Brazil, and Buenos Aires, Argentina.

In May 1965, the Council of the First Presidency and the Twelve approved the recommendation that the world be divided into areas for missionary purposes and that members of the Twelve be appointed to supervise them, assisted by designated Assistants to the Twelve. Two weeks later, on

May 18, 1965, Elder Kimball received a letter from the First Presidency appointing him to supervise the missions in South America. Elder Franklin D. Richards was appointed to assist him. During the next two and a half years, Elder Kimball conducted six lengthy tours of South America. His main focus was threefold: to train and motivate the missionaries and their leaders to accelerate the growth of the Church, to inspire the members to keep the commandments, and to instruct branch and district leaders about their duties once stakes were organized. In an effort to create a good climate in which the Church could thrive, he also befriended local government officials. He always emphasized in meeting them that in addition to its eternal objectives, the Church prepares its members to be better people and more loyal citizens of their respective countries.

The South American tour conducted in April and May 1966 was perhaps the most significant one to Elder Kimball. He and Elder Richards, accompanied by their wives, flew to São Paulo, Brazil, on April 26. During the next four days, they interviewed the local leaders. "My little Portuguese is coming back," wrote Elder Kimball after many hours of interviewing. "I was delighted with the leaders I interviewed. Wonderful spirit." After study, analysis, and spiritual confirmation, Elder Kimball called Walter Spat, a German national who had lived in Brazil most of his life, as the stake president. President Spat selected Osiris Cabral Tavares as his first counselor and Antonio Carlos de Camargo as the second.

Fifteen hundred members of the Church gathered in São Paulo on May 1 to participate in the organization of the first stake in South America. Elder Kimball could not conceal the joy he felt. "Organization day!" he wrote exultantly. "Today was glorious, the organization of the first stake of Zion in Southern Zion in South America, and in the Portuguese language." He referred to it as "a stake in the southern wing of the two winged bird, Zion, . . . one wing in North America and the other in South America." He saw this as merely the first step in an extraordinary growth of the Church in South America, looking toward the fulfillment of Elder Melvin J. Ballard's prophetic vision. A salient reason for Elder Kimball's confidence in the continued growth of the Church in South America was the depth and dedication of its leaders. For instance, he made special reference to the bishop of one of the wards in São Paulo, Helio da Rocha Camargo, who, he said, "could have filled any position in the stake." Nineteen years later Elder Kimball, then the President of the Church, called Bishop Camargo to the First Quorum of the Seventy; Elder Camargo was the first native Brazilian to be called as a General Authority.

On the return trip to the United States, Elder Kimball stopped in Quito, Ecuador, where he met the president of the country, Cemente Yerovi, "a very gracious and jovial" man who, the apostle was interested to learn, had a son in Wyoming and a daughter in Arizona. Two days later, on May 11, Elder Kimball was in Bogotá, where, in El Parque Nacional, he dedicated the country of Colombia for the preaching of the gospel.

Later in the year, Elder Kimball returned to South America, where, on November 20, 1966, he organized a stake in Buenos Aires, Argentina. Installed as the president of this, the second stake in South America, was Angel Abrea, a future General Authority of the Church. Sustained as counselors in the stake presidency were Hugo Angel Catron and Juan Carlos Avila. In the remarks Elder Kimball made on this "dedication day," he recalled the experiences of Elder Parley P. Pratt of the Twelve in the early 1850s, when he spent several months in Chile in an unsuccessful attempt to establish the Church in South America. He also related the experience of Elder Melvin J. Ballard's December 1925 dedication of the continent of South America for the preaching of the gospel. Now that there were two stakes on the continent and several other areas were rapidly moving toward stakehood, the growth of the "acorn" planted by Elder Ballard was evident.

During a trip to South America the following year, 1967, Elder Kimball again visited the people around Otavalo, Ecuador, whom he considered to be pure Lamanites. To reach the remote community, he was first met in Quito, Ecuador, by businessman Robert E. Wells, a future General Authority of the Church, who provided him with a car. Then it was a four-hour drive through rugged, mountainous country of astonishing beauty and grandeur to the community of Otavalo, whose inhabitants spoke both Spanish and Quechua. Elder Kimball again had the feeling he was among "real native Indians" and was anxious "to get a foothold" here. He spoke to them through an interpreter at a large gathering arranged by the missionaries. "Of all the meetings I have ever attended," he wrote later, "none has ever quite eclipsed this one. As I stood and spoke to them, I could visualize the . . . people sitting around on the ground, listening to this voice from the heavens and then hearing His messages; and I told these people they were now hearing a brief summary of some of the messages that the Lord himself gave to their ancestors." Later, in reflecting on the experience, he added: "This may be the beginning of a great new day among the Indian people, for these seem so sincere and are somewhat isolated and very progressive." Fourteen years later, a new stake was organized in Otavalo.

After leaving Otavalo, Elder Kimball traveled to Lima, Peru, where in a meeting with priesthood leaders he discussed "stakehood, explaining what they should do in preparation." Then in La Paz, he dedicated the country of Bolivia for the preaching of the gospel, after which he traveled to Argentina via Santiago, Chile. There was a three-inch snowstorm in Santiago on June 5 that snarled traffic, broke tree limbs along the boulevards, and was followed by bitterly cold winds that made the meetings in the unheated chapel most uncomfortable.

Crossing the Andes to Argentina, the Kimballs found the weather more pleasant. At Mendoza, they were met by President Richard G. Scott, a future member of the Twelve, who was the president of the mission headquartered in Córdoba, Argentina. President Scott had been directing the work of several missionaries stationed in southern Bolivia. Since Elder Kimball was anxious to visit the area, he and Sister Kimball, the Scotts, and others drove north from Córdoba toward the border, stopping at Salta. There they purchased cloth, seeds, thread, wool, soap, first-aid supplies, medicines, and other items to take to the Bolivian members. Before crossing the border at Villazon, they parked the mission cars and rented a Jeep for the trip to Quiriza, their destination to the north. With eight passengers, their gear, and the items purchased at Salta, the Jeep was crowded. The winding, primitive road, portions of which lay in the riverbed, took them past several small Bolivian villages and occasional herds of llamas. Elder Kimball noted that President Scott frequently downshifted the Jeep, and he learned later that this was the vehicle's main braking mechanism, the conventional brakes being practically gone. Arriving in Quiriza, Elder Kimball was astonished to see painted on the face of a sheer cliff in bold letters "Bienvenidos Elder Kimball." He learned that a resourceful missionary had attached a paintbrush to a long pole in order to reach the cliff face.

Following a meeting in Quiriza, Elder Kimball saw two men standing near the doorway, quietly waiting for him to exit. When he reached the door, they approached him hesitantly, extending toward him a box they held. It contained a dozen small eggs, a gift of great economic value to them. To Elder Kimball it was, by his own admission, a gift that meant as much to him as almost any other gift he had received. He was deeply touched, not only by the significance of the gift but also by the humble, loving attitude of the men who gave it to him.

Before Elder Kimball left the area, a ground-breaking ceremony was held for a small chapel to be constructed. Elder Kimball lifted the first shovelful of dirt, followed by President Scott and several of the local priesthood leaders.

Then one of the men waved to the women, who had been standing aside with their children, to come participate. They all came running, some carrying their babies, and each one in turn, women and children alike, lifted some dirt in celebration of the great event.

Elder Kimball returned to South America in November. It was his last tour as the area supervisor. On November 12, 1967, he organized a stake in Montevideo, Uruguay, fulfilling his goal of three years before. Vincente Carmelo Rubio was selected as stake president, with Ariel Alcides Fedrigotti and Washington Gonzalez as counselors. Because Brother J. Thomas Fyans had done so much to prepare the area for stakehood, Elder Kimball invited Brother Fyans to participate in the organization even though he had been released as the mission president. Before returning home, Elder Kimball also held another series of meetings in Brazil.

A few months before this tour of South America, Elder Kimball attended a historic meeting in Salt Lake City with members who represented minority congregations of wards or branches in the city. These included Japanese, Indians, Germans, Dutch, Norwegians, Chinese, and Mexicans. Elder Kimball, assisted by Elder LeGrand Richards, had spearheaded a program whose object was to enable newcomers who did not speak English well or who wanted to keep their national roots alive to mingle together in a church setting. Meanwhile, they were encouraged to affiliate with conventional wards once it was feasible to do so. Later, when the Brethren began to encourage new converts to remain in their native countries where their strength was so needed, less emphasis was given to these minority units.

Throughout this period, Elder Kimball continued to give special attention to the Lamanites. His influence among them was increased when the Utah state governor appointed him to the Utah Indian Affairs Committee. And the Lamanites' fondness for him increased, as evidenced by two special recognitions he received. The first was at Pine Ridge, South Dakota, in October 1963, when Sister Two

Dogs conferred a new name upon him: Wamb Lee Ho Waste, whose English translation was, roughly, "Good Voice Eagle." Sister Two Dogs explained the meaning of the name to Elder Kimball: "Because [you] fly all over the world like an eagle and use [your] voice for the teaching of the good gospel truths." The second was at Provo, Utah, the following month, when Elder Kimball was made a chief of the Tribe of Many Feathers and was given the name Hosteen Yazzie. "I sang my Navajo song to them," he explained, "and spoke to them, urging the Indian boys and girls to make good grades and to magnify their opportunities at the university and to live the gospel."

Chapter 20

Changes, Travels, and a Book about Repentance

D uring the time Elder Kimball supervised South America, President David O. McKay called Joseph Fielding Smith and Thorpe B. Isaacson as additional counselors in the First Presidency to help him and his first and second counselors, Hugh B. Brown and N. Eldon Tanner, carry the extra load caused by President McKay's declining health. Previously, Presidents Brown and Tanner had replaced Presidents J. Reuben Clark and Henry D. Moyle, who had passed away. When Thorpe B. Isaacson suffered a debilitating stroke not long after his call, President McKay called Alvin R. Dyer as another counselor in the First Presidency a few months after Elder Kimball completed his South American assignment.

These major changes, along with the passing of Elder George Q. Morris, had created vacancies in the Quorum of the Twelve which had been filled by Elders Gordon B. Hinckley and Thomas S. Monson. These junior members of the Twelve had been assigned to work with Elder Kimball on the Missionary Executive Committee, which had overall responsibility for the Church's global missionary program. The committee supervised the work of the Missionary Department at headquarters, which included the calling and assignment of missionaries under the direction of the First Presidency. The committee had a major responsibility in the selection, calling, and training of new mission presidents and in handling problems connected with missionary illnesses and discipline. The committee also worked with government officials of various nations to help resolve difficulties with missionary visas and missionary quotas.

On August 23, 1965, all three members of the committee conferred with two draft officials about the effect on missionary work of increased drafting caused by the Vietnam War. "It looks like our forces will decrease," Elder Kimball wrote after this meeting, "and that many of our fine young men may have to go to war instead of in the mission field." The scope and intensity of missionary work and the frequent, worldwide turnovers in personnel made the Missionary Department the most active, aggressive, and pressure-filled department at Church headquarters. At the heart of this was the committee chaired by Elder Kimball. There can be little doubt that the key role he played here provided special insights and motivations that helped drive the extraordinary acceleration of missionary work later when Elder Kimball became the President of the Church.

After his release from the South American assignment, Elder Kimball was assigned to supervise Great Britain, assisted by Elder John Longden. Before beginning his new duties, however, he received an assignment to return to Australia to hold several stake conferences and to visit Singapore, Hong Kong, Japan, and Korea. Accompanied by Sister Kimball, he left Salt Lake City on January 28, 1968, to fly to Hawaii, where he went through the temple to help prepare spiritually for the duties ahead. En route to Melbourne, his first assignment in Australia, he stopped over in Pago Pago, where he met the governor, and in Apia, where he held a meeting with the missionaries. After conducting a stake conference in Melbourne, he traveled to Hobart in the south of Tasmania and to Sydney for special meetings before going to Adelaide for another stake conference. He then flew across the continent to Perth on the west coast. Because this stake had been in existence for less than three months, Elder Kimball spent much time training the leaders as part of their stake conference. "I hope I gave them much new vision in their first conference with new goals. They were very receptive," he wrote.

The Kimballs flew from Perth to Singapore, where they spent the night. The desk at the hotel failed to call them early, as they had requested, notifying them only when the limousine for the airport was waiting. They hurriedly threw their things together and left before Elder Kimball could shave. Their flight to Hong Kong was via Bangkok. As the plane crossed Vietnam, he was "anxious" because of the ground war that still raged. They were met in Hong Kong by mission president Keith Garner, who hosted them overnight, took them on a quick shopping tour, and accompanied them to a special meeting with members and missionaries.

From Hong Kong they flew to Tokyo, Japan, where they were met by mission president Adney Y. Komatsu, a future General Authority. Over a three-day period, meetings were held in Tokyo, Kyoto, and Osaka. Elder Kimball was favorably impressed with the Japanese. "They are a kind, receptive, ambitious people. I think we may well look at this ambitious people of the 'Rising Sun.'" He found kindred spirits among these industrious, hardworking people.

In Korea, missionary work was still in its incipient stages. The first mission in the country had been organized only six years prior to this visit, and the Book of Mormon had been published in Korean the previous year. "We find the Koreans are ravenous in their appetite for knowledge and many of them have degrees, and some of them doctors' degrees. They are well-groomed and attractive." One of the key Church leaders in the country was Han In Sang, who later would be called to serve as a General Authority of the Church. He headed the translation department in Korea at the time of Elder Kimball's visit, and it was he who had translated the Book of Mormon into Korean.

Aside from handling some matters by correspondence and telephone, Elder Kimball did not begin his work as the supervisor in Great Britain until August 1968. He and Sister Kimball were met at London's Heathrow Airport on August 30 by mission president Reed Callister. Because of cramped quarters in the mission home, the travelers checked in at the Cumberland Hotel, where they remained for six days. They were joined there by Elder and Sister John Longden. During the London stay, Elder Kimball presided at a conference of the London Stake and conducted a seminar for mission presidents and their wives. The apostle met specially with President George I. Cannon of the British Central Mission to counsel about his work. Brother Cannon would be called as a General Authority in 1986, eighteen years later.

Leaving London, Elder Kimball toured the Scottish Mission. The customary meetings of missionaries and members were held in Edinburgh, Aberdeen, and Dundee. In between, he held a stake conference in Glasgow, where the stake presidency was reorganized, and dedicated a new chapel at Dumfries. Here in Scotland still lived the reputations of David O. McKay, who had served as the conference president in Glasgow as a young man, and David B. Haight, who had served as the Scottish Mission president a few years before Elder Kimball's tour and whom he would call as a member of the Twelve when he became the President of the Church.

With no pause to catch his breath, the apostle began the tour of the North British Mission the day following the last series of meetings in Scotland. In five days he held the usual meetings in Sunderland, Leeds, and Liverpool. He also presided at a stake conference in Leicester, dedicated a new chapel in Liverpool, and made a special trip to Preston, where his grandfather Heber C. Kimball had commenced the work in Great Britain in the summer of 1837. Here in Preston, the first nine English converts had been baptized in the River Ribble on Sunday, July 30, 1837. The first of these, George D. Watt, who later became a scribe and clerk to both Joseph Smith and Brigham Young, raced a friend to the river's edge to see who would be first. Through the years, Elder Kimball visited this place many times, but he never tired of doing so and reflecting on the significant events in Church history that occurred there and the consequences that flowed from them. During this trip to Great Britain, he also toured the South British Mission, visited the London Temple, and over the last weekend, September 21 and 22, conducted a stake conference in Manchester.

In his meetings with missionaries during this trip, Elder Kimball urged them to work with more concentration and persistence, to follow the mission rules exactly, to work cooperatively with the local leaders and members, and to make sure investigators were taught thoroughly and were ready for baptism. A decade before, some converts had been baptized hurriedly after their participation in Church sports, which had caused critics to refer to them derisively as "baseball baptisms." Elder Kimball deplored the use of this term as unfairly casting a shadow on everyone baptized during this period. While he did not condone careless or slipshod proselyting that may have occurred, he openly lauded those who had presided then for the aggressive, purposeful way the work was conducted, which he felt had significantly altered local attitudes of inertia and had contributed to the strength and vitality of the Church. This view was confirmed when he conducted area conferences in England in 1976 and found that many of the promising young leaders were part of the harvest of almost twenty years before.

In his meetings with Church members, Elder Kimball repeated the counsel he had given to the British people before: to remain in their homes and build up the Church there, to keep the commandments fully, to teach children the gospel in their homes and prepare them for missionary service, to pay an honest tithing, to reach out to their neighbors and friends and to work cooperatively with the full-time missionaries, and to make their voices heard and their influence felt in civic affairs. Important keys in attaining these ends were described by Elder Kimball in a general conference talk he delivered shortly after returning from this trip. "God and His program," he told a Tabernacle audience, "will be found only in deep pondering, appropriate reading, much kneeling in devout, humble prayer, and in sincerity born of need and dependence."

Elder Kimball conducted two lengthy tours in Great Britain during 1969. Leaving Salt Lake City in mid-February, he traveled to London via Frankfurt, Germany. Beginning in London, he then held a series of missionary and member meetings in Glasgow, Aberdeen, Dundee, Bristol, Birmingham, Belfast, Dublin, Sunderland, Harrogate, Manchester, Liverpool, Leeds, and Preston. In Belfast, Ireland, he was impressed by a young woman who led the singing and conducted the meeting and who, he learned, was a product of the aggressive proselyting effort that had been so much maligned by some critics. While he and Camilla were in the Midlands with President and Sister George I. Cannon, they spent some time visiting places of interest in Stratford-upon-Avon, Shakespeare's birthplace, and in the surrounding area, rich in historic importance. He did not do this with any sense of enthusiasm, but mostly out of deference to the wishes of Camilla and the urging of their hosts. And in Leeds, both grandparents were proud, in a Latter-day Saintly way, to find grandson Randall Kimball Mack serving faithfully and ably as a district leader.

The second British tour of 1969, conducted during August and September, was distinguished by special regional meetings held in London and Leeds where local and missionary leaders were given detailed instructions about a cooperative, integrated proselyting effort and other matters of importance. Then followed a whirlwind tour of many British cities, including Bristol, Cardiff, Southampton,

Redding, Sunderland, Harrogate, Liverpool, Manchester, and Preston, where instructional and motivational meetings were held. As he had always done, Elder Kimball carefully analyzed the conditions that existed in the Church units in these cities and gave specific instructions about needed changes. While he was not unaware of local circumstances that might have justified lowered performance, he was careful to encourage members and leaders to continue striving for improvement. Driven by a sense of urgency that his many physical disabilities had produced and by a feeling that the time was short, he prodded, cajoled, and implored the Saints to do more, to do it better, and to do it faster than they had ever done the work before. A meeting held with Spencer W. Kimball was never an occasion for a relaxed, contemplative, scholarly review of a gospel principle. It was a call to action, to self-improvement, to selfless service. He did not want people to go away from one of his meetings merely with a glowing feeling of gratitude and appreciation for the gospel plan and for the rewards offered to the faithful. He wanted them to leave with a determination to do something, whether to repent of misconduct, to challenge a neighbor to receive the missionaries, to start paying tithing, to start saving money for a mission, or whatever. He was a preacher of righteousness, cast in the ancient, traditional mold: positive, energetic, unyielding. Yet he was not a nag. Underlying all his preachments was a clear sense that he had the best interests of his listeners at heart. It was as the pleading of a concerned, loving parent who wanted the best for his children, even if it involved taking a little medicine now and then, medicine he sweetened with his infectious enthusiasm.

A significant event of Elder Kimball's last lengthy tour of Great Britain occurred on September 15, 1969, as he was in Herefordshire in the Malvern Hills. It was in this area in the early 1840s that Elder Wilford Woodruff performed his notable missionary work among the United Brethren, baptizing hundreds of members of the sect. Nearby was the pond on the farm of John Benbow where most of these baptisms were performed. And near also were the remains of the Gadfield Elm Chapel, which the United Brethren gave to the Church after their mass conversion. Since chapels as such were never constructed by the Saints in Ohio, Missouri, or Illinois in the early years, this reputedly is the first chapel of the restored Church, a building where not only Wilford Woodruff but also Brigham Young and Willard Richards had spoken to the United Brethren who had become Latter-day Saints.

Elder Kimball was aware of this background and of the fact that these three early apostles had a special place on the Herefordshire Beacon, one of the higher peaks of the Malvern Hills, where they retired to be alone, to pray, and to make decisions about the work. It was here, for instance, on May 20, 1840, that they decided, after prayer and counsel, to publish the Book of Mormon and a collection of hymns in England. Because of this and Elder Kimball's understanding that in 1838 in Chatburn his grandfather had dedicated that region of England for preaching the gospel, he went into the Malvern Hills on September 15, 1969, presumably to the Herefordshire Beacon, where he encouraged the missionaries to make greater efforts in preaching the gospel during their missions.

During these travels, Elder Kimball worked at odd moments on a manuscript he had been composing for several years, which he originally referred to as a book on repentance, but which he ultimately named *The Miracle of Forgiveness*. It was based on thousands of interviews he had conducted over a period of fifteen years with members of the Church who had serious moral problems. These interviews arose originally due to an assignment he had received from the Brethren to provide counseling for homosexuals. Later, Elder Mark E. Petersen was appointed to assist him. In turn, Harold I. Bowman was recruited to help. In time, those who came to Elder Kimball for counsel included not only homosexuals but individuals, both single and married, who had moral problems of almost every description and degree. He could never say no to those who pleaded for his help, which he gave unstintingly, sometimes almost to the detriment of his personal well-being. As he spent time in this work, he began to see that more members of the Church than he had imagined were burdened with feelings of guilt and remorse resulting from misconduct. He also became aware that the problems were worldwide in scope, that he had been exposed only to a small percentage of those who were troubled, and that there was an urgent need for a definitive writing to help those in trouble and to assist leaders, bishops especially, who had the responsibility to counsel transgressors. He was prompted to begin writing the book when representatives of a Salt Lake publisher came to him to urge that he write it. He was reluctant at first, typically disclaiming any writing ability. As they persisted, however, and as he perceived there was really no one else but him who had the depth of knowledge and the motivation to write such a book, he assented. Then followed the tedious process of assembling and organizing the voluminous material, which he used without divulging identities, and of writing the narrative. The many hours needed to accomplish the task were fitted into an already overcrowded work schedule or were stolen from what might be called Elder Kimball's vacations.

When the completed manuscript was first submitted to the publisher, it was much too long for a commercial product. So over a period of two years, Elder Kimball laboriously reworked it, condensing and trimming while preserving its essential core. It was published in the fall of 1969, several weeks after he returned from his last tour in Great Britain. On the day it came off the press, he autographed five hundred copies of the book, which was destined to go through numerous printings and to be translated into several different languages for use around the world. It stands today as the equivalent of a textbook in counseling Latter-day Saints burdened with the weight of moral transgression.

A companion book was later published. Entitled *Faith Precedes the Miracle,* this book consists of excerpts from Elder Kimball's talks and writings, arranged and edited by his son Edward in cooperation with representatives of the publisher. It too has received wide distribution and fills an important need in teaching the principle of faith in a practical, understandable way. Elder Kimball's other published book, *One Silent Sleepless Night,* chronicles in a dramatic way an ordeal through which he passed following one of the operations on his throat. Despite Brother Kimball's strong protestations that he lacked literary ability, this little volume reveals a powerful, poetic style suggesting he could have had a successful career as a writer had he been inclined to pursue it.

Chapter 21

Acting President, Then President of the Twelve

Three weeks after Elder Kimball's book *The Miracle of Forgiveness* came off the press, he went to Doctor Cowan for another checkup. "There is a spot on the left side of the throat which worries me," he wrote afterward. "It has not changed much since first we discovered it three months ago. My voice seems to have deteriorated some." The doctor shared his concern and had another biopsy performed. The laboratory reports on the specimens were inconclusive. Three of five doctors concluded the growth was not malignant; two disagreed. One of these was Doctor Cowan, the lead doctor. Elder Kimball reported these results to the First Presidency to seek counsel. The next Thursday at the regular council meeting in the temple, the Brethren joined to administer to him, Elder Gordon B. Hinckley anointing and President N. Eldon Tanner sealing the anointing and conferring a special blessing. "As I was administered to by all the brethren, I tingled all over," Elder Kimball reported. A sense of calm and peace also came over him, a feeling that seemed to pervade the room. When President Tanner had finished, Elder Harold B. Lee was the first to take Spencer in his arms to embrace him and express his love. Others followed. "It was a day of days," he wrote, which gave him confidence and a sense of direction, even though the biopsy had left him without a voice. From past experience, he knew his voicelessness was not permanent.

With strong urging from the First Presidency, Elder Kimball and Camilla left Salt Lake City two days after Christmas for a midwinter break in Hawaii. With no conference assignments and freed from the pressure of committee meetings and interviews, Elder Kimball relaxed in the warmth of Hawaii's tropical climate. Slowly his voice came back.

When he returned in January, Elder Kimball learned that President McKay's condition was critical. The ninety-six-year-old prophet had been in declining health for several years. The end came for him on January 18, 1970. His apostolic service had spanned almost sixty-four years, longer than any apostle of this dispensation. When Elder Kimball considered President McKay's long and distinguished career, his solid accomplishments, and his fragile health, he felt only that sadness at his passing that was occasioned by the temporary loss of President McKay's companionship. At age seventy-five, faced again with the spectre of cancer, Elder Kimball felt that the length of the separation for him might not be too long. Events of the next year seemed to reduce it to almost no time at all.

Elder Kimball was appointed to the committee for funeral arrangements. In counsel with the family, the funeral was set for January 22 in the Salt Lake Tabernacle. The building was packed, with an overflow in the Assembly Hall. The speakers extolled President McKay's life and character. With a mane of flowing, white hair and his tall, rugged good looks, President McKay was to some the embodiment of what a prophet ought to look like. Elder Kimball admired him for that but, aware he could never grow to that physical stature, instead sought persistently to rise to President McKay's spiritual stature.

The day after the funeral, the Twelve gathered in the upper room of the temple to counsel regarding a reorganization of the First Presidency. President McKay's death had dissolved the old presidency, automatically releasing his five counselors, Hugh B. Brown, N. Eldon Tanner, Joseph Fielding Smith, Thorpe B. Isaacson, and Alvin R. Dyer. There was unanimity that the First Presidency should be reorganized as soon as possible.

The critical question in the minds of some members of the Church was whether Elder Joseph Fielding Smith, President of the Twelve and the senior living apostle, would succeed President McKay. There was speculation that he would not be selected because he was almost ninety-four years old. Those who thought so misunderstood the role of a prophet, equating his position with that of the chief executive officer of an international corporation. They did not understand that a prophet's essential role is to have the discipline and the spirituality to receive God's revelations for the guidance of His people. President Smith had those qualifications in rich abundance. Therefore, there was no doubt among the Brethren that President Smith was the one. After discussion and on motion duly seconded and carried unanimously, he was sustained by his brethren of the Twelve and then ordained and set apart as the tenth President of the Church. He selected Elders Harold B. Lee and N. Eldon Tanner as his first and second counselors. Because Elder Lee was then the second-ranking apostle in seniority, he was also sustained and set apart as the president of the Twelve, with Elder Spencer W. Kimball as the acting president. President Smith invited President Lee to set apart Elder Kimball, who would act for him in directing the affairs of the Twelve. The blessing included these insightful words: "You have been tried and tested, Brother Kimball, and you

Elder Spencer W. Kimball in the 1970s.

have not been found wanting. The hearts of the people in this church have been drawn toward you, perhaps as to few other men in our day, because of the kind solicitude, the anxious concern, and your never-ceasing zeal in reaching out to the high, the low, the rich, the poor, the young, the old; and many are those who call your name blessed." The hearts of the members also were drawn to him because of the way he had fought back against the heart attack and the cancer. Stern physical tests still awaited, trying his patience and endurance to the limit and swelling the volume of public empathy and support for him.

Elder Kimball's new role increased his authority and responsibility and gave him greater control over his own activities. He now oversaw the work of all the members of the Twelve, making their stake conference and mission tour assignments and coordinating their work as area supervisors. He also had the responsibility to direct the work of the regional representatives and prepare training materials for their periodic seminars. He now moved to a larger suite of offices that housed the quorum records and accommodated the administrative staff who would assist him.

Although Elder Kimball now had authority to limit his stake and mission assignments, he did not do so. If anything, he increased them. During an assignment to attend meetings on the east coast in mid-February 1970, he stopped in New York City to consult with Doctor Hayes Martin. During the first interview, Doctor Martin called Doctor Cowan in Salt Lake City to discuss the results of the biopsy the previous October. Doctor Cowan affirmed his conclusion that the new growth was malignant. Doctor Martin said that according to established medical rules, the growth should be removed and the doctor given discretion to perform other surgeries during the operation to the extent deemed necessary. This could have resulted in a complete loss of voice. However, because of "very exceptional reasons" in Elder Kimball's case, the doctor indicated he would not oppose a decision not to undertake further surgery. This forestalled any action as to his throat for twenty months. During that time, except for occasional spells of hoarseness that limited his speaking, Elder Kimball conducted his work in a normal way. He was sustained in his new position at the solemn assembly held as part of general conference in April 1970. This acceptance by the general membership of the Church filled him with enthusiasm and a new sense of purpose. "Again we went to the temple with a long agenda and many things to do," he wrote shortly afterwards. "It was a glorious day with my brethren. My heart is singing." Part of his sense of elation derived from the new freedom he found in setting his own schedule and in exerting greater influence on the work of his quorum. His freedom of action was enhanced when he was released from supervising the work in Great Britain. His replacement was Elder Boyd K. Packer, a longtime associate in his work with the Lamanites, who was sustained as a member of the Twelve at the solemn assembly.

During this period, Elder Kimball was troubled by a decision to discontinue the policy of separate units for cultural minorities. He was afraid Lamanites and others would be intimidated by membership in conventional units and would not have opportunities to serve in leadership positions. He was also concerned that the inability to speak English fluently would be inhibiting to some. He marshalled all the facts, and at a council meeting on July 1, he made a persuasive presentation in support of the previous policy. A committee was appointed to study the matter further. While the initial report of the committee recommended that arrangements for cultural minorities be handled on a ward or stake basis, further discussion resulted in a policy to decide requests for separate units for cultural minorities at the general level on a case-by-case basis.

At the time Elder Kimball was set apart as the acting president of the Twelve, there was bitter agitation nationwide against the Vietnam War. Also, angry criticism was being directed toward the Church because of its policy on priesthood. Much of it originated on university campuses. Shortly before President McKay died, three incidents had dramatized the depth of feeling the issue on priesthood had generated: the president of Stanford University announced that Stanford would discontinue intercollegiate athletic competition with Brigham Young University because of the Church's policy on priesthood; activist Jerry Rubin said in a speech delivered on the campus of the University of Utah that the Church would be destroyed unless the policy was changed; and at a basketball game at Colorado State University in Fort Collins, the school administration allowed a militant black group to hold a public prayer vigil that turned into a condemnation of the Church and in turn caused intimidating action against the BYU team and the Cougarettes, BYU's cheerleading team. These and other circumstances caused Church leaders to seek ways to defuse the controversy and to anticipate and prepare in advance against attacks on the Church rather than to react to them after they had occurred. The first significant step in this direction was taken in February 1970 while Elder Kimball was in New York visiting Doctor Martin. President Lee asked him to join a group of Church leaders and prominent Latter-day Saint businessmen to discuss how the Church could respond to these attacks to the Church. Out of this meeting came initiatives that ultimately resulted in the creation of two new Church departments: the Department of Public Communications (now known as Public Affairs), whose purpose was to apprise the public of the policies, aims, and activities of the Church and to respond to questions raised about the Church and to attacks made on it; and the Department of Internal Communications (now merged into other departments), whose purpose was to coordinate and direct the preparation and distribution of Church instructional materials around the world.

Meanwhile, the attacks on the government because of the war and on the Church because of its policy on the priesthood continued and even accelerated. Interestingly, these two sources of public dissent came together on July 24, 1970, when President Richard M. Nixon paid a courtesy call on the leaders of the Church. When the president arrived at Church headquarters, 47 East South Temple Street, Salt Lake City, thousands of people had gathered to greet him. Also in the crowd were anti-war protesters, some dressed in nondescript garb and carrying provocative signs, and militant blacks whose protests were directed toward the Church leaders who greeted Mr. Nixon on the steps of the Church Administration Building.

Inside, Elder Kimball joined the First Presidency and the Twelve in the First Presidency's council room, where President Nixon briefed them on issues facing the country. Those gathered around the council table included Joseph Fielding Smith and the three men who, in turn, would succeed him as Presidents of the Church: Harold B. Lee,

Spencer W. Kimball, and Ezra Taft Benson. Also present were Latter-day Saints David M. Kennedy and George Romney, members of President Nixon's cabinet. This is one of the few occasions when a president of the United States has personally briefed the Council of the First Presidency and the Quorum of the Twelve.

During the general conference in October 1970, Elder Kimball again was concerned about his physical condition. This time, however, his concern was unrelated to his heart or his voice. The new problem was solved when he underwent prostate surgery on October 26. There was no malignancy. Although he felt good afterward, the doctor insisted he remain in the hospital for six days. After four days, he tired of the inactivity and began wandering the halls, calling on other patients to visit or to bless them if they requested it. One of the patients was President Thorpe B. Isaacson, who occupied an adjoining room and still suffered from the stroke he had had shortly after being called to the First Presidency. He soon was relieved of the anxieties of his condition, passing away quietly less than two weeks after Elder Kimball was released from the hospital.

During early 1971, Elder Kimball was on the road again, visiting Tonga, Samoa, Hawaii, and Fiji in the Pacific, where he held stake conferences and met with missionaries. He also traveled to Mexico for the same purpose. Everywhere he went now, Elder Kimball urged leaders to provide the missionaries necessary to handle the proselyting work in their own countries. He foresaw this as a means of stimulating vigorous growth locally as missionaries returned to their homes to provide leadership.

By July, he was weary. The pressure of fourteen- to fifteen-hour days was increased by threats made against the First Presidency and Elder Kimball by apostate groups. For a while during July, security personnel followed him everywhere. To get away from it all, he and Camilla went to Aptos Beach in California for a vacation. She did not find it restful. "Spencer insisted that we take long vigorous walks,

*Spencer and Camilla
during the 1970s.*

down the beach and over the hills every day. He really pushed us both past what old folks should endure."

Throughout the summer, Elder Kimball had noticed more soreness on one side of his throat. After returning from the beach, he was examined by Doctor Cowan, who thought the cancerous spot detected eighteen months earlier had grown. It was decided to postpone any therapy, however, until the patient returned from the area conference in Manchester, England, scheduled in late August. An intervening crisis would make further postponement necessary.

The Manchester conference, the first of its kind, brought together members of the Church from all over the British Isles. It was to be the model for other area conferences to be held around the world. Technicians had been sent ahead of time to prepare the arena where the main sessions would convene. Elder and Sister Kimball arrived in Manchester on August 26, checking into the Piccadilly Hotel, where members of the official party were staying.

He was told on arrival that a special meeting had been scheduled in a conference room of the hotel that evening. It turned out to be a historically significant gathering. In attendance, among others, were two members of the First Presidency, Joseph Fielding Smith and Harold B. Lee, and seven members of the Twelve: Spencer W. Kimball, Marion G. Romney, Richard L. Evans, Howard W. Hunter, Gordon B. Hinckley, Thomas S. Monson, and Boyd K. Packer. Since a quorum was present, it became an official meeting of the Council of the First Presidency and the Twelve, the first ever held outside the United States. In the early 1840s, official meetings of the Twelve had been held in England when a majority of its members were present, but never before had a meeting of the Council of the First Presidency and the Twelve been held abroad.

After details of the conference were discussed, the Brethren shared testimonies. Elder Kimball, who had reviewed the diaries of Heber C. Kimball before traveling to Manchester, told how his grandfather, twice during a certain day while walking near Preston, was so overwhelmed with emotion he had to go to a nearby stream to wash his face. Unable to understand this phenomenon, he later asked Joseph Smith about it. The Prophet told Heber he was emotionally touched because he was in an area where the Savior had walked and taught, an explanation that lends some credence to ancient traditions about the appearance of Jesus Christ in the British Isles.

Before leaving England, Elder Kimball made another pilgrimage to Preston to ruminate again about the significant events that occurred there at the opening of the work in Great Britain. The fifteen thousand Saints who had assembled in Manchester and the tens of thousands of other British Saints who had migrated to the United States over the intervening years validated the significance of the pioneering work Heber C. Kimball and his associates had performed, work that was a constant spur to the grandson.

Elder Kimball was weary when he returned from

England. Sleep did not restore his energies. He was listless, occasionally dozed off during working hours, and sometimes suffered shortness of breath. Seeing Doctor Russell M. Nelson in the hallway one day, he took him aside and described these symptoms. Doctor Nelson recommended an immediate and thorough physical examination. The results were devastating. "BLACK DAYS," wrote Elder Kimball. "I could die any moment." The prognosis was that unless corrective steps were taken, his life expectancy was five to six years at best. Given his age and physical condition, the chances of successful surgery were fifty-fifty.

Following the October general conference, Doctor Nelson performed a preliminary surgical probe to test and analyze the functioning of the heart. Soon after, Doctor Cowan was alarmed at the condition of Elder Kimball's throat and recommended another biopsy. Two days later, October 15, 1971, the First Presidency urged Spencer and Camilla to go to the coast to spend time at the Laguna Beach cottage, where they could prayerfully sort out the options and decide on a course of action. They were met by Ferron Christensen, the local stake president, who looked after the cottage and who, uncharacteristically for a stake president, was wearing a pink shirt. That evening as the Kimballs talked, Spencer said facetiously that he would like a pink shirt like that before he died. Camilla passed the word to President Christensen, who soon afterward presented Elder Kimball with a bright pink shirt. The apostle was pleased and wore it occasionally at home but never to the office.

After the Kimballs returned from Laguna Beach and consulted with the doctors, heart surgery was deferred until the throat problem had been resolved. The earlier recommendation of a biopsy was abandoned when a series of twenty-four cobalt treatments was administered between November 9 and December 24. After Christmas, the Kimballs returned to Laguna Beach for another stay at what Elder Kimball called "the Home of the Prophets," a home, incidentally, that he insisted be sold after he became the

Spencer W. Kimball, front center, in 1972 when he was serving as acting president of the Quorum of the Twelve. Standing, left to right: Elders Marion G. Romney, Howard W. Hunter, Thomas S. Monson, Boyd K. Packer, Delbert L. Stapley, Marvin J. Ashton, Hugh B. Brown, and LeGrand Richards. Seated: Elders Ezra Taft Benson, Gordon B. Hinckley, Spencer W. Kimball, and Mark E. Petersen.

President of the Church. Apparently he could not reconcile his concept of "lengthen your stride" with the idea of a beach cottage whose main purpose was to provide the prophet with a temporary getaway from the pressures of office. He was adamant that the cottage be sold, even over the gentle remonstrance of his counselors, whose advice he usually followed.

Lowered energy levels restricted Elder Kimball's activities to a minimum during early 1972. He was able to attend and speak at the dedications of the Provo and Ogden, Utah, temples, but it was a great exertion. "I am losing ground," he wrote despondently the last day of February. "Time shortens." By mid-March, it was decided that Elder Kimball's throat condition had normalized to the point at which decisions could be made about heart surgery. A "surgical consultation" was held on the thirteenth, attended by Elder and Sister Kimball, Doctors Russell M. Nelson and Ernest Wilkinson, and Presidents Harold B. Lee and N. Eldon Tanner. "Yes is the answer," Elder Kimball wrote afterward. With the blessing of his brethren, and being prepared to face the odds cited by his doctors, he was prepared to risk his life in the hope of extending it a few more years. The surgery was scheduled to take place after the April general conference, a conference distinguished by the sustaining of Elder Marvin J. Ashton as a member of the Twelve to fill the vacancy caused by the death of Elder Richard L. Evans.

Following the last session of conference, Sunday, April 9, 1972, the Council of the First Presidency and Quorum of the Twelve gathered in the upper room of the temple. There the Brethren conferred a special blessing on Elder Kimball, who was scheduled to undergo open-heart surgery on the twelfth. He entered the hospital the next day. On Tuesday the eleventh, on the eve of the operation, Doctor Russell M. Nelson, who would perform the operation, went to Presidents Harold B. Lee and N. Eldon Tanner for a special blessing. Because President Tanner was scheduled to leave on Thursday for an international trip, the weekly council meeting was held on Wednesday, the day of the surgery. President Lee left the council room during the meeting to take a telephone call. On returning, he said in a quavering voice, "The Lord has heard and answered our prayers; the operation on Spencer was a success." It was one of the few times President Lee openly manifested deep emotion.

The Brethren were elated with the announcement, assuming all was well with the patient and that he would soon return to his place in the circle and resume his responsibilities. But how was it with the patient? He went through a most stressful period. There were the pain and discomfort that followed the surgery, bouts of depression, uncertainty about whether he would recover, and nagging feelings of guilt because he was not doing his job. Aware of his turmoil, the First Presidency persuaded him and Camilla to go to Laguna Beach again, which they did in early June. When the Brethren received word through Camilla that Spencer was restless and sometimes agitated because of inactivity and being out of the loop, President and Sister Lee traveled to Laguna Beach, where they spent the weekend of June 17 and 18. President Lee carefully briefed Elder Kimball about everything of significance going on at Church headquarters, which greatly revived his spirits. They lagged again, however, when later he awakened to find that one side of his face was paralyzed. Remembering his experience as a boy, he assumed it was another attack of Bell's palsy. The doctor, however, shocked him when he diagnosed it as a stroke. This, on top of everything else, would have been a crushing blow. He had seen how President Isaacson's stroke had rendered him incapable of doing his work. However, that depressing diagnosis was soon changed. The effects of the Bell's palsy, which apparently was indeed the illness causing his facial paralysis, were only temporary and soon disappeared as they had done before.

Soon after he returned from Laguna Beach, Elder Kimball's life and career entered a new phase. On Sunday, July 2, 1972, President Joseph Fielding Smith quietly passed away, only a few days before his ninety-sixth birthday. Five days later, following the funeral, the First Presidency was reorganized. President Harold B. Lee was sustained and ordained as the eleventh President of the Church. He selected N. Eldon Tanner and Marion G. Romney as his counselors. Elder Kimball was sustained and set apart as the president of the Quorum of the Twelve.

This change in status did not greatly affect Elder Kimball's work in the Quorum of the Twelve, except that now general reports of the activities of the quorum were made to the First Presidency at the weekly council meetings in the temple rather than to President Lee, as had been the case when Elder Kimball was acting president of the Twelve.

Before President Smith died, arrangements had been made to hold an area conference in Mexico City. President Kimball joined the official party, which traveled there the last of August. Included in the official party were Elder Bruce R. McConkie of the First Council of the Seventy and his wife, Amelia, one of President Smith's daughters. After the conference, Elder McConkie was called to the Quorum of the Twelve, filling the vacancy caused by the call of Marion G. Romney as a counselor in the First Presidency. Elder McConkie was sustained as a member of the Twelve at the October general conference and afterward was ordained and set apart. At the time, this junior member of the Twelve was fifty-seven years old, tall, powerful, athletic, and in robust health. The senior member of his quorum, President Spencer W. Kimball, was twenty years older than Elder McConkie, was recovering from open-heart surgery, was still suffering the effects of throat cancer, had recently suffered another attack of Bell's palsy that had affected his hearing, and not too long before had undergone major abdominal surgery. How curious it is that President Kimball outlived his vigorous young colleague.

President Kimball made another lengthy trip to the Orient in March 1973. While at a conference meeting in Fukuoka, Japan, he reflected that there were only forty-five Japanese missionaries in all the Japanese missions. "I seemed to see a vision," he wrote, "of the future from 45 to 450 . . . and maybe thousands of Japanese missionaries, joined by large numbers of Korean missionaries moving to Manchuria, Siberia, China, and westward to Moscow to join thousands from the islands, Australia, New Zealand, Philippines to attack the great Asian countries with the gospel, and . . . all of these missionaries, moving westward and meeting the thousands of missionaries from America and Western Europe to proselyte . . . Eastern Europe and Russia." This foreshadowed the determined missionary effort he would soon launch after becoming the President of the Church.

The following August, President Kimball joined the official party attending the area conference in Munich, Germany. Afterward, he held special meetings in Brussels, Amsterdam, Hamburg, and Stuttgart before returning home. And three months later, he and Camilla traveled to South Africa, where they toured the mission, holding the usual meetings with members and missionaries. They returned home by way of Rio de Janeiro, where several meetings were held with the Brazilian Saints.

This ended President Kimball's world travels before he became the head of the Church. They had taken him to all parts of the earth except those under communist domination. They had given him insights into people and places and into the global operation of the Church. He was ready for the call that he had assumed would never come to him.

Chapter 22

President of the Church

Present Spencer W. Kimball never thought he would outlive President Harold B. Lee. He was four years older than his friend and had suffered serious, life-threatening illnesses, major surgeries, and numerous minor physical problems. Had he known the details of President Lee's condition, he might have thought differently. But he didn't know and therefore assumed he would go first. When President Lee died unexpectedly on December 26, 1973, President Kimball was shocked.

Earlier in the evening, President Lee's secretary, D. Arthur Haycock, had called to say President Lee lay critically ill in the hospital. He had gone there for a routine physical checkup. Later he had become seriously ill, and when Arthur called, he was near death. President Kimball rushed to the hospital to find the patient's room crowded with doctors, nurses, and medical equipment. All the efforts to save President Lee failed. He died about 9:00 P.M.

At the moment of President Lee's death, Spencer W. Kimball, who until then had been the president of the

President Kimball delivering an address at general conference, 1973.

Twelve, instantly became the head of the Church. He was made acutely aware of this when, following the announcement of President Lee's passing, Marion G. Romney, second counselor in the First Presidency, turned to President Kimball and asked for direction. So well established had the process of succession in the presidency become that all the Brethren understood and accepted it without question or discussion.

"President Lee is gone," said President Kimball at the funeral. "I never thought it would happen. I sincerely wanted it not to happen. I doubt if anyone in the Church has prayed harder and more consistently for a long life for President Lee than my Camilla and myself." These sentiments were not feigned. President Kimball felt a genuine sense of inadequacy, reflected in his reference to President Lee as a "giant" and to himself as a "pygmy." Such disarming frankness magnified his character in the eyes of the people, while perhaps blinding them to his immense potential.

When the reorganization of the First Presidency took place on December 30, 1973, in the upper room of the temple, President Kimball was ordained and set apart as the twelfth President of the Church. He selected N. Eldon Tanner and Marion G. Romney as his counselors. President Ezra Taft Benson became the president of the Quorum of the Twelve. At the press conference the next day, President Kimball gave no hint of the determined action he would take later to advance the Church and motivate its members. He endorsed the work of his predecessors and said he would emphasize the home, the family, and the training of youth, while promoting missionary service. Questioners were told that he was in relatively good health, that women who could do so should give priority to child rearing, and that the Church policy on priesthood would not change unless by revelation.

President Kimball found his new duties more demanding than he expected. The enormous volume of meetings, correspondence, invitations to speak, and requests for interviews was burdensome. Many issues came to him for final decision, and the fact that he was the final arbiter created a sense of isolation and aloneness. It also increased his dependence on divine direction and sharpened his spiritual sensitivities. One night his father appeared to him in a dream or a vision. Another time he awoke with a sense that President Harold B. Lee was in the room. Both experiences gave him feelings of comfort and an assurance that he was not alone.

For some time President Kimball had suffered some impairment in the hearing in his left ear. So in early February 1974, he traveled to Los Angeles to be operated on by an ear specialist. However, the doctor was reluctant to operate, because the prophet's blood had been thinned so much because of his heart condition that he bled easily and excessively. The doctor asked him to return in a month for further examination. The patient was too busy to return and never went back.

President Kimball unveiled the first phase of his prophetic initiative on April 4, 1974. The prophetic mantle clearly fell on President Kimball that day as he spoke to the General Authorities and regional representatives of the Twelve. He outlined an ambitious program for strengthening the stakes and accelerating the missionary effort. He envisioned that stakes and missions in foreign countries would soon begin to provide more than enough missionaries to proselyte their own people so that, for example, missionaries from Mexico might be sent to Indonesia and missionaries from England be sent to Australia, and so on. He urged stakes to take a more aggressive approach to the task of involving less-active members, and he told the story of a man who whipped his friend who was freezing to death and thereby saved his life by getting his circulation going again.

His presentation was illustrated by a large map of the world with colored strings tying country with country, visually demonstrating the unity and linked relationships among Church units around the world. President Kimball also sounded his call to the members of the Church to lengthen their stride, to leave the plateau on which they had rested too long and move upward in a significant way. The effect was electrifying. If anyone had the mistaken idea that his would be a caretaker administration, this presentation dispelled it. Everyone present became aware that a new prophet was at the helm, prepared to lead the Church in new ways and along new paths dictated by his experience and his inspiration. His new role was confirmed and finalized two days later when he was sustained as the Presiding High Priest and the President of the Church at a solemn assembly held in the Salt Lake Tabernacle.

President Kimball's itinerary for the coming year demonstrated what he meant by a lengthened stride.

Instead of a single area conference, as was held during each of the three preceding years, he scheduled seven—in Scandinavia, São Paulo, Buenos Aires, Tokyo, Manila, Taipei, and Seoul. He explained the reason justifying these conferences. "This church belongs to the people," said he, "so we bring the conferences to you. We want people to stay where they are and build Zion." This was consistent with practices the leaders of the Church had followed for several decades, practices that would see their most effective application during the administration of President Kimball. During the restored Church's first century, the admonition of leaders to new converts was to gather to America, the land of Zion. Here the center stakes were to be built solidly before rebounding to establish stakes around the world. Then, as the Church became an effective international organization, the call would be for converts to gather to spiritual Zion within stakes either inside or outside the United States. This was the key message given at the first area conference in Manchester, England, in 1971, dramatized by the concluding musical number "This Is Our Place," composed by local members.

At the regional representatives' seminar held in October 1974, President Kimball expanded on the talk given at the April seminar. In his keynote address, "Lengthening Our Stride," he focused on his recurring theme of accelerating missionary work. He called for more and better-trained missionaries. He was anxious to see more missionaries called from outside the U.S. He saw in this a means both of expanding missionary work and of laying the groundwork for stronger leadership abroad in the next generation. Then in his address during the first general session of the conference, he touched on more than a dozen subjects of importance. These included a campaign to clean up homes and farms, the coming election, a warning against polygamist cults, the Word of Wisdom, Sabbath shopping, card playing, food storage, the virtues of work, frugality, living within our means, the evils of blasphemy and profanity, avoidance of

President Kimball leading scripture study with members of the Kimball family during the 1970s.

pornography, the destructive effects of abortion and adultery, the disturbing trend toward sameness in the appearance of the sexes, and the shrewd and evil influence of satanic forces. This address signaled to the world a fixed determination to adhere to the high standards of conduct for which the Church had become noted.

Shortly after the October general conference, President Kimball was distressed when he was served with a subpoena to give a deposition in a case brought by the National Association for the Advancement of Colored People against the Boy Scouts of America and Troop 58, organized in one of the wards of the Liberty Stake in Salt Lake City. There were two black Scouts in the troop. One of them complained to the black ombudsman for Utah because he was deprived of the chance to become the senior patrol leader of his troop because of the Church procedure that the senior patrol leader had to be the deacons quorum president. It was contended that this violated the young man's civil rights. This procedure had been put into effect as part of the effort to bring about more complete coordination and correlation between the priesthood and the activity programs for young men. While the Church was not a party to the suit, the Church's practice was a key issue in the litigation. It was for this reason the subpoena was issued to President Kimball. And because it was a subpoena *duces tecum,* he was directed to bring to the deposition every document relating to the Church's policy withholding the priesthood from blacks. Because he had had little to do with litigation during his life and was uncertain about what faced him, President Kimball was distraught. He could not sleep. He could talk of little else in the meetings with his counselors. Long sessions were held with the First Presidency, the Twelve, and the Presiding Bishopric where the implications of the suit and the subpoena were considered at length. The Brethren were reluctant to change the procedure because it served an important need to coordinate the priesthood and activity programs. Yet they also were reluctant to sever connections with the Boy Scouts of America, ending a relationship that had lasted amicably and profitably for both parties for more than sixty years. After prayerful deliberation it was decided to change the Scouting procedure in Church-sponsored troops so as not to require that the senior patrol leader also be the deacons quorum president. This removed the basis for the suit and it was soon dismissed, much to the relief of President Kimball. He had found that the subpoena so dominated his thoughts he was unable to focus on anything else for long. And there was much to do.

The seven area conferences President Kimball conducted through August 1975 allowed him opportunities to strengthen the themes he had identified in the October 1974 general conference, as well as themes peculiar to local conditions. He admonished the members to lengthen their

Spencer and Camilla at an area conference, 1975.

stride by developing greater faith, obedience, and diligence; by preparing their children for missions and temple marriage; by becoming active in civic and political affairs; and by reaching out to share the gospel with neighbors and friends. Occasionally, if he detected any sense of laxity or obstinacy in his listeners, he would speak out forcefully. "We are not playing games," he would say. "This is serious business." He made it clear that he wanted every worthy and qualified young man to fill a mission. And if there were temporary reasons why one was not qualified, he urged that one become qualified.

President Kimball continued to hold area conferences for five more years, the last being a series of conferences held in the Far East during October 1980. During the interim, he was in the South Pacific twice; in the British Isles again; in Europe, Central America, Hawaii, South Africa, and Canada; and in South America twice. He also held a series of area conferences in the United States, in Texas; Illinois; Wisconsin; Washington, D.C.; Georgia; New York; Missouri; Florida; and Michigan.

Arranging for an area conference entailed much planning. Once the general itinerary was decided on, travel schedules and hotel reservations were arranged and meetings were set. In consultation with local leaders, adequate security and transportation to and from the meetings were provided for the prophet. President Kimball carefully reviewed everything before leaving Salt Lake City. If he discovered large gaps of time between meetings or appointments, he wanted to know why. If he learned that the reason was to provide time for relaxation or a nap, he usually insisted the gaps be filled with meetings or interviews. He was relentless. This was an area where he would not take counsel. He continued to drive full speed ahead, rejecting any suggestion to ease up or to provide any latitude in his schedule. He seemed to have the absolute determination to spend himself in service. And the example of an eighty-year-old man who spoke in a whisper because of cancer of the throat, who had recently undergone open-heart surgery and major abdominal surgery, who had a hearing problem, who stood at the head of a family, and who carried the burdens of a worldwide church—the example of such a man driving at full speed lent powerful force to his injunction to "lengthen your stride."

President Kimball had an interesting interpretation of the term *rest* as used in the scriptures, which he explained at the general priesthood session in October 1975. He said the word was not synonymous with relaxation but rather pertained to the feelings of joy and satisfaction one receives from doing his duty. It was this concept that caused the prophet to speak out against Sunday afternoon naps. He believed the time could be better spent studying the scriptures, visiting the sick, preparing Sunday School lessons, or holding family council meetings. Sleeping was out of the question. He was even heard to say that he looked forward to the time when the temples would be open around the clock to enable the Saints, in shifts, to be continuously performing vicarious work for the dead.

Those who accompanied President Kimball on these trips naturally shared in the vigor and excitement of his schedule. His entourage usually included Camilla, a secretary, a security man, a personal physician, and several General Authorities and their companions. It is suspected that most of them were exhausted when they returned. Not the prophet.

In March 1976, for example, President Kimball and his party returned from the South Pacific one night at about 8:30 P.M. He was at the First Presidency meeting at 8:00 A.M. the following morning and attended the meeting of all General Authorities at 9:00 A.M. in the temple. He had caught a bad cold while he was gone and was very hoarse that day, so he asked President Romney to conduct the meeting in the temple. President Tanner said that Doctor Russell M. Nelson, who went along as the prophet's personal physician, told him that he had learned one important thing during the tour—that the article of faith that states that we believe in being subject to kings, presidents, rulers, etc., does not include doctors.

Often these trips included visits with local dignitaries and meetings with the press. President Kimball disliked this aspect of the work. He once explained that it was contrary to his nature and inclinations to participate in these formalities but that he was willing to do so if the Brethren felt that it would help advance the work.

The prophet's antipathy toward media interviews was illustrated during his trip to Great Britain in the summer of 1976. In London he granted a personal interview to a radio talk show host for one of the local stations. The host's questions focused mainly on the issues of prophetic infallibility and the priesthood. At a press conference that followed, the reporters centered their attention on a scandal involving a Latter-day Saint politician in the United States, the Howard Hughes will, and the Church's policy on the priesthood. These, of course, were the "hot" issues that the media representatives were most interested in, but they were not the things the President would have preferred to discuss.

During this trip he conducted separate area conferences in London and Manchester, England, and Glasgow, Scotland. The party was driven from London to Manchester on a chartered bus. The original schedule would have taken the bus through Stratford-upon-Avon to enable the travelers to visit the home of William Shakespeare and other points of historic and cultural interest. No one was surprised, however, when, en route, the schedule was changed so as to bypass Stratford-upon-Avon. Instead, President Kimball decided to save time to enable him to attend a special gathering in Preston prior to the organization of the Preston stake.

At Manchester, the party was joined by several others, including Bishop H. Burke Peterson and his wife, Brookie, and mission president Royden G. Derrick and his wife, Allie. President Derrick was later called to the Seventy. Also on the bus were representatives of the *Daily Mail*, the British Broadcasting Company, and the *Church News*. En route to Preston, President Derrick distributed copies of a brochure he had prepared, entitled *Truth Will Prevail*, which told the story of the first missionary effort in England, extracted from the journals of Heber C. Kimball and Joseph Fielding.

President Kimball had visited Preston several times before. This visit had special meaning, however, because of plans to organize the Preston England Stake. Although the work in England started in Preston in 1837, it was one of the last areas in the country to be included within the boundaries of an organized stake.

Arriving in Preston, the party went first to the River Ribble, where the first baptisms in England were performed by Mormon missionaries. Assembled there were a number of local people, adults and children, attired in the dress customarily worn in 1837. After a session of picture taking, the members of the party again boarded the bus and were driven around Preston, visiting places of historic interest to the Church—a building on Wilfred Street reported to stand on the site of the building where Heber C. Kimball and his associates witnessed a frightening display of satanic power; Vauxhall Chapel; the Cockpit; and the Preston Market Place. With these things in mind, and doubtless others gleaned from a study of his grandfather's journals, President Kimball led the party to nearby Blackburn, where the meeting to organize the Preston stake was held. There was not a building large enough in Preston to accommodate the crowd of over eight hundred who attended the meeting.

Elder Mark E. Petersen of the Twelve had preceded President Kimball to Preston. There he had conducted interviews and had made tentative decisions about the composition of the stake presidency, which would consist of Eric Cryer, president, and Brothers Trebilcock and Bishop, counselors. The prophet reviewed and approved what Elder Petersen had done, and Elder Petersen then conducted the business portion of the meeting. Following talks by the new leaders, Sister Kimball, Elders Bernard P. Brockbank and Robert D. Hales, and Bishop Peterson, President Kimball was the concluding speaker. It was an emotional and historic occasion for the prophet as he, in a sense, put the capstone on the work started in England by his grandfather 139 years before. The President spoke for over an hour, tracing the missionary activities of Heber C. Kimball, enjoining the members to support the missionary cause, declaring that the Church was established in the last days in fulfillment of Daniel's interpretation of the king's dream, and exhorting the members to seek exaltation by learning and living the principles of the gospel.

President Kimball elaborated on the same themes in his major addresses delivered at the area conferences in

Manchester, London, and Glasgow—on the need for more missionaries and for the members to put on the whole armor of God by being chaste, paying an honest tithe, keeping the Sabbath day holy, and regularly holding family prayer and family home evenings. However, in Glasgow he bore down much more strongly than he had previously done in admonishing the members to fulfill missions and to put on the whole armor of God. When, for example, he enjoined parents to prepare their sons for missions, he declared, raising his whispery voice to its highest pitch, "Every worthy boy should fill a mission, *every* one." Similarly, when he urged the regular holding of family home evening, he whispered out the injunction that they should be held every Monday night, *every* one. Then, after ticking off the different commandments and principles he expected the members to keep, he added with vigorous finality, "We are not fooling; this is no game; this is *exceedingly* important."

It is difficult to assess the full impact of these area conferences. It is safe to say, however, that no other President had spoken directly and personally to so many members of the Church in most parts of the world about things of fundamental importance to the Church and its members. And it is clear that the image of honesty, sincerity, and dedication he projected unfailingly had a positive impact upon his listeners. Moreover, the power of the messages he delivered had a motivating, elevating effect on his audiences, encouraging if not provoking them to live better lives and to be more active in Church work. More important than these things, however, was the inspiring impact he had on others merely because he was the prophet, the mouthpiece of God on the earth. This aspect of his influence was most clearly revealed at the London area conference. The Esso Hotel, where the prophet stayed, is adjacent to the Wembley Centre, where the meetings were held. However, because of the crowding, it was necessary to travel back and forth by bus. At the end of each session of the area conference, the

Saints thronged around the President to get a good glimpse of him, to shake his hand, to say a word to him, or in some instances, to plant a fraternal kiss on the cheek. It was touching at the end of the second session to see the looks of love, awe, and excitement on the faces of the men, women, and children who crowded around the bus merely to touch the hand of the President, who had extended it out of a small front window as he waited for the bus to get under way.

Beyond the impact these conferences had on the members of the Church, they also had a compelling effect on President Kimball. They buoyed him up and gave him the incentive to go forward despite his many physical disabilities.

Still another affliction loomed a few months after the prophet returned from Great Britain. He learned that cataracts were impairing his sight. The doctor recommended that they be removed. Yet this resilient man moved from one physical crisis to the other without complaint, without fanfare, without a break in his lengthened stride. At times it seemed as if some malignant fate were trying to stop the voice, the eyes, the ears, and the heart of God's mouthpiece. But he paid little attention to his ailments. Shortly after his cataracts were discovered, he went to Florida to see the BYU football team play in the Tangerine Bowl. Never at ease, never in neutral gear, never balked or baffled, he was constantly in motion, constantly trying to improve, to remedy faults, to stimulate others, to banish inertia and sloth, to convert the world, to prepare a community of Saints worthy to receive the Lord at his second coming.

In a further effort to anchor Church members to their home countries, President Kimball inaugurated an extensive program of temple building so the temple ordinances would be readily available to members living outside the United States. During his administration, twenty-six temples were either dedicated or rededicated. Many of these were smaller temples, as in Tonga, Samoa, and Tahiti. Regardless of their size, the prophet looked on all temples with reverence. "A temple," wrote he, "is the Lord's house, and when we enter his house, we enter as his guests. Thus, we should do everything possible to keep the Lord's house holy, unpolluted, clean, and sweet." (*Ensign*, Jan. 1977, p. 6.) He was insistent that those who enter the temple meet high standards. "Because of the sacred nature of the endowment and the other ordinances performed in the temple," he wrote, "those who go to the temple to receive them must be prepared and worthy. People who are converted to the Church often feel enthusiastic about going to the temple immediately after their baptism. But it takes time for them to adjust their lives so that they are prepared and worthy when they do attend the temple. Thus, we have counseled stake presidents and bishops not to recommend people to go to the temple to receive their endowments until they are sufficiently mature in the gospel." (Ibid.) And the prophet looked on temples as workplaces, not merely as sanctuaries for contemplation. "In the book of Revelation," he told the audience at the dedication of the Fair Oaks California stake center on October 9, 1976, "it speaks of serving the Lord 'day and night in his temple.' (Revelation 7:15.) So I am looking forward to the day when a temple will not close. They won't have any holidays, ever, and there won't be any night or day. The temple will have its lights on all night long and will be going night and day and full all the time. When vacation time comes, they [will] let people go on vacations but they [won't] let the temple go on vacation."

This is but another manifestation of President Kimball's ingrained attitudes toward the principle that dominated his life, the principle of work. Such manifestations were numerous and diverse. Mention already has been made of his novel interpretation of the word *rest* and of his stricture against Sunday afternoon naps. His preference in music for songs like "Put Your Shoulder to the Wheel" (*Hymns*, no. 252) and "Have I Done Any Good?" (*Hymns*, no. 223) reflected his bias. And when preparations were being made to republish the hymnbook, he insisted that in "I Am a Child of God" the phrase "teach me all that I should know" be changed to "teach me all that I should do." To him mere knowledge was sterile unless it was wedded with work—hard, productive work. We have President Kimball to thank for the fact that the hymn "In Our Lovely Deseret" was included in the hymnbook when it was republished. Aside from the nostalgic memories of his childhood that the song evoked with its repeated chorus of "hark, hark, hark," he strongly endorsed the sentiment of the final stanza in the hymn: "That with all their mind and might they may love him and may learn to do his will."

It is undoubtedly true that the action President Kimball took on May 10, 1978, was dictated in large part by his desire to avoid any implication that he spent time lolling around on the beach. On that day, against the strong recommendation of his counselors to the contrary, he directed the sale of the Laguna Beach, California, cottage that had been used for several decades by Presidents of the Church as a hideaway where they could spend a few quiet, uninterrupted days away from the pressures of their calling. President Kimball had used the cottage off and on for several years. One wonders why he decided to dispose of it after more than four years in office. It is suspected the reason was tied up with the area conferences he was holding. Everywhere he went throughout the world, he admonished Church members to lengthen their stride, to quicken their pace, and to extend their reach. These words and his hectic schedule were, to him, incompatible with the idea of spending time on the beach. The conflict was easily resolved by selling the cottage.

Of all the temples dedicated during his tenure, perhaps the most significant one to President Kimball was the Jordan River Temple. Several things underscored its significance: it was the first temple constructed in the Salt Lake Valley since pioneer days; it was financed entirely by member donations; modern technology was utilized in the presentations within the temple; and the temple's name conjured up images of

President Kimball, Camilla, and family in front of the Laird Drive home in Salt Lake City, 1977.

the Holy Land. It was President Kimball who insisted on the name despite negative reactions from some who were concerned that the deteriorated condition of the Jordan River and its environs would detract from the sanctity of the temple. President Kimball predicted this would not be so and that the temple, bearing that name, would alter the public perception of the Jordan River, a prediction which has proven to be true. An additional significance attached to the Jordan River Temple was the unconventional ground breaking on June 9, 1979. After he had delivered the main address and offered a dedicatory prayer, President Kimball mounted a giant Caterpillar tractor and, manipulating the controls, moved a huge shovelful of dirt. At this, resounding applause went up from the more than ten thousand people who had gathered for the ceremony. When the temple was dedicated on November 16, 1981, President Kimball attended in a wheelchair, as did President Tanner. In the interval between the ground breaking and the dedication, President Kimball underwent three head operations. The dedication was the first public meeting he had attended since September 5, 1981, when the last of these three surgeries had been performed.

Accompanying the effort to establish the Church globally by means of the area conferences and the construction of temples worldwide were steps to decentralize some authority and responsibility. Stake presidents, for instance, were authorized to ordain bishops and patriarchs. And before the First Quorum of the Seventy was reestablished, stake presidents were authorized to call and ordain seventies and to call and set apart the presidents of seventies quorums. Area presidencies were organized and given broad authority to direct the work within their areas. And general auxiliary conferences were discontinued while area, regional, and stake auxiliary gatherings were encouraged.

Meanwhile, in order to lift the spirituality of priesthood leaders and to instruct them in their duties, President Kimball organized fifty-eight solemn assemblies for priesthood leaders in the United States and Canada, held over a period of several years. At these meetings, which were held in temples when possible, counsel was given about special issues facing the Church: abortion, gambling, incest, homosexuality, adultery, apostates, and child and spouse abuse, among others. Highlights of a solemn assembly were the administration of the sacrament by the General Authorities, special counsel given by members of the First Presidency and the Twelve, and testimony bearing.

These activities entailed extensive travel and many absences from home. President Kimball took them all in stride while maintaining a positive, exuberant attitude. His work was seasoned with occasional flashes of good humor. As he and a companion returned from one assignment, the flight attendant asked them if they wanted a cocktail. When they declined, she asked, "Well, would you like some tea, or coffee, or perhaps a Coke?" Receiving a negative response, she said almost with disbelief, "Gentlemen, is there *anything* I can get for you?" President Kimball spoke up, "Do you have a little lemonade?" "No," she said, "but I could squeeze you a little." Raising his hands in mock defense, President Kimball answered, "Don't you dare touch me." This was accompanied by the quiet, lyrical chuckle that was so much a part of his personality.

President Kimball's sense of humor also was reflected in an encounter he had with a highway patrolman. The officer saw a car driving without lights on State Street in Salt Lake City. He pulled the car over and on approaching saw that President Kimball was the driver. "Sir," he said, "did you know you were driving with your lights off?" "Yes," he answered, "I just noticed it." "President Kimball," he said, "please let me see your driver's license." "I was in hopes you wouldn't recognize me," President Kimball said. "I was in hopes it wouldn't be you," the officer said. Writing out only a warning ticket, he handed it to President Kimball, who said, "Now, young man, do not fail, merely because of my position in the Church, to give me a ticket if I deserve one." Said the officer, "All right, President Kimball, if you insist." "I don't insist," President Kimball said. All the while this was going on, Sister Kimball sat chuckling on the passenger side of the front seat.

As Church growth spiraled and the number of local units multiplied, the need to expand and streamline the headquarters organizations became urgent. For many years, there had been discussions about activating the First Quorum of the Seventy, a body defined by the Doctrine and Covenants as being "equal in authority to that of the Twelve special witnesses or Apostles." (D&C 107:26.) The discussions ended at the October 1975 general conference, when President Kimball announced that the First Quorum of the Seventy had been reconstituted. Charles Didier, William R. Bradford, and George P. Lee were presented and sustained as members of the Seventy to serve with the other seven presidents of the quorum. At the following general conference in April 1976, four additional members of the Seventy were presented and sustained: Carlos E. Asay, M. Russell Ballard, John H. Groberg, and Jacob de Jager. That this

President Kimball with counselors at general conference, about 1977.

group included men who previously had been ordained high priests ended a long-standing discussion regarding whether high priests could be called as seventies. Finally, at the October general conference in 1976, all of the Assistants to the Twelve were sustained as members of the First Quorum of the Seventy. Thus were in place the three governing quorums of the Church: the First Presidency, the Twelve, and the Seventy, which, with the Presiding Bishopric, were prepared to direct the rapid growth of the Church.

Another organizational change was made in March 1982, designed to streamline Church administration worldwide. Three supervisory groups were created at Church headquarters: the missionary, the priesthood, and the temple and genealogy (later family history) executive councils. Each council included three members of the Twelve, two presidents of the Seventy, and a member of the Presiding Bishopric. Grouped under each council were related departments and activities at headquarters that were to report through the executive councils to the Council of the First Presidency and the Quorum of the Twelve. To each

291

council fell the responsibility to oversee various areas of the world, working through the area presidencies and subject to the ultimate control of the First Presidency and the Twelve.

Though these were important steps needed to strengthen the fast-growing Church, they were overshadowed by the action taken by President Kimball on June 9, 1978, when he made the priesthood available to all worthy male members of the Church. Such an action had been discussed for decades. Until President Kimball acted, however, the discussions always ended as they had in the early 1960s during President David O. McKay's tenure. At that time, as already noted, numerous letters were received from Nigeria and Ghana in West Africa, pleading for the Church to send missionaries. The Brethren refrained from granting these requests. Instead, they sent literature and equipment and urged the people to be patient and prayerful. President McKay noted in his diary that the issue facing the Church was not unlike the issue that faced the first apostles over whether the gospel should be taken to the Gentiles. The earlier issue was resolved when Peter baptized the gentile household of Cornelius after receiving the extraordinary vision recorded in the tenth chapter of Acts. President McKay said the issue regarding the priesthood would be resolved only in the same way—namely, by a revelation from heaven. It remained for President Spencer W. Kimball to fulfill that prediction many years later.

While he and his brethren had talked about the priesthood restriction often and had speculated as to when the Lord would lift it, President Kimball did not begin to focus on it intensely until more than a year before the revelation was announced. Several factors seem to have prompted him to do so: he had genuine concern for those affected by the restriction, a concern intensified by his experiences in South America; he was concerned about the conflict between the restrictions on priesthood and his admonition that members join in prayer that the doors of all nations be opened to the preaching of the gospel; and he was concerned about administrative complications leaders would face in Brazil, when the temple was completed in São Paulo, in determining qualifications for temple recommends, given the uncertainties about ethnic origins in that country. These and other grave issues drove President Kimball to his knees, seeking a spiritual solution to a problem of tangled complexity.

A string of related events provides insight into the lengthy process by which President Kimball received the revelation he sought. His concern for those deprived of priesthood blessings due to racial origin was typified by his concern for Helvécio Martins, a black member of the Church in Rio de Janeiro. Brother Martins, who would later be called to the Second Quorum of the Seventy, joined the Church several years before the revelation on priesthood. In 1977, while serving as the public communications director for the Church in Brazil, he attended the cornerstone laying of the São Paulo Temple. President Kimball motioned to Helvécio, who was in the audience, to take a seat beside him on the stand. Through an interpreter, he told Brother Martins that if he remained faithful, no blessing of the Church would be withheld from him. Later that year, one of the General Authorities assigned to a stake conference in Rio de Janeiro contacted Helvécio and said President Kimball wanted to be sure Helvécio understood the implications of what President Kimball had said at the cornerstone laying ceremony. Helvécio said he understood. (Conversation of author with Elder Martins.)

Meanwhile, President Kimball had begun to discuss the priesthood question with his brethren and to pray for spiritual direction. This included fervent and frequent prayers alone in the Salt Lake Temple. On March 23, 1978, President Kimball advised his counselors that he had had a wakeful night struggling with the question of priesthood restrictions and felt they should be lifted. No action was taken at the time. On April 20, 1978, the prophet advised the Twelve of his prayerful efforts to receive divine guidance on the issue and asked them to join him and his counselors in their prayers to that end. There followed personal interviews between President Kimball and members of the Twelve to discuss the matter. President Kimball continued to spend many hours alone in the temple, imploring the Lord for guidance.

On May 4, 1978, following a council meeting, Elder LeGrand Richards asked President Kimball for the privilege of saying a few words. He told the Brethren that during the meeting, he had seen a personage seated in a chair on the organ. He said he thought it was President Wilford Woodruff. "He was dressed in a white suit and was seated in an armchair," reported Elder Richards. "I thought at the time that the reason I was privileged to see him was probably that I was the only one there who had ever seen President Woodruff while he was upon the earth. I had heard him dedicate the Salt Lake Temple and I had heard him give his last sermon in the Salt Lake Tabernacle before he died." (Lucile C. Tate, *LeGrand Richards: Beloved Apostle,* p. 292.) The significance and timing of this appearance are apparent. Here, appearing through the veil in the upper room of the temple, was the prophet who, almost a hundred years before, had wrestled with a critical problem, plural marriage, which was resolved by revelation, the same way the problem President Kimball faced would be resolved.

The week following this incident, President Kimball again spent several hours alone in the Salt Lake Temple, asking the Lord for guidance. On Tuesday, May 30, 1978, President Kimball read to his counselors a tentative statement he had written in longhand removing all priesthood restrictions from blacks except those restrictions as to worthiness that rest upon all alike. He said that he had a "good, warm feeling" about it. There was a lengthy review of the statements of past leaders about the restrictions on blacks. It was decided that this aspect of the matter should be researched in detail. Elder G. Homer Durham, who was serving as the Church historian, was asked to do this. Also, the luncheon in the temple for the following Thursday was canceled. Instead of eating lunch, the Brethren were asked to fast and pray that the Lord would make his mind and will clear in this matter.

On Thursday, June 1, 1978, following the meeting of all General Authorities, the First Presidency and the Twelve (Elders Mark E. Petersen and Delbert L. Stapley were absent) counseled for two hours about the restrictions on the priesthood. Each member of the council expressed himself freely on the subject. In the discussion, the feeling was unanimous that the time had come to lift the restrictions. And following the prayer at the end of the meeting, which was offered by President Kimball, several present mentioned the powerful, confirming spirit they felt.

On Wednesday, June 7, 1978, President Kimball advised his counselors that through inspiration he had decided to lift the restrictions on priesthood. At that time, letters were read from three members of the Twelve, which President Kimball had requested, containing suggested wording for the public announcement of the decision. Using these three letters as a base, a fourth statement was prepared and then reviewed, edited, and approved by the First Presidency. This document was taken to the council meeting with the Twelve on Thursday, June 8, 1978. At this meeting, President Kimball advised the Twelve that he had received the inspiration to make the priesthood available to all worthy male members of the Church, whereupon the document was read and, with minor editorial changes, was approved. Later in the day Elder Mark E. Petersen approved by telephone from South America, and Elder Delbert L. Stapley approved when President Kimball visited him in the hospital. The statement, of course, was merely a memorandum of the revelation President Kimball had received by the spiritual means already described.

The next day, Friday, June 9, 1978, all the General Authorities who were in the city and available assembled at 7:00 A.M. President Kimball announced the decision to lift priesthood restrictions, had the statement read, and invited the comments of the Brethren. All sustained the decision and approved the statement. The members of the Seventy who were out of the city on assignment were advised of the decision by telephone. Following the meeting, the statement was released to the press.

The reaction to the announcement was prompt and, with a few exceptions, was overwhelmingly positive. Within minutes after the news hit the street, the telephones in the First Presidency's office began to ring, and they rang incessantly for hours. There were hundreds of calls, calls from England, from Hawaii, from Florida, from Maine, and from countless points in between, calls (but for two isolated exceptions) that expressed feelings of exuberant joy.

The announcement of this revelation irrevocably altered the future of the Church. Its impact was felt almost immediately in the missions of the Church. During the first full year after the revelation, convert baptisms were up almost 20 percent. Two years later, that rate of growth had almost doubled. The growth was most pronounced in South America, Mexico, and the Caribbean. In Brazil, for instance, of the 1989 membership of more than 300,000, approximately 85 percent had joined the Church after the revelation.

But the increase in numbers does not tell the full story of the impact of the revelation. Most important was the fervor and strength added to the Church by those, like Elder Martins, who had waited so long for the blessings they once had been denied. The period of deprivation made the blessings more sweet and meaningful, opening new opportunities and new vistas of thought and reflection through the sacred temple ordinances. And the discipline and training to be gained through the exercise of priesthood authority enlarged the capacities of its new recipients, better qualifying them as heads of families, as Church leaders, and as contributing participants in the social and political life of their respective countries.

The revelation also deprived certain critics of the Church of one of their main weapons of attack. No longer could

The prophet speaking during general conference in the Tabernacle, October 1978.

they point to priesthood restrictions as supposed evidence of bigotry and repression in the Church. However, revealing a typical adroitness, these critics sought to claim or suggest that their criticisms inspired the revelation. The background of the revelation detailed above demonstrates the fallacy of this contention.

The impact of the revelation on the members of the Church generally was significant. It seemed to relieve them of a subtle sense of guilt they had felt over the years, guilt caused by the fact that some among them were barred because of racial origin from the priesthood blessings others enjoyed. The enormous outpouring of happiness among the members of the Church which followed the announcement of the revelation seemed to reflect members' genuine joy that the gospel could now be freely shared with all inhabitants of the earth.

Chapter 23

The Final Years

L ater in June, after the revelation on priesthood was
announced, President Kimball presided at the dedication of the women's monument in Nauvoo,
Illinois. Joining him were leaders of the Relief
Society and other women's auxiliaries, many of the General
Authorities, and civic leaders from many areas, including
the governor of Utah, Scott M. Matheson. A representative
of the governor of the state of Illinois also was present, and
she offered an apology for the conduct of Illinois officialdom
in expelling the Latter-day Saints in the 1840s and then,
stretching her arms outward, pleaded, "Come back."

President Kimball had an enlightened, sanguine attitude
toward women and their role in society. Camilla's character
and achievements undoubtedly influenced this outlook. She
was college-trained, had taught in the Church school system, was a voracious reader, and had wide-ranging interests. He applauded her efforts at intellectual development
and sought the same for all Latter-day Saint women. And he
was anxious to change the narrow view some men had of

the roles of their wives and daughters. While he maintained that the principal role of a mother was to bear and train children, this did not mean she should lose sight of her own identity and well-being in that process. After all, the years of childbearing and child rearing for a woman with normal life expectancy represents only about a third of her life span. President Kimball was anxious that a woman not assume her life's work was completed when the last child left the home; he felt she should recognize that beyond her core duties lay responsibilities of self-improvement and self-enrichment. He elaborated on some of these ideas at the general women's fireside held in mid-September 1978, three months after he dedicated the women's monument in Nauvoo. "Let us create a climate," he told the women, "in which we encourage the sisters of the Church to have a program of personal improvement. It ought to be a practical and realistic program, which is determined personally and not imposed upon them. Yet it ought to cause them to reach for new levels of achievement. . . . We should be as concerned with the woman's capacity to communicate as we are to have her sew and preserve food. Good women are articulate as well as affectionate. One skill or one attribute need not be developed at the expense of another. Symmetry in our spiritual development is much to be desired. We are as anxious for women to be wise in the management of their time as we are for women to be wise stewards of the family's storehouse of food." (*Ensign,* Nov. 1978, p. 104.)

These remarks were especially significant, given as they were during the period of intense effort by some to extend the time during which states could ratify the Equal Rights Amendment (known as the ERA) to the U.S. Constitution. The opposition of President Kimball and his brethren to the ERA did not represent an opposition to women's rights. From its inception, The Church of Jesus Christ of Latter-day Saints has been in the forefront of those groups endeavoring to advance the rights and privileges of women. The Relief Society, established in 1842 by the Prophet Joseph Smith,

President Kimball greeting the Saints following a general conference session in the Tabernacle.

was one of the first organizations created in the United States exclusively for women. And Utah was among the first of the territories or states to grant suffrage to women, a policy that had the unqualified support of the Church.

At the general conference following the general women's fireside, President Kimball announced the creation of an emeritus status for several members of the Seventy who originally had been called to lifetime service as General Authorities. Later, other lifetime-service members of the Seventy were given similar status when they reached age seventy. Afterward, when seventies were called for a specific term of years and had completed their service, they were released but not given emeritus status. The purpose of this action was to prevent the buildup of a large number of seventies who, because of age or infirmity, might be unable to meet the heavy demands of travel and administration that service as an active seventy entails. The emeritus designation was not given to those who held the apostleship, however, because at the time one is ordained as an apostle and a member of the Quorum of the Twelve, he is given, in a suspended form, all the authority necessary to lead the Church, conditional upon two events—that he survive to become the senior living apostle and that the other living apostles join to ordain him as the prophet and President of the Church. President Kimball was in full accord with this orderly procedure governing succession in the presidency.

In October 1978, President Kimball presided at ceremonies dedicating the Missionary Training Center in Provo, Utah. A year later he dedicated the Orson Hyde Memorial Gardens in Jerusalem. And in April 1980, he presided at ceremonies in Fayette, New York, to commemorate the sesquicentennial anniversary of the organization of the Church. On April 6, he spoke by satellite transmission from the rebuilt log cabin that once belonged to Peter Whitmer Sr. to the members of the Church gathered in the Salt Lake Tabernacle for the annual general conference. Later, President Kimball dedicated and delivered an address from the new Fayette chapel.

It was a mark of President Kimball's resiliency that he was able to participate in these sesquicentennial events even though seven months earlier he had undergone an operation for a subdural hematoma. On Thursday, September 6, 1979, the prophet had felt weak and unstable in both the First Presidency meeting and the council meeting in the temple. Despite this, he left immediately after the temple meeting to be driven to Brigham City, Utah, about seventy miles north of Salt Lake City. His purpose in going there was to comfort his younger sister, Alice, who was mourning the recent death of her husband, George Nelson. He talked animatedly to Alice, apologizing for not having taken better care of his "baby sister." On the return trip to Salt Lake City, Arthur Haycock was concerned to see the President's left arm and hand hang to his side as if they were lifeless. He called ahead and arranged for Doctor Ernest Wilkinson to meet the President at the Salt Lake Clinic. After a cursory examination at the clinic, President Kimball was hospitalized at the LDS Hospital at 7:00 P.M. A lengthy battery of tests, including a brain scan, revealed a subdural hematoma on the upper right side of his head. Between 1:00 and 2:00 A.M. Friday, the President underwent surgery in which a hole was bored through his skull and the area was drained and then irrigated.

Remarkably, President Kimball was well enough to speak briefly at the opening session of the regional representatives' seminar on Friday, October 5, just a month after his surgery. He then spoke at the morning and priesthood sessions of general conference the next day. His voice was exceedingly weak, so much so that he barely was able to complete his brief remarks to the brethren at the priesthood session. During the Sunday morning session of general conference, he dwelt upon themes that had by that time become his trademark, almost: moral cleanliness, gardens, neatness in and about homes and dwellings, the evils of abortion and birth control, and the need for love and unity. He was overflowing in his gratitude to the Lord for raising him up once again and to the people for their prayers and expressions of love and support. In the priesthood session, he admonished the brethren to be loving, kind, and thoughtful to the sisters, not in a condescending way but in recognition of the fact that wives and mothers are full and true partners and that no man will ever be exalted singly. The President delivered a poignant sermon at the last session of conference on Sunday, October 7, in which he related the story of Caleb and Joshua, expressing the hope that the kind of spirit that moved Caleb would actuate him.

The prophet underwent another operation for a subdural hematoma two months after the first one. And in September 1981, he underwent still another similar operation. For several months before the last operation, President Kimball's physical condition had worsened significantly. His eyesight had weakened to the point that he could read only the largest print. His hearing, which had been affected by the attacks of Bell's palsy in 1972, had become progres-

President Kimball with his counselors in 1982. Standing, left to right: N. Eldon Tanner, Marion G. Romney, and Gordon B. Hinckley.

sively worse. It was necessary for him to wear a brace inter-mittently to support his weakened back, and twin trusses supported a double hernia. Meanwhile, his voice had become more whispery, and his equilibrium occasionally was shaky. His ailments were doubly worrisome because of the weakened condition of Presidents N. Eldon Tanner and Marion G. Romney, both of whom suffered serious eye problems. President Tanner also suffered from Parkinson's disease. In these circumstances, President Kimball called Elder Gordon B. Hinckley as a third counselor in the First Presidency in July 1981. Elder Neal A. Maxwell then filled the vacancy in the Twelve caused by President Hinckley's call. Later, after the death of President N. Eldon Tanner in November 1982, President Romney was installed as the first counselor in the First Presidency and President Hinckley was installed as the second counselor.

Because of a continued deterioration in the health of President Marion G. Romney, President Kimball delegated to President Hinckley full authority to carry out the day-to-day activities of the Church. While President Kimball's health was fragile and he lacked the energy to fulfill heavy administrative duties, he retained the capacity to make decisions. Therefore, President Hinckley took no action, beyond the scope of policies and procedures already approved, without the express authorization of President Kimball. During this period, President Hinckley went regularly to the prophet's apartment in the Hotel Utah to report on the work and to seek his direction as to special matters. So it was that President Kimball directed the call of Elders Russell M. Nelson and Dallin H. Oaks to the Twelve in April 1984, the call of additional members of the Seventy during the same month, and the call of Elder M. Russell Ballard to the Twelve in October 1985.

President Kimball faced a stressful challenge during these last days. While his physical capacities waned, his desire to work remained constant, if, indeed, it did not increase. The inability of his body to respond to the demands of his will created a sense of restlessness and unease. How could the head of the Church, who had admonished the members to lengthen their stride, be justified in remaining idle in his apartment? To him, it was unthinkable. He fretted over it, yet there was nothing he could do about it. The infirmities of age had caught up to him. He continued to struggle against the inevitable until November 5, 1985, when he slipped away. He was ninety years old at the time of his passing from this life.

On the day before the funeral, the Saints began lining up before 8:00 A.M. in a drizzling rain to view President Kimball's last remains, even though the public viewing was not scheduled to begin until 9:30. All day they came, men and women, young and old, rich and poor, to pay their last respects to God's prophet. Over 41,000 of them came to see the beloved leader lying in state in the rotunda of the Church Administration Building. The bier was placed in the center of the room with carpet runners on either side so as to expedite the procession. Otherwise, the mourners would have been streaming by long after the 9:00 P.M. closing hour.

The eulogies offered at President Kimball's funeral in the Tabernacle the following day appropriately lauded his character and achievements. Nothing was said, however, or could have been said, to memorialize him better than the example he had set during his constant, concerned, and unwearying work in the cause to which he had dedicated his life.

Bibliography

PRIMARY SOURCES

Gibbons, Francis M. Diaries, 1970–85.

Kimball, Spencer W. Journals, 1914–74, 1978–85. Archives of The Church of Jesus Christ of Latter-day Saints, Salt Lake City.

————. Manuscripts. Archives of The Church of Jesus Christ of Latter-day Saints, Salt Lake City.

Official Reports of the General Conferences of The Church of Jesus Christ of Latter-day Saints, 1943–85.

NEWSPAPERS

Church News, Salt Lake City, Utah, 1943–85.

Deseret News, Salt Lake City, Utah, 1943–85.

Salt Lake Tribune, Salt Lake City, Utah, 1943–85.

PERIODICALS

Articles by or about Spencer W. Kimball in the *Improvement Era, Ensign, New Era,* and *Friend.*

Bibliography

BOOKS

Cowan, Richard O. *The Church in the Twentieth Century.* Salt Lake City: Bookcraft, 1985.

Dew, Sheri L. *Ezra Taft Benson.* Salt Lake City: Deseret Book Co., 1987.

Durham, G. Homer. *N. Eldon Tanner: His Life and Service.* Salt Lake City: Deseret Book Co., 1982.

Gibbons, Francis M. *David O. McKay: Apostle to the World, Prophet of God.* Salt Lake City: Deseret Book Co., 1986.

———. *George Albert Smith: Kind and Caring Christian, Prophet of God.* Salt Lake City: Deseret Book Co., 1990.

———. *Heber J. Grant: Man of Steel, Prophet of God.* Salt Lake City: Deseret Book Co., 1979.

———. *Joseph Fielding Smith: Gospel Scholar, Prophet of God.* Salt Lake City: Deseret Book Co., 1992.

Goates, L. Brent. *Harold B. Lee: Prophet and Seer.* Salt Lake City: Bookcraft, 1985.

Howard, F. Burton. *Marion G. Romney: His Life and Faith.* Salt Lake City: Bookcraft, 1988.

Kimball, Edward L., and Andrew E. Kimball. *Spencer W. Kimball.* Salt Lake City: Bookcraft, 1977.

Kimball, Edward L., ed. *The Teachings of Spencer W. Kimball.* Salt Lake City: Bookcraft, 1982.

Kimball, Spencer W. *One Silent Sleepless Night.* Salt Lake City: Bookcraft, 1975.

Miner, Caroline Eyring, and Edward L. Kimball. *Camilla.* Salt Lake City: Deseret Book Co., 1980.

Tate, Lucile C. *David B. Haight: The Life of a Disciple.* Salt Lake City: Bookcraft, 1987.

———. *LeGrand Richards: Beloved Apostle.* Salt Lake City: Bookcraft, 1982.

Index

Index

Delta, Utah, 154
Denmark, Church tour of, 189
Depression, Great, 93–96
Derrick, Royden G. and Allie, 282
Didier, Charles, 290
Diphtheria, 30
Dipty, Mongoldan, 231
Doxey, Graham, 145, 185
Dreams: of ancestors, 142; of
    Lamanites, 160; of father, 202, 274;
    of Harold B. Lee, 274
Duncan, Ariz.: chapel dedication,
    xi–xii; flooded, 126, 128, 132
Durham, G. Homer, 294
Dyer, Alvin R., 246

Ear infections, 50–51
Eastern States Mission, 157, 211
Ecuador, Church members in, xii
Edmunds, John K. and Jasmine
    Romney, 155
Edwards, Caroline, 155
Edwards, Catherine, 155
Edwards, Catherine Eyring, 155
Edwards, Robert, 155
Edwards, Weston, 155
Edwards, William F., 155
Ellsworth, Homer, xiii–xiv
Ellsworth, William, 108
Emeritus status instituted, 300
England: vacation to, 115–16; Church
    tour of, 190–91; SWK assigned to
    supervise, 247–53
Europe: vacation to, 109–16; tours of,
    188–93, 234
Evans, Ralph, 159, 161, 265
Evans, Richard L., 182, 195, 268
Eyring, Camilla. See Kimball,
    Camilla Eyring
Eyring, Caroline (sister of Camilla),
    191
Eyring, Caroline Romney (mother of
    Camilla), 68–69, 71, 84, 196
Eyring, Catherine (sister of Camilla),
    155
Eyring, Ed (brother of Camilla), 69,
    89
Eyring, Edward Christian (father of
    Camilla), 68–69, 71, 84, 208
Eyring, Emma Romney, 84

Eyring, Evelyn, 89
Eyring, Henry (brother of Camilla),
    69–71, 155
Eyring, Henry B., 155, 225
Eyring, Joe, 179, 191
Eyring, Mary (sister of Camilla), 99,
    109, 117; 196–97
Eyring, Ted, 155

Faith Precedes the Miracle, 255
Fast offerings, 33
Fedrigotti, Ariel Alcides, 244
Finland, Church tour of, 189
First Quorum of Seventy, 290–91
Flake, Eugene, 166
Flint, Mich., trip to, 124–25
Flooding, of Gila River, 126–28,
    130–32
Fotheringham, Billy, xii
France: vacation to, 110, 115; Church
    tour of, 191, 193
Fugal, Roy, 211
Fyans, J. Thomas, 239, 244

Gates, Susa Young, 26
Germany, tour of, 188–89, 191–92
Gheen, Ann Alice. See Kimball, Ann
    Alice Gheen
Gibbons, J. Smith, 46
Gila Academy, 24, 37–38
Gila Junior College, 144
Gila Monster, 11
Gila River, flooding of, 126–28,
    130–32
Gila Valley: early conditions in, 6–7;
    SWK's affection for, 11; effect of
    Depression on, 91–92; SWK revis-
    its, 178–79
Gillespie Ranch, 63
Golden jubilee, 102–3
Gonzalez, Washington, 244
Graduation, of SWK, 41
Grant, Heber J.: at death of Andrew,
    81–82; at golden jubilee, 102–3;
    receives spiritual confirmation
    about SWK, 135; greets SWK, 147;
    background of, 151; passes away,
    157–58
Greenhalgh, Joseph W., 85–86, 109,
    120

311

Index